Convivencia

Challenging Migration Studies

This provocative new series challenges the established field of migration studies to think beyond its policy-oriented frameworks and to engage with the complex and myriad forms in which the global migration regime is changing in the twenty-first century. It proposes to draw together studies that engage with the current transformation of the politics of migration, and the meaning of 'migrant,' from the below of grassroots, local, transnational and multi-sited coalitions, projects and activisms. Attuned to the contemporary resurgence of migrant-led and migration-related movements, and anti-racist activism, the series builds on work carried out at the critical margins of migration studies to evaluate the 'border industrial complex' and its fall-outs, build a decolonial perspective on global migration flows, and critically reassess the link between (im)migration, citizenship and belonging in the cross-border future.

Series Editors:

Alana Lentin, Associate Professor in Cultural and Social Analysis at Western Sydney University

Gavan Titley, Senior Lecturer in Media Studies at the National University of Ireland, Maynooth

Titles in the Series:

Radical Skin, Moderate Masks: De-Radicalising the Muslim and Racism in Post-Racial Societies
Yassir Morsi

The Undeported: The Making of a Floating Population of Exiles in France and Europe
Carolina Sanchez Boe

Race in Post-Racial Europe: An Intersectional Analysis
Stefanie C. Boulila

Contemporary Boat Migration: Data, Geopolitics, and Discourses
edited by Elaine Burroughs and Kira Williams

Reproducing Refugees: Photographia of a Crisis
Anna Carastathis and Myrto Tsilimpounidi

Disavowing Asylum: Documenting Ireland's Asylum Industrial Complex
Ronit Lentin and Vukašin Nedeljković

Convivencia: Urban Space and Migration in a Small Catalan Town
Martin Lundsteen

The Politics of Alterity: France, and her Others
Sarah Mazouz and Translated by Rachel Gomme

Convivencia

Urban Space and Migration in a Small Catalan Town

Martin Lundsteen

ROWMAN & LITTLEFIELD
Lanham • Boulder • New York • London

Published by Rowman & Littlefield
An imprint of The Rowman & Littlefield Publishing Group, Inc.
4501 Forbes Boulevard, Suite 200, Lanham, Maryland 20706
www.rowman.com

86-90 Paul Street, London EC2A 4NE

British Library Cataloguing in Publication Information Available

Library of Congress Cataloging-in-Publication Data

Names: Lundsteen, Martin, 1983- author.
Title: Convivencia : urban space and migration in a small Catalan town / Martin Lundsteen.
Description: Lanham, Maryland : Rowman & Littlefield, [2022] | Series: Challenging migration studies | Includes bibliographical references and index. | Summary: "This book analyzes the local-global transformation of migration and societies in a small Catalan town through a multi-scalar ethnography, connecting the local processes of space- and place-making with the more extensive processes of migration, economic crisis and social transformation, and finally, the socio-political responses to these changes"—Provided by publisher.
Identifiers: LCCN 2022002851 (print) | LCCN 2022002852 (ebook) | ISBN 9781786614520 (cloth) | ISBN 9781786614537 (epub)
Subjects: LCSH: Migration, Internal—Spain—Catalonia. | Catalonia (Spain)—Emigration and immigration. | Catalonia (Spain)—Social conditions.
Classification: LCC HB2080.C3 L86 2022 (print) | LCC HB2080.C3 (ebook) | DDC 304.809467—dc23/eng/20220307
LC record available at https://lccn.loc.gov/2022002851
LC ebook record available at https://lccn.loc.gov/2022002852

∞™ The paper used in this publication meets the minimum requirements of American National Standard for Information Sciences—Permanence of Paper for Printed Library Materials, ANSI/NISO Z39.48-1992.

To the people of Salt

Contents

Acknowledgments

I am indebted to so many friends, colleagues, and mentors who made this work possible in one way or another. Although it is impossible to mention them all here, I want to express my deepest gratitude to everyone who has made it possible and for making me grow as a person.

That being said, I feel that some of these people must be made visible. Therefore, in the first instance, I would like to thank all the people from Salt with whom I have enjoyed meeting, speaking, debating, and arguing. The way you have welcomed me and made me see what Salt is all about, and allowed me to feel at home despite my strange presence and curious questions, has been valuable for the research and me as a person.

In particular, I would like to thank Birame, Laye, Kadijatou, Salif, and Rashid, flatmates and informants, but above all friends; the entire group of *vidilla saltenca* for taking me in and thus letting me delve into their private lives; Judit and Mosta for the emotional and personal support, the intellectual stimulation, for the contacts, in short, for everything; Ignasi for the more theoretical debates and field trips. I would also like to thank all the interviewees, spontaneous informants, and temporary neighbours to pay attention to me and answer my questions, despite everything. And last but not least, Rosa and Barry for their happiness and openness.

In another vein, I would like to express my deepest gratitude to those professors and mentors who have made me think and enjoy since I first began my academic journey at the age of 21, laying the foundations, sometimes implicit, of the present work. I especially want to thank the profound influence and encouragement of some of the professors at Roskilde University (RUC) and University Jaume I. In the past, I was unaware of the fascinating world of anthropology, and it was essentially thanks to them that I later decided to join the cult and allow myself to be possessed by those ancient spirits of anthropology. However, at the University of Barcelona, I took the steps on the irreversible path towards that other being that I am today, which would best be described as an anthropologist. This is why I would like to express my deepest gratitude to the professors of University of Barcelona, my fellow researchers, and the members of Grup d'Estudis de Reciprocitat (GER). You have all played a crucial role.

Beyond mere formalism, I owe special thanks to my official supervisors, Susana and Mikel and Jaume. You have all guided me in one way or another. I sincerely appreciate your comments and criticisms, as well as your support in critical moments.

Likewise, I would like to thank the people of the Observatory of the Anthropology of Urban Conflict (OACU) and those surrounding *La Reina de África* for sharing all kinds of moments and experiences, projects and activisms throughout all these years.

I am also grateful to my friends with whom I have shared beers, hugs, tears, laughter, getaways, soccer games, parties, and much more; you are the basis on which this project has been carried out.

Several institutions supported the realization of this thesis financially. In the first place, the University of Barcelona, which granted me an APIF scholarship for the years 2009–2011. Second, the Ministry of Science and Innovation, which awarded me an FPU scholarship for the years 2011–2013. Thirdly, GER helped economically with the copyedit of the book via the grant *2017 SGR 1307*. Finally, GRITIM-UPF has offered me office and indexing software in the final stage of writing.

On the other hand, several centres welcomed me during the process: in Barcelona, the Grup d'Estudis de Reciprocitat and the Department of Social Anthropology; at Oxford, the Center on Migration, Policy and Society and the Institute of Social and Cultural Anthropology at the University of Oxford.

Vanessa, my partner in life, also deserves a special mention. We have shared a large part of this journey together, with all the good and the bad things that this entails. But the support you have given me during these years has been essential and is much appreciated.

Finally, although equally important, I would like to thank my parents for the support, understanding and affection, and material help given throughout these years. Also vital in all these years is my family, both in Denmark and Spain; you are fundamental to me—and especially the young ones, who give me yet another motivation to change this world for a better place.

Introduction

The Emergence of the Problem: Cultural Conflicts

> [A]ny emancipatory social science faces three basic tasks: elaborating a systematic diagnosis and critique of the world as it exists; envisioning viable alternatives; and understanding the obstacles, possibilities, and dilemmas of transformation. In different times and places one or another of these may be more pressing than others, but all are necessary for a comprehensive emancipatory theory. (Wright 2010, 7)

We are living in an age of migration. In the last decades, the number of migrants and refugees arriving in Europe has been on the rise, which, in addition to those already settled, has only led to an ever-growing sociocultural complexity of Europe. A reality that has collided with the until recently dominant (desired) ideas of monoculturalism, thereby forwarding debates on integration, multiculturalism, and interculturalism, belonging and nationality, and a questioning of the origins and the fundamental ideas of what Europe is, through the return of its colonial past and, more specifically, the colonial subjects. These issues are certainly present in recent social conflicts emerging in relegated and stigmatized spaces such as the French banlieues (Dikeç 2007), conflicts often branded 'cultural conflicts' or as they were labelled in Catalonia, 'conflicts of *convivencia*' (where *convivencia* refers to an idea of living together in peace). Know this rhetoric is not arbitrary, while the analyses of these conflicts have often been limited to the symbolic or ideological aspects of these, thereby ignoring other relevant economic, political, and ideological factors, and especially the inherent spatial logics.

In fact, this book deals with this exact question: How is it that otherwise complex and often contradictory social conflicts in Catalonia, and Spain at large, have been branded 'cultural conflicts'; a characterization that only a small minority seemed to question? Through a comprehensive and ethnographically informed analysis, based on several years of fieldwork in a small Catalan town, it shows that these conflicts are more than just cultural conflicts and, more importantly, that such a reading is a biased interpretation often influenced by economic and political interests. Instead, throughout the book, we will see how the so-called 'conflicts of *convivencia*' emerge as the iceberg tip of a deeply complex phenomenon—a web of social conflicts articulating such varying themes as urban transformation, migration, race/ethnic relations and marginalization, the informal economy, and public policies on poverty and cultural diversity.

First, let us start by taking a step back in the whole process of problematization (i.e., 'how and why certain things (behaviour, phenomena, processes) become a problem', Foucault 1985, quoted in Bacchi 2012, 1)[1] of the social conflicts and migration in Spain and Catalonia, to place the question within a concrete historical and geographical context of the paradigmatic small town, Salt, located in the region of Girona (Catalonia).

CONFLICTS OF CONVIVENCIA: A NEW SOCIAL QUESTIONING?

> [I]t is imperative to submit to radical questioning all the presuppositions inscribed in the reality to be thought and in the very thought of the analyst. (Bourdieu, Wacquant, and Farage 1994, 2)

In 2010, my attention was captured by Salt while I was doing field work for my master's degree in another small Catalan town, Premià de Mar (see Lundsteen 2015). While the field work in Premià de Mar had reached a point of saturation, Salt was the focus of a lot of media attention; thus, it seemed reasonable to change the setting for my doctoral degree to develop my research further. However, it was not until the beginning of 2011 that I was able to visit Salt for the first time.

Earlier that year, 8 January, Mohammed Reda, an 'unaccompanied minor' of Moroccan nationality whom the Generalitat de Catalunya was tutoring, was seriously injured after falling from a fifth-floor during a police chase. Mohammed, 16, was said to be known by the police as a petty criminal (now labelled a 'multiple offender') who, according to the accounts of the police, had a 'habit' of climbing out of windows and buildings when trying to escape the authorities (he was known as 'spiderman'). According to the police, he had been driving a stolen motorbike.

A week later, while he remained hospitalized in the intensive care unit, on the evening of 14 January (6:00 p.m.), a group of around 50–100 youngsters gathered in front of the local police department and town hall, protesting against the police intervention and demanding the suspension of the two police officers. The demonstration soon dispersed and evolved into riots, and seven containers were set on fire. By the end of the riots, at around 9:00 p.m., three people had been arrested for public disturbance, one adult of Maghreb origin, and two minors of South American and Maghreb origin (Barrera 2011). They were later released with charges. The media discredited the agency of the young protesters and spoke about the possible involvement of two adults. One of them, Morad El-Hassani, was an ex-convict who had been heavily involved in the first social conflict described.

The following night, on 15–16 January, new incidents took place, during which five vehicles and seven motorbikes were burned. Several newspaper articles linked these acts directly to the uproar from the previous day (ACN, El Punt 2011). Nonetheless, three days later, during the night of 19 January, a neo-Nazi was accused of setting fire to containers and arrested (Europa Press 2011a).

Notwithstanding, the response from the mayor was a clear rejection of what she dubbed 'vandalism'. She requested more police to be deployed with harsher rules in place (VilaWeb 2011a). It seems clear that the local administration was afraid they were losing control of the situation, believing that it might have evolved into a social explosion similar to that of the French *banlieues*, as some commentators had predicted. This analysis now seemed to confirm itself and thus became more popular (see, e.g., Pastor 2011). There also seems to have been a latent fear that other mostly right-wing political formations and associations would exploit the situation, now that the elections were only five months away.

Furthermore, as a reaction to the incidents, a group of residents had started gathering signatures and were planning a large demonstration under the slogan: 'Basta ya. Queremos una solucion' ('Enough. We want a solution'), in front of the town hall by the end of February, coinciding with the anniversary of the first social situation and demonstration in 2010 (Julbe 2011). However, this first mobilization was displaced by another one, which had been organized by many local associations and was announced on 18 January. This led to the proposal of a 'united demonstration', as they called it, on 22 January with the slogan: 'Volem viure a Salt en pau i bé' ('We want to live in peace and harmony in Salt'). The spokesperson of the organizing associations, and the president of the neighbourhood association of the Centre, Toñi, explained that one of the aims of the demonstration was to show the unity of the majority of residents of Salt against the incivility of a few and to disassociate crime from migration (ACN 2011; Oller and Julbe 2011), as she said on *Catalunya Radio* on 19 January 2011:

> This Saturday we have to go together like we were one, with a pacific demonstration we make a statement of civility, and if anybody is pretending to break it I am now calling for the security forces, *els mossos*, I will not accept that this demonstration will be broken which is the voice of a people, the voice which demands to be able to live in peace and well.

On 20 January, Mohammed Rena died in hospital and, consequently, the police forces were reinforced and in a state of high alert for two days (Soler 2011b; VilaWeb 2011b). Meanwhile, the mayor called for calm and serenity (ACN, ARA 2011). Instead of conflicts of any significance, the 'united demonstration' took place on a cold, sunny afternoon in January 2011. As mentioned, this was when I started my observations in the town.

On 22 January, various neighbourhood and migrant associations organized a demonstration in favour of *civismo* (civility) and *paz social* (social peace). Although 2000–3000 residents participated, including almost all the local associations and various people, I perceived a certain tension and heard several critical voices. A fact that made me question the supposed homogeneity of the discourse. It is telling that the demonstration, according to the leading organizers, was to be a *silent* one. One of its objectives was to achieve unity through the denial and negation of differences and disagreements, possibly out of fear of what was perceived as the potentially negative consequences of opening Pandora's box. The demonstration silenced the critical and dissident voices to achieve equilibrium or social cohesion. In fact, it aimed at putting an end to what was perceived as a potential social fracturing of the local community, and the slogan of the demonstration was literally, 'We want to live in Salt in peace and harmony.'[2] This was a response to what had been described as 'loutish' protests started by a group of young 'trouble-makers'.

The main focus was on convivencia and on efforts to maintain the supposedly fragile social cohesion in town. It seems there was an attempt at silencing the critical voices from the right-wing parties (such as PxC,[3] MSR,[4] PP,[5] and GPS[6]) by dismantling their discourse of equating migration with crime and insecurity, but at the same time, they excluded other critical voices such as those of the marginalized youngsters. By doing this, I believe that the organizers of the demonstration, perversely and implicitly, confirmed the latent hypothesis of the anti-immigration and fascist parties; instead of talking about the underlying problems of the conflicts, significant concerns were expressed to avoid a 'social fracture' and, in this way, cancelling the social protests that the youngsters had led. In a similar take to other riots or protests around the world, the tensions have been interpreted as a symptom of a dysfunctional and unequal society, where 50% of young people are unemployed and facing a somewhat uncertain future and, at the same time, are targeted by the police and indirectly blamed for the town's problems. Consequently, the inherent structural racism was utterly ignored.

It is clear that these instances in Salt, if judged by the set-up, insert themselves within a larger history of similar cases of what has been termed 'ethnic conflicts/upheavals', such as the Brixton riots of 1981, Broadwater Farm in 1985, Los Angeles in 1992, Bradford in 2001, Clichy-sous-Bois in 2005, and later, Tottenham in 2011, and Malmö in 2013 (Wacquant 2009a; Cachón Rodríguez 2008, 2011). On a more local scale, social conflicts in Spain related to migration are not a new phenomenon. As immortalized in the film *La piel quemada* [*Burnt Skin*] by Josep Maria Forn (1967), and as López Sánchez (1986) shows in the case of Barcelona, the people who arrived in Catalonia during the decades 1950–1970 primarily from the southern part of Spain (Andalucía and Murcia) and the north-western region (Galícia) were often considered migrants and ill-received; as Júlia, 55, a 'migrant' from Valencia, recalls:

> People traditionally from Catalonia had little in common, and less in the 50s, with people traditionally from Murcia, they weren't precisely similar. So, this also created some conflicts because there have been some and from which words such as *xarnego* are pretty illuminating and above all in this derogatory way of saying it, so now we apply it to another kind of social group.

Although the opposing social groups were often described as Spanish migrants and 'native' Catalans, we should not forget that the latter were also often newcomers from other regions of Catalonia, nor that some of the 'Spaniards' had arrived decades before (principally from Aragon and the Valencia Community). What might be surprising to some (those who sustain that cultural racism is a contemporary phenomenon) is that these conflicts were often explained in cultural terms (Fernández et al., 2009). Therefore, one might say that there is a continuation between these and the current conflicts analysed here, where the hegemonic reading is that there is a problematic convivencia. It is a concept that mediates several historical times and different scales, as it both sends us back in time and constitute the main issues of today's integration of migrants in Spanish society.

Indeed, convivencia has become a key concept when talking about migration in contemporary Spain. Although during the historic period named *la Transición* (1975–1982) and in its aftermath, convivencia was employed to address the (desired) reconciliation of, on the one hand, the two Spains (thus referring to the 'winners' and the 'losers' of the civil war) and, on the other hand, supporters of a united Spain (unionists) and the supporters of independence (pro-independents), as well as the different use of languages and, up to a certain point, different cultures, in the Basque Country and Catalonia. It was first employed by the medievalist philologist Ramón Menéndez Pidal to describe the competition and coexistence of various phonetic forms of early Romance languages in the Iberian Peninsula, although its use can be dated as early as the 17th century (Szpiech 2013). One of his disciples, Américo Castro, later further developed this to describe the ideally peaceful interaction and cohabitation of medieval Jews, Muslims, and Christians in the heyday of Al-Andalus (Erickson 2011), also known as Muslim Spain (790–1495). Although the concept has been subject to several critiques since then, the academic debate has mainly focused on the veracity of the claim to peacefulness and the actual interrelatedness of the social interrelations back then (Akasoy 2010; Glick and Pi-Sunyer 1992; Soifer 2009).

Despite these conceptualizations, in contemporary use and vernacular understanding of convivencia (Erickson 2011; Suárez-Navaz 2004), a direct coupling among convivencia, social cohesion, and migration has emerged. One which implies a plurality of cultures, habits, language, religion, and so on, and a mutual acceptance and cohabitation between the various communities. Moreover, convivencia is employed to refer to a situation beyond mere 'coexistence' and is characterized by peace, mutual tolerance, and an apparent lack of conflict. Or, rather, on the contrary, it is often used when there is a lack of it.

In fact, in the 1990s, with the increasing arrival of people from outside of Spain and Europe, the idea of new urban scenarios often stigmatized as 'powder kegs' emerges, places with a high concentration of cultural plurality that (so goes the self-fulfilling prophecy) will inevitably lead to racist and cultural confrontations and unrest (Aramburu 2002): 'convivencia conflicts'. This idea—indeed an anthropological oxymoron—is often employed in a vernacular speech to describe conflicts in the neighbourhood community or the everyday interactions in public space. This we see clearly in the following description of the purpose of the *Convivencia* Unit of the Guardia Urbana de Tarragona:

> Is the specialized unit for mediation, counselling and information when handling conflicts of '*convivencia*'. Its objective is to help to reach a peaceful solution when there is no need to file a complaint or when filing a complaint is not considered a suitable way of resolving the problem. It works above all in the field of the neighborhood communities.

However, in practice (although often implicitly), it has come to serve as a substitute for ethnic conflicts, racial conflicts, or cultural conflicts. Other similar ways of describing these tensions include 'intercultural convivencia conflicts', wording often used by non-governmental organizations (NGOs) and such, but not so popular in the media. Interestingly it seems to have replaced racism, just as 'intercultural convivencia' seems to have replaced 'multiculturalism'.

These depictions of disturbing images and tropes are systematically invigorated every time a similar sequence of events to the ones described here takes place. In this way, immigration as a social phenomenon is recurrently presented as a problem or a challenge that could potentially endanger the current state of convivencia. It is not surprising that people start to fear the presence of migrants, even if they have not experienced any prior problems; their mere presence seems to entail conflicts.

So, although these tensions have been forgotten in the memory of many inhabitants in Catalonia, it is clear that cultural conflicts do not simply arise with extra immigration from the European Union (EU). Then, what is new about these conflicts? In this sense, the conflicts in Salt are just the latest in a line of similar social conflicts in Catalonia and Spain, with the common denominator that they are perceived as conflicts related to migration. When considering the beginning of the 21st century retrospectively, it is remarkable how many similar conflicts took place. In my view, these conflicts mediate and allow us to understand how migration was dealt with at the trans-local level; what unite these seemingly isolated events are how they were perceived and interpreted. Indeed, when dealing with conflicts of convivencia, I believe we can discern and analyse the emergence of a new rhetoric concerning social conflicts and migration in Spain—a new social questioning. In this sense, the following cases of Ca n'Anglada, El Ejido, and Premia de Mar, which all took place late in the 1990s to 2000, are crucial. They allow us to detect the changing discursive practices and the subsequent institutionalization and hegemonization of certain discourses and policies, which will be fundamental for how we should analyse the issue through recourse to the case of Salt.

Accordingly, I will analyse the key factors, ideas, and actors at play in the following. I will then draw out the topics that will make up the body of the thesis. This is a mode of procedure that has been fundamentally inspired by the extended case method introduced by Gluckman in his famous study of the inauguration of a bridge in Zululand (1940), later developed in Turner's study of the political changes in a Ndembu village (1996), and recently 're-discovered' by Burawoy (Burawoy 2000, 2009).

SOCIAL CONFLICTS AND MIGRATION IN 21ST-CENTURY SPAIN

The first significant conflict detected by the media between natives and migrants in Spain occurred in the neighbourhood of Ca n'Anglada, Terrassa, in 1999. A working-class neighbourhood made up of 20,000 residents, of whom a large majority are 'old migrants' from the rest of Spain, often elderly people, and a small proportion of 'new migrants', chiefly from Africa and mainly of Moroccan nationality. The events have never been investigated thoroughly, and until recently, it was unclear what had happened. However, I have been able to recover articles from the period, on which I base the following short description.[7]

On the evening of 11 July 1999, two neighbourhood residents got into a fight during a local festival; other fights followed between groups of native youngsters and Moroccans. According to a journalist, a pogrom took place, with natives persecuting Moroccans. The windows of a Moroccan bar and butcher were broken, as was a property that served as a mosque, and where the local Moroccans (and other Muslims) would congregate (Rodríguez 1999a). In the following days, similar occurrences took place. The police attempted to protect the Moroccans until 14 July, when a racist demonstration of around 1,300 people protested the presence of Moroccans in the neighbourhood. Several 'skinheads' were present, and during the upheaval, a Moroccan boy was heavily injured and left unconscious from attacks with sticks and motorcycle helmets (Rodríguez 1999b). Later, another was stabbed (Rodríguez 1999c).

Two days later, an anti-racist demonstration was held, and three persons were arrested in other neighbourhoods of Terrassa, two of which were related to the stabbing and the other to an accusation of incitement of racist violence (the accused had appeared on television waving knives and inciting others to go kill *moros*), as well as two 13-year-olds who had attacked a '10-year-old black boy' (Rodríguez 1999d). In the following days, more arrests (a total of 11) were carried out; many linked to disturbances and public-order offences (Rodríguez 1999e).

Some weeks later, on 27 July, the mayor led an anti-racism demonstration with 2,200 attendees, with the slogan, 'The Town of All People' (de Orovio and Rodríguez 1999). Moreover, just a few days after, the Catalan parliament (Generalitat de Catalunya) signed a statement condemning the racist attacks and supporting the demonstrations, urging 'the local governments to implement policies that prevent the formation of ghettos and calling on citizens to collaborate actively with respect and tolerance towards the social integration of everyone living in Catalonia' (La Vanguardia 1999). Half a year later, the town council proposed several urban renewal projects with the primary objective of 'getting rid of the neighbourhood's stigma as marginal' and, thus, aiming at stimulating private entrepreneurial investment in the area, which again should tackle the problem of urban degradation (Rodríguez 2000).

Not surprisingly, in the following years, continuous references were made to Ca n'Anglada. In fact, the case is interesting precisely because it is often referred to as the first conflict between 'natives' and 'migrants'. In my view, history shows us that this idea is inaccurate; however, I do believe that this was the first time the media echoed such a conflict, and it might have been the first conflict to be described as a convivencia-cultural conflict; just like one of the town councillors stated: '"We are aware that there are different groups" and that this could produce *convivencia* conflicts'[8] (Rodríguez 1999a). Hence, this linked migration and diversity to social conflicts in a causal relation—a tendency that would persist when dealing with similar issues since then.

Furthermore, this was not the only path-breaking tendency. At one point, some of the people affected expressed a desire to demonstrate peacefully in the neighbourhoods, but the town council and the police convinced them not to do so (Rodríguez 1999e). The attacks were directed at the symbols of the social integration of the new migrants, such as the Islamic butchers and the mosques. Moreover, instead of defending the integration of these elements, racism was not confronted overtly and was only condemned rhetorically. The tendency here has thus been to want to pace out the conflicts instead of attacking the roots of them, a tendency that ends up accepting the implicit and explicit racism of some neighbours and their claim to exclusive belonging. As one of the residents of Moroccan nationality who, at that time, had been living in Terrassa for 12 years, put it:

> it was a fight between youngsters that somebody has been in charge of manipulating, a cultural and racist conflict has been organized . . . the neighbours are being manipulated because the people are demonstrating with the skinheads who are both our enemies and their enemies, they are the scum of society. (de Orovio 1999)

But first and foremost, it is an interesting case because it brings together a large proportion of the elements present in the succeeding cultural-convivencia conflicts: subjective insecurity (contrasted with the lack of official recognition of an objective change), informal economy (petty crime and such), rumours concerning the provision of social benefits for migrants only, the fact that the major parties involved were 'Moroccans' and 'old migrants', and the setting in a working-class neighbourhood with a prior history of community bonding (i.e., a history of struggle against social relegation and marginalization, first during the Franco regime, and later with the social consequences of the crisis during the Transition).

Another critical event took place in El Ejido (Almería), south-eastern Andalucía, in February 2000.[9] Several weeks of violent unrest followed a murder allegedly committed by a Moroccan resident. The 'native' Spanish residents, many of whom were tenant farmers, held demonstrations 'against the foreign presence' with physical attacks unleashed on the Moroccan population and heavy damage inflicted on import stores, besides the burning of a mosque. At first sight, another conflict between natives and (Moroccan) migrants, let us see how it was interpreted by academics, institutions, and the media, among others.

Many anthropologists, such as Ubaldo Martinez Veiga and Emma Martin, who had researched the area (Narotzky 2005), took part in the debate. However, one, in particular, played a significant role. Mikel Azurmendi, a Basque anthropologist, emerged as a spokesman during and after the events in El Ejido and played a fundamental role in the culturalization of social conflicts and migration in Spain (Lundsteen 2010, 2020a, 2020b).

In 2000 the Popular Party (PP), then the ruling party in Spain, created an institutional body called the Forum for the Integration of Immigrants and appointed Azurmendi as chairman (Narotzky 2005, 46–48). Through this organ, Azurmendi helped institutionalize a view on migration, particularly from the Maghreb, in line with the party's views. According to this, the attacks were an almost natural defensive strategy against what the 'native population' perceived, in Azurmendi's words, as undemocratic habits of people who did not want to be assimilated into the 'democratic culture' of Spain (Azurmendi 2001, 2002a, 2002b). He also rejected any accusations of racism.

One might argue that what we see in his writings, apart from a justification of the policy measures and the new (stricter) Alien Act implemented by the government, is a translation of the famous neoconservative preachings of Samuel P. Huntington (1996) that explain the social conflicts of Spain in cultural terms.

Another important outcome of this conflict and its interpretations was the projection of an image of Moroccans, which had until then been the majority migrant population in Spain, as problematic, unassimilable, and a threat to the cultural values of Spain, which reinforced the old stereotypes and imagery of *el moro* (Lundsteen 2018). This hypothesis would confirm itself in subsequent conflicts, such as in the clash around the construction of a mosque in Premià de Mar (Lundsteen 2020a, 2015). As Martínez Veiga (2001) shows us, one of the main reasons was labour-market exploitation. The Moroccans, then the primary labour force, were perceived as less docile than the capitalist agricultural enterprises would want them to be; they did not merely succumb to the force inflicted on them and had recently been protesting and striking regularly. Indeed, the conflicts would inaugurate a new era of Spanish migrant policy concerning the labour market.

The interpretations made by the institutional and administrative bodies do not fundamentally disagree concerning the background factors; most of the interpretations were based on a concern for cultural factors. Moreover, among the neighbours, we see similar arguments, although some suggest outright racial explanations. However, in this regard, I believe it is essential that most of the participants in the conflict—whether or not they were tolerant of cultural differences, racist or not—shared the view that the conflicts arose basically due to convivencia or '(inter)cultural conflicts'. This fact, in my opinion, shows a generalized concern with the cultural differences and the problems that could erupt among some of the native population in response to encounters with migrants. This interpretation in cultural terms seems to have become the most common attitude, both in the media and among people in general. Indeed, as we have seen so far, this interpretation has been applied to any social conflict related to migration.

Now, this serves as a point of entry. As will become apparent throughout this book, a variety of conflicts occur in Salt, some of which are more transcendent and reiterative than others. However, the main questions when studying these conflicts should, according to Cachón Rodríguez (2015, 98), rather be: *Which* conflicts are made essential and *why*? *What* do they catalyse? *What* kind of conflicts are ignored? In this book, I will focus on social conflicts and convivencia in Salt, and, more importantly, what these, their outcomes, and how they are handled tell us about contemporary society. Therefore, the main objective that has guided this research has been to inquire into the material and ideological foundation of the so-called cultural conflicts; to scrutinize the relations between cultural diversity and social conflicts; and to consider why some social conflicts exist are said to be inherently cultural.

To address this, there is a need to restrict the limits of the area of study to a particular geographical location that will provide a guiding case that should reveal the relevant themes to analyse to answer the question of what is new about these convivencia conflicts. In this sense, the mentioned features and contradictions in the case of Salt make it a privileged case for an urban ethnography of the relations between migration and space, with specific attention to everyday intergroup relations, conflicts, and coexistence, all of which are happening in an engaging social context of a small town—a setting to which little anthropological attention has been granted, especially within the broader fields of urban anthropology and anthropology of migration (Goebel 2011).

Because this research inserts itself within a theoretical tradition that conceives space and time as social constructions, the field is a socio-spatial abstraction, and thus, the delimitation of an area of study must also be included in the analysis (Franquesa 2007b). Therefore, although officially Salt consists of eight neighbourhoods (Barri Vell [Old District], Veïnat [The neighbourhood], Barri Centre [Centre District], la Massana, Grup Sant Cugat, Barri Mas Masó, Barri Pla de Salt and Polígon Torre Mirona), I have chosen mainly to put the focus on the spatial units of the neighbourhoods Barri Centre and Barri Vell. This delimitation is all but natural nor completely arbitrary, and in vernacular terms, various neighbourhoods—that is, the social understanding of its constitution and its borders or limits—might even coexist, as Franquesa (2007b) shows in the case of Palma. Consequently, I have attempted to bring into the analysis the different delimitations and not limit the observation to these neighbourhoods.

SALT, A SEMI-RURAL TOWN IN THE NORTH OF CATALONIA

Salt is a small town located in the Girona region of North Catalonia, one of 17 Spanish autonomous communities situated in the northeast of Spain. Catalonia is home to about 7.675 million inhabitants, of which 1.159 million (15.11%) are of a nationality other than Spanish (Statistical Institute of Catalonia, henceforth IDESCAT, 2019). Although in absolute figures the most significant portion of foreigners lives in the big cities, a more significant percentage is often found in smaller and rural towns (see table 0.1).

Table 0.1. Catalan municipalities with the largest percentages of foreign populations. Elaborated by the author from figures IDESCAT 2019.

Municipality	*Province*	*Population*	*Number of foreign nationals*	*Percentage*	*Main nationalities*
Guissona	Lleida	7,136	3,700	51.85	Romania, Ukraine, and Senegal
Castelló d'Empúries	Girona	10,906	4,721	43.29	Morocco, France, and Germany
Salt	Girona	31,362	12,246	39.05	Morocco, Honduras, and Gambia
Portella, la	Lleida	728	279	38.32	Ukraine, Romania, and Senegal
Lloret de Mar	Girona	38,373	13,989	36.46	Russia, India, and Morocco
Sant Pere Pescador	Girona	2,042	736	36.04	Morocco, Romania, and Gambia
Ullà	Girona	1,153	395	34.26	Morocco, Gambia, and Colombia
Jonquera, la	Girona	3,290	1,113	33.83	Morocco, Ecuador, and Romania
Salou	Tarragona	27,476	8,983	32.69	Senegal, Russia, and Dominican Republic
Aitona	Lleida	2,591	843	32.54	Morocco, Romania, and Mali

The municipal area of Salt is one of the smallest in the region, with about 6.64 km^2, half of which is not urbanized. It has a population of 31,362 inhabitants, of which 15,516 were born in Catalonia, 3,584 in the rest of Spain, and 12,262 outside of Spain (IDESCAT 2019). This gives a population density of about 4,723 inhabitants/km^2 and around 9,200 inhabitants/km^2 if only the habitable surface is considered. It is double the size of Girona, and Madrid has a population density of about 5,198 inhabitants/km^2. The highest in Spain is l'Hospitalet de Llobregat, with about 20,046 inhabitants/km^2.

In geographical terms, it borders small towns such as Sant Gregori, Taialà, Vilablareix, Fornells de la Selva, and Bescanó, and to the east, with Girona (see Figure 0.1). Distinguishing Girona from Salt at an urban level is a difficult task, only possible thanks to the municipal signs while, apart from the urban continuum, the urban morphology is practically the same on both sides.

However, once in Salt and exploring the urban and social fabric of the town, I discovered how varied it really is. It has a peculiar urban fabric with the neighbourhoods constituting sediments of different historical periods; a harsh socio-spatial segregation; a rich rural-urban patrimony; and an active and vibrant life in the squares, streets, and parks.

If we follow the most current socio-spatial administrative arrangement of Salt we can distinguish the following neighbourhood units: (a) Barri Vell, (b) Veïnat, (c) Pla de Salt, (d) Sector Center, (e) la Maçana, (f) l'Eixample, and (g) Torre Mirona (industrial estate), which are drawn on the following map (Figure 0.2).

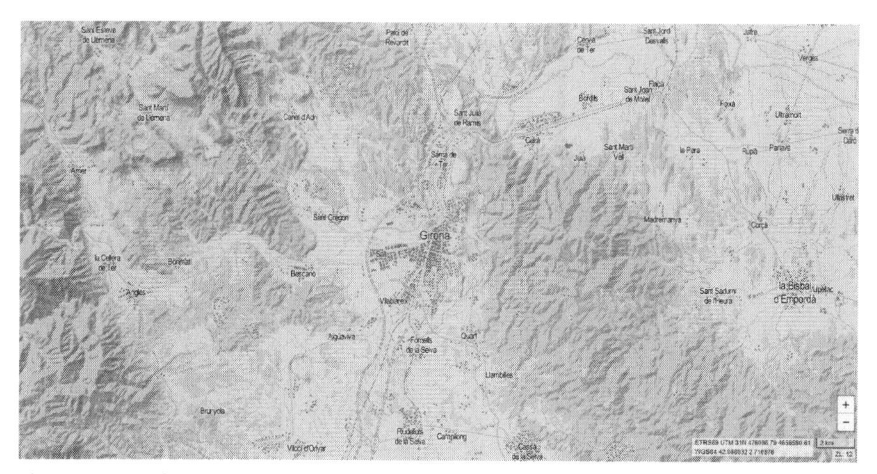

Figure 0.1. The Girona Region. *Source*: The Cartographic and Geological Institute of Catalonia.

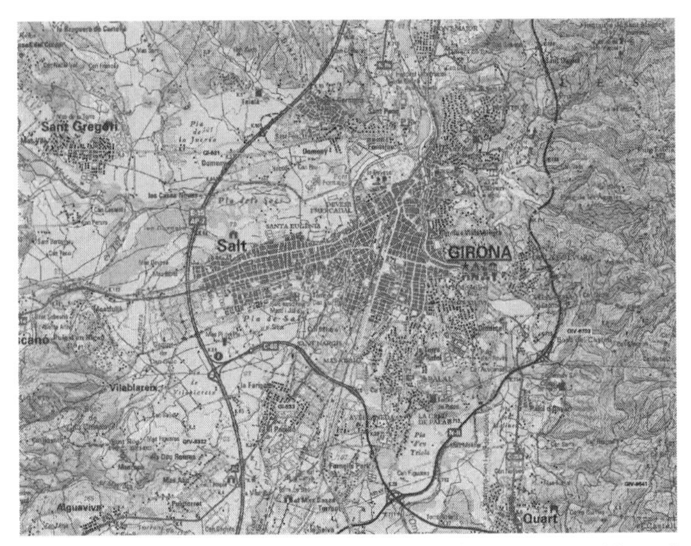

Figure 0.1-2. The Girona Region. *Source*: The Cartographic and Geological Institute of Catalonia.

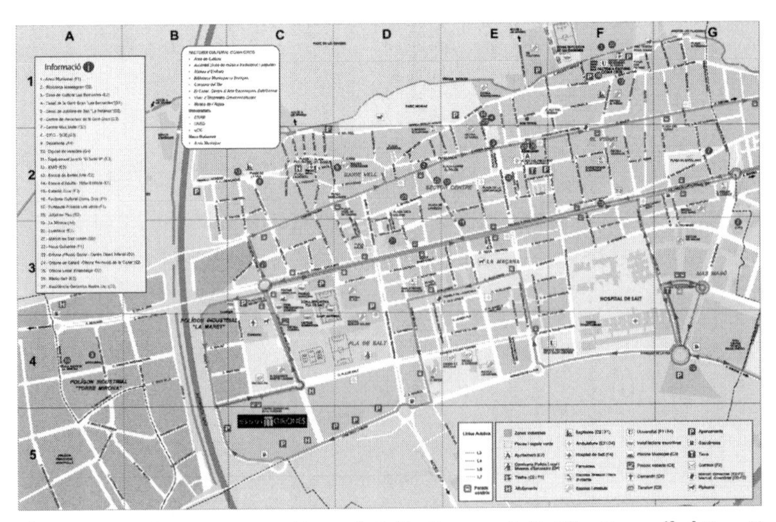

Figure 0.2. Contemporary Map of Salt. *Source*: Salt City Council: https://viusalt.cat/informacio-salt-girona-costa-brava/mapes-planols-de-salt/zagct analisis_territorialcapescarrererplanol_cadcarrerer/

However, these are administrative differentiations which, as Franquesa (2007a) argues in the case of Palma, does not always coincide with the residents' perception. In fact, the official names of units d, e, and f, differ from the names used by the neighbourhood associations, which are (d) Barri Centre, (e) la Massana, and (f) els Escriptors. Furthermore, others could be added, such as the new Mas Masó (previously called Can Masó) and the area of Plaza Catalunya, both located in the south-eastern region. Particularly relevant is Plaza Catalunya, with an important history of territorial stigmatization and neighbourhood struggles (see Figure 0.3).

When analysing the urban transformations that have given rise to the configuration of Salt, it is important to bear several factors in mind. First, the geographical proximity to Girona; second, its location beside the river Ter;

Figure 0.3. Buildings according to the decade of construction. *Source*: www.foro-ciudad.com

third, the continuous arrival of the labour force for the industry, agriculture, and the service sector in the region; and, finally, the land ownership regime. To comprehend the inherent urban transformations in the town, it is vital to bear in mind that the local socio-spatial organization essentially responds to the productive and reproductive needs of the political-economic system, which is why some authors speak of a 'geography of capitalism' (Franquesa 2007b; Harvey 2001)especially in the field of urban planning. Combining theoretical discussion with the presentation of a case study of the old centre of Palma (Majorca. The underlying premise of this idea is that space is the continuous production of social processes (Lefebvre 1991), which means that space is, in the end, a social construction (Harvey 1996). It follows that capitalism, as a mode of production, seeks to ensure a particular space (i.e., socio-spatial organization) that is adapted to its (re)productive needs.

In this case, given the cumulative and inherent logics of capitalism, space in its abstract form needs to be both a means of production and a product. However, this does not imply a homogeneous or complete process. On the one hand, there are initial configurations of each area, geographical-historical specificities, and on the other, conflicts of interest between different modes of production and the different classes and social groups involved. Nevertheless, continuous and previous domination and immobilization of space are required to achieve and perpetuate this end. That is, space must be conceived in abstract terms (contrary to its daily and social use and production), something that is achieved through the employment and display of a variety of urban planning technologies. Therefore, to understand the current socio-spatial configuration of Salt, we must adhere to a set of processes linked to geographic-historical development, among which I will highlight: (1) migratory movements, (2) urban planning, (3) the labour market, and (4) the real estate market.

This short historical review will also reveal how other factors play a part in these processes. In fact, these processes are not unidirectional nor homogeneous, but rather the result of several sometimes conflictual decision-making processes, usually based on political and economic interests. We will see that the ordering and production of space not only follows a cumulative logic but that it also intervenes specific trends of social thought or movements such as those of 'social hygiene' and 'social mixing'.

THE FIRST PERIOD

Three factors are essential to understand the subsequent historical-geographical development from the pre-industrial era. In the first instance, the favourable location right next to the Ter River, and, above all, the technological development that irrigation put into practice through the creation of the Rec Monar (built in the 10th century) undoubtedly represented the base on which the textile factories of the area were developed. Second, the distribution of land tenure. Until the mid-19th century, as a rural town, Salt had an extensive agricultural area scattered throughout medium-sized properties. A total of 70 percent of the land was divided among five families. Among these was the family of the future Marqués de Camps, who owned seven farmhouses in the area and 40 percent of the total land, and the Cigarró family, still visible in some names of places in the town, such as l'Era de Cal Cigarró. The rest of the land (30 percent) was distributed in small properties (75 percent of which did not even exceed 0.005 hectares), mainly destined for a subsistence economy (Boades i Raset 1988). Third, colonialism, both colonial exploitation and colonial and the slave trade, meant a growth of capital in the hands of the feudal classes, which later made possible a considerable investment of capital in the land and the means of production necessary for industrialization (Williams 1944). Additionally, the trade in the Iberian Peninsula made the necessary sale and consumption possible (Sánchez 2010).

It was not until the middle of the 19th century that the urban structure changed radically. The industrialization of Salt was undoubtedly an essential axis for the regions of Girona until the point that, according to some historians, it formed its most important industrial centre (Alberch and Portella 1978). Taking advantage of the hydraulic resources of the Monar canal, several textile factories were founded in the last period of the colonial era. In total, there were three, although during the years 1910–1923 Joan Comas i Cros became the owner of all of them—hence the name of the factory complex of today: Coma-cros.

The arrival of workers attracted by the industrial activity, moving in from the Girona region, in particular, Banyoles (in fact, the first businessman to install a factory in Salt, Pere Ramió, moved his yarn factory from Banyoles to Salt), motivated the construction of new houses in the vicinity of the factories and separated from the Vila de Salt (an old settlement broadly coinciding with what is currently Barri Vell). These new constructions constituted the urban base of the neighbourhood, which is known today as Veïnat (back then, also known as Raval de Sant Antoni), thus starting a tradition of socio-spatial segregation of the town. Veïnat was then the working-class neighbourhood for the newly arrived. According to historical estimates, there were about 800 workers out of 2,000 inhabitants by the end of the 19th century (Bover i Pagespetit 2003). Although Salt (now Barri Vell) was the area where the original *Saltencs* (the demonym of people from Salt) lived, including both farmers and the agrarian and industrial bourgeoisie, this segregation was still clearly visible in the 1956 map drawn just after the inauguration of Les Cases Barates. Compare this with the other map from 1990, where the urban continuum still present today, is evident (see Figure 0.4).

Figure 0.4. aereal view of Salt 1956. *Source*: The Cartographic and Geological Institute of Catalonia.

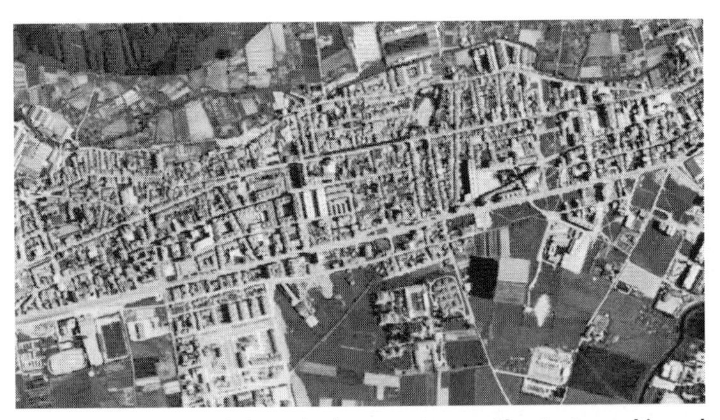

Figure 0.4-2. Aereal view of salt 1990. *Source*: The Cartographic and Geological Institute of Catalonia.

During this time of industrial growth, the population of Salt saw the first important and transformative increase, going from around 362 people in 1842 to 1,316 in 1857. At first glance, this may seem an insignificant number, but according to contemporary historians, it caused a substantial change in the social life of the town (Alberch and Portella 1978; Boades i Raset 1988; Clara 1977; Nadal i Farreras 1978). From 1900 onwards, the population grew continuously by about 1,000 inhabitants per decade, reaching 5,196 inhabitants in 1930. At that time, Salt was already defining itself as the working-class town for the region whose vast majority (80%) worked in Girona. Many of these first immigrants came from other parts of Catalonia, although some also came from other parts of the Spanish State, especially the Valencian community.

THE SECOND PERIOD

Due to both the Civil War and the Great Depression, during the 1930–1940s, Salt did not experience any significant change in the population, and it was not until the post-war period that the town entered the second period of migratory movements and structural transformations of the town. This era was marked by the socio-economic effects of the Civil War: Some regions of Spain were having supply problems, whereas others would prosper at an industrial level, following the Stabilization Plan of 1959 (Conversi 1999). In some areas, mainly Madrid, Catalonia, and the Basque Country, the industrial basis, founded in the colonial era, was already in place, and more labour force was needed in this new stage of reconstruction. These two phenomena generated a socio-spatial and human reconfiguration at the State level with emigrations from the countryside and more desolate areas of Spain to the emerging industrial and tourist areas, such as Catalonia and the Basque Country. A development that, in Salt, being as it was the industrial centre of the area, meant a new socio-spatial configuration with the arrival of migrants, mainly from Andalusia and the interior Girona regions. This translated into a spectacular increase in inhabitants: from 5,956 in 1950 to 7,077 in 1960, reaching 11,467 in 1970. Of these, only 25% were born in Salt. Half of them were born in the Girona region and province, and more than 20% were born in the rest of Spain, of which more than half were Andalusian (Alberch and Portella 1978, 391).

These new inhabitants settled mainly in Veïnat and Barri Centre, the working-class neighbourhoods of the town. This marked a significant change for Salt because it intensified its position as a place of residence for workers in the Girona region. Urban planning in the area was initiated to relocate populations who had previously been dwelling in self-built housing, such as the *Barraques de Montjuïc*, and some of these went to live in *Les Cases Barates*, built in 1956 on the outskirts of the municipality of Salt (Cervera, Ventura, and Montsalve 2001). Simply put, the land was cheaper in Salt and the outer areas surrounding Girona, and so in similar ways to other European metropolises, a 'red belt' around Girona emerged: *Font de la Pólvora*,

Pontmajor, *Santa Eugènia*, *Sant Narcís*, and *Can Gibert i Plà*. A strategy for creating a 'greater Girona' was promoted through progressive expansion of the municipal area, thus annexing the neighbouring towns. Moreover, although Salt was not annexed until 1974, the incorporation was initiated in 1963, and both Salt and Sarrià de Ter were listed in the General Urban Development Plan of 1955 as areas of influence—'true suburbs of the capital'. According to the plan, these territories were to become places of industry and residency for the working classes of the region (Comisión Superior de Ordenación Urbana de la Provincia de Gerona 1956).

Despite the proposed planning, the actual urban growth and development took place with little or no control. In the case of Salt, this meant highly rapid growth with wide-ranging heterogeneous urban planning and tall buildings. Little by little, what is known today as Barri Centre (see figures 0.2 and 1.1) was developed. However, many of the homes were subsidized by the Spanish Ministry of Housing, such as *Grup Verge María*, *Grup Sant Jaume*, and *Grup Sagrada Família*, to name just a few. Barri Centre became an internal periphery within the periphery of Girona, Salt, in a space relegated to the residence and recreation of the home-owning working classes. A historic process driven by Francoism promoted ownership of flats instead of renting, which had prevailed until then (Palomera 2014). A shift in the culture helped to create working-class neighbourhoods and, later, through the sale of properties due to the 'real estate boom', migrant working-class neighbourhoods (Lundsteen, Martínez Veiga, and Palomera 2014).

The processes of urban transformation and migratory movements continued their course in the following decade when a certain generalized stigmatization and deprivation took root. The arrival of these migrants had not gone unnoticed, and as mentioned elsewhere (Aramburu 2002; López Sánchez 1986; Fernández González et al. 2009), the new populations were often held in suspicion. When discussing this, the media often emphasized the difficulties in adapting or assimilating these migrants and their children (Maluquer Sostres 1963). Starting in the 1970s, a social problem was formulated that would later constitute the first socio-political concern for immigration in relation to the social and urban crisis of the 1980s (La Farga 1981b, 9). In the case of Salt, one conclusion drawn by Alberch and Portella (1978, 393) was rather exemplary. There is a 'progressive denaturalization and depersonalization of Salt, due to the continuous foreign immigration and the current scarce capacity to assimilate.'

As is well known, the economic crisis of the 1970s brought with it significant cultural and economic inequalities and, with them, marginality and associated social problems, such as drug addiction due to heroin, which had a huge effect on marginalized and poorly structured neighbourhoods. This was also the case in Salt, as ex-mayor Iolanda Pineda recalls:[10]

We have always had some problems in Salt; there were problems in the 80s, late 80s and 90s with drugs and drug addiction. Some people from my generation ended up with some serious issues, I mean, it wasn't exactly peace and glory back then.

The growing unemployment and the lack of prospects affected young people, especially from the most vulnerable and precarious social strata, who would often resort to the informal economy to subsist or simply entertain themselves. It was then, in the midst of Transition, that the discourse on 'citizen insecurity' and 'peripheral neighbourhoods' emerged (Álvarez-Uría and Varela 1989; Zuloaga 2014; Hurtado Martínez 1999). As a result of the systemic crisis, tensions rose among the inhabitants, and institutional violence became daily (see, e.g., El Punt, Redacció 1986; Diari de Girona 1986a, 1986b, 1987). And so, in the Girona region, territorial stigmatization was constituted by some of the residents in the town and in the surrounding areas too.

In Salt, the planning of the 'great Girona' continued beyond its independence from the municipality of Girona (1983). This was due to the failed attempt to create a General Urban Development Plan for Salt (17-PG1971) to end what was perceived as uncontrolled, speculative urban planning and that had only focused on the needs of Girona, which left the previous plan (17-PG1955) in effect. And it was not until 1987 that the first General Urban Development Plan of Salt was finally agreed upon. The marked objectives were (1) to end the urban dependency of Girona, (2) to homogenize the areas, (3) attain another type of house and heterogenize the urban construction of Salt overall, and (4) attract young people and offer attractive housing for the 'children of Salt' (PGOU-1987). As a result, a new expansion of Salt was planned, this time towards the south with the creation of La Massana. According to Albert (a 40-year-old resident of Barri Vell originally from Salt), this opened a new horizon of progress and prosperity:

It was a time when, I don't kid you, my parents, who started growing up and out of misery, to buy a house, in three years, they already had a house. And they worked in a textile factory, where half of this neighbourhood worked, people could suddenly prosper economically.

At this time, in the mid-1990s, the material conditions for the real estate bubble of the 21st century were established due to both the liberalization of the land and the new migratory movements. Undoubtedly, the fact that many of the flats and houses in Barri Centre were VPOs (subsidized housing) had also been of great importance. Throughout the years, many old residents could purchase homes and become owners. A revaluation of properties occurred after the incorporation into the European Community and the introduction of the euro. This, together with the real estate bubble, enabled the socio-urban rise of homeowners. In the words of Ramon Artal, a municipal planner from 1985 to 2011, 65 years old, and resident in Barri Vell:

> In general, all the public housing in Spain has followed a similar pattern. At some point, the State or the Provincial Council or the Town Council or whoever was the owner at that time has rescinded the contract and put them up for sale to its inhabitants in very favourable conditions. One thing is Official Protection, and another is property. In Spain, a real estate developer could make a private housing block under Official Protection if I applied for it. He would then receive official aid to do it, and those homes would be officially protected for 30 years or 35 years. What does this mean? The developer has a few years during which he cannot resell it, and if he rents it, he has to rent it at a limited price. Moreover, once he can sell it, after some years, it's always at a limited price, until these 35 years have passed. Another thing is Houses of Public Promotion, such as the Cases Barates or Grup Verge Maria, property of the Provincial Patronage, or the flats in front of the town council originally from the Obra Sindical del Hogar [a Spanish Public organism created under the Franco Regime just after the Civil War to offer cheap housing]. These properties have been passed from one administration to another as the political powers are passed from one administration to another. However, in the end, all the administrations have adopted the same policy, and at a given time, there is a public initiative to get rid of these properties and put them for sale to their inhabitants.

THE THIRD PERIOD

In the 21st century, the urbanization of the town would continue. At the same time, concerns were expressed regarding the degradation of Barri Centre. Thus, in 2000–2010, a third period of significant impact occurred. Spain had not become a country of immigration, that is, with a positive migratory balance until the early 1990s (Ortuño Aix 2006). Although immigration of people from other countries had already started in the 1970s, it had not been numerically significant until then. However, migration did exist, and in Salt, I met several people from Africa who had lived in Spain for more than 20 years. In contrast, many Spaniards I met had not lived there for more than a decade. Nonetheless, the former would often immediately be identified as foreigners, and the latter would quickly be considered *saltencs*, a phenomenon that I will further deal with in chapter 2 and that has to do with ethnocultural logics of belonging, imagined or symbolic communities, and issues of formal (legal) and informal citizenship.

In the 1990s, a new era in the history of migratory movements commenced leading to impetuous growth in the Spanish economy. It was driven partially by an increase in the demand for the labour force, primarily due to the boom in the construction sector and productive changes in agriculture (Martínez Veiga 2001). However, most political-economic factors in the countries of origin also facilitated the mass departure of people, especially young people, who would leave to improve their social and economic situations. For instance, much of the Senegalese people who have settled in Catalonia are originally from the Kolda region of Lower Casamance, a region with a high rural population rate (85%) and an economy based on agriculture and cattle. This is a poor area compared with other regions of Senegal, somewhat marginalized within the economic-political geography of this country and with a young population, with more than half of them being younger than 20 years of age (Solé Arraràs 2014).

The arrival of people, mainly from Africa and later Latin America and Asia, caused a significant increase in foreign nationals. From around 350,000 in 1991, the numbers rose to about 2,700,000 in 2003, and 5,663,525 in 2010 (National Institute of Statistics [INE] and EUROSTAT). In Catalonia, the corresponding numbers went from about 60,800 (1%) in 1991 to 124,550 (2%) in 1997 and reached 1,198,500 in 2010, of which 237,007 were of Moroccan nationality and the most important national community in the autonomous region (IDESCAT). In Salt, this translated to a rise in the population from 20,000 to 30,000 in 2000–2010 (see figure 0.5). In general, this was due to a significant increase in foreign-national residents, originally from Africa (Morocco, The Gambia, Mali, and Senegal) and South America (Honduras in particular), an inward migration that coincided with an outward emigration of Spanish nationals, especially after 2004.

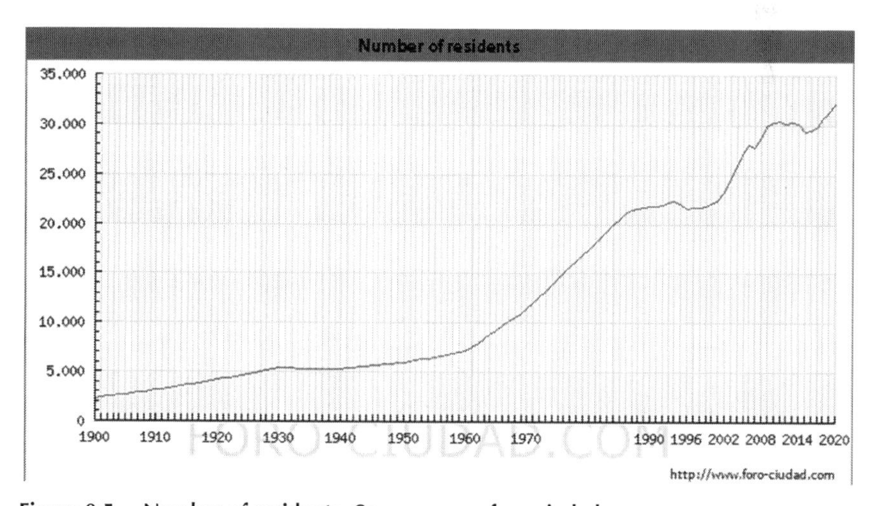

Figure 0.5. Number of residents. *Source*: www.foro-ciudad.com

Though it may be true that many newcomers are from outside of Spain, it is often ignored that many other residents arrived from other parts of Catalonia, Spain, or other European countries. In 2008 alone, 1,772 people moved to Salt, of which 771 were from the same region, 416 from the province, 321 from Catalonia, and 264 from Spain (figure 0.6). In comparison, during the same year, 2,133 people emigrated (954, 456, 330, 393, respectively); 1,537 people came from abroad: 53 from the EU, 58 from Europe, 754 from Africa, 312 from America, 88 from Asia; and 272 were not recorded (IDESCAT 2009). These movements often go unnoticed, or their influence on the social fabric is simply disdained. However, these persons are ethnoculturally heterogeneous, and although they supposedly bring positive changes to the town, in chapter 5, I will show how as agents of gentrification, they play an essential role in many of the changes in the urban fabric, often indirectly, which do not necessarily benefit most inhabitants.

However, there is a statistical problem here. When we look at the figures of the resident populations in the neighbourhood, we discover that Alim, who has lived in Salt for 12 years, is considered a foreigner because he has Moroccan nationality. On the contrary, Francesc, despite having recently arrived and originally being from Mataró, is considered a 'natural' of the town because he is Spanish when in cultural terms, he is far more foreign to the town than Alim. However, if we study the municipal register, this methodological na-

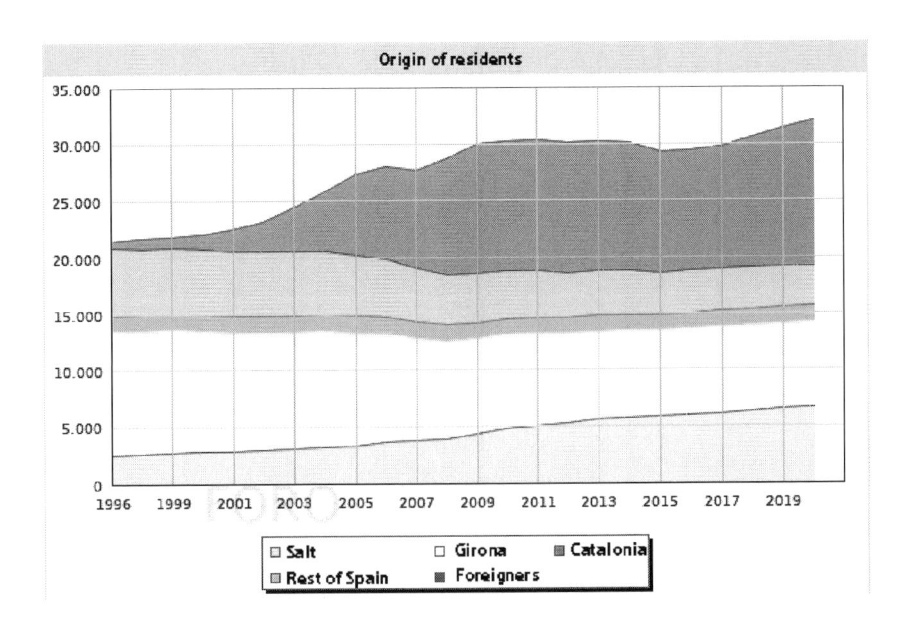

Figure 0.6. Origin of residents. ***Source*****: www.foro-ciudad.com**

tionalist image is complicated because it shows what region and town each new inhabitant comes from. Thus, we can observe how many of the so-called newly arrived foreign nationals do not come directly from the country where they were born. Furthermore, we see that recently, many people have arrived from other parts of Catalonia or Spain. However, two factors make these trends invisible: people without residence permits do not register due to fear of being discovered, and the period of residence is not reflected in the census.

The increase in foreign nationals can be explained thus. First, the real estate market made housing in Salt much cheaper than elsewhere in the Girona area, partly due to the stigmatizing image that has been projected onto Salt. Second, Salt offered good living conditions and a particular centrality regarding the region's important centres of work and leisure. There was also high demand for labour in the region back then. The men mostly found work in the construction or industrial sector, especially the meat industry, and many women would work as domestic workers in the informal sector and the service industries, such as the hotels.

This confluence of social and economic factors—migrations and changes in the real estate and labour markets—would enable the completion of La Massana, whereas the social fabric and the socio-human structure of the Barri Centre would transform into a 'ghetto'. The physical degradation of the neighbourhood continued, and because of the new economic crisis, a social deprivation followed in which many inhabitants lost their jobs, especially those who worked in the construction sector. This situation mainly affected the young and foreign nationals, with unemployment rates higher than 50%. Moreover, the planned construction plummeted, leaving deserted areas such as Mas Masó (see figure 0.7).

At the same time, the rehabilitation of Barri Vell would take place. In the 1990s, part of the Barri Vell had started to mobilize. It is a historically significant neighbourhood, especially in commercial terms. The old urban fabric, however, was undergoing a process of degradation. Against this backdrop, the neighbourhood association AVV Barri Vell was born. Their main aim was to process the complaints in the neighbourhood. However, this was not until early 2003 when the shy mobilizations paid off with the implementation of a Special Plan for Internal Reform (PERI of Barri Vell 2002/5799). The main objective of this was to make the neighbourhood a more attractive area, and a residential and quiet neighbourhood: 'The reduction of noise and easy pedestrian access, will maintain the condition of a mainly residential area, and confirm its peaceful character as a one of its main attractiveness for its revitalization' (PERI de Barri Vell 2002/5799, 8). Restoration and maintenance of 'the cultural-historical heritage' were proposed to attain this. To achieve this, reform and rehabilitation of the space were split into two: the public

Figure 0.7. The Urban Desolation Anno 2012. *Source*: Martin Lundsteen

space, where the aim was to promote green spaces and viability, and the private space, protecting the elements included in the Plan for the Protection of Patrimony. In the words of ex-architect Ramon Artal:

> It basically has two objectives: one, to better specify the protection of the diffuse architectural patrimony, i.e. Salt does not have an architectural patrimony, important in punctual buildings: it does not have Gothic cathedrals, it doesn't have any Sagrada Familias, nor any important works. However, what it does have, specifically the Barri Vell and Veïnat, some of the streets here, have an urban atmosphere caused by a particular shape of the houses and the streets, which is of a certain quality, but which is diffuse, you do not see it in anything concrete. And, on the other hand, some streets were quite degraded, where specific action was recommended, to fix them, and fix the narrow streets with traffic and therefore very narrow sidewalks. So, the PERI concretized the protection of the buildings, and it defines how the streets must be when they are re-urbanized, not a lot more. It is certainly not an instrument designed to encourage commercial reimplantation.

So, with it, a regeneration and consequent revitalization of Barri Vell was proposed to homogenize the neighbourhood while maintaining the low height of the buildings. Although PERI may have helped rehabilitate the urban space, it also promoted a gentrification process still underway today, which has undoubtedly had a significant effect on the neighbourhood. This phenomenon promoted the settlement of a young population with high purchasing power and cultural capital. As Ramon Artal says, before 'it was a bit abandoned, and now, in addition to having seen a repopulation, it has also been but rejuvenated. Now I see young people buy bread or go to his house, while before it was only old people or people who went to Caritas.' Even today, the housing prices in Barri Vell are considerably higher compared to other parts of the town.

On the other hand, for the rest of the town, part of which was also still in the process of degradation, the local government proposed to carry out urban development actions to reverse a supposed situation of socio-urban degradation through projects financed by the regional and state institutions, such as the so-called *Llei de Barris*, primarily focused on the Barri Centre.

Some years later, in 2010, a macro-project for urban transformation was approved for Salt. The project, signed by the architects Ricard Pié and Josep Maria Vilanova, was presented with all the other municipal groups in the town council and envisaged a radical change. This was mainly in the urban fabric of Barri Centre, over a period of 12 years and with an expected global cost of 200 MEUR (Ramon Mòdol 2010). However, the opposition of some neighbours, the implementation of austerity, and the opacity surrounding the project brought it to a halt. We will have a much closer look at the urban developments in chapter 5.

Likewise, here we have seen how vital geographical and historical transformations have shaped Salt to be the way we see it now. It has explained the underlying processes of urban planning, the functioning of the real estate sector within the market economy, and human mobility. We have seen how migration patterns can be explained through housing development and transformations in the real estate markets, closely linked to several important urban planning projects in Salt during the late 1990s and the beginning of the 21st century. In chapter 1, I will present the town in ethnographic terms, the results of these historical-geographical changes as they appear to the human eye. First, I will explain how I have produced the data on which the descriptions and the following analysis are based.

RESEARCH METHODS

The ethnographic fieldwork is a complex process that includes a positioning in the field (consciously or not) and the employment and selection of a whole array of methods, among which the interview and participant observation are the most famous, a process that requires a certain savoir-faire (Olivier de Sardan 1995). Due to space limits, here I will limit myself to describing the different methods employed (see Lundsteen 2015, 36–55, for any further detail).

Field Work

The more abstract methodological considerations mentioned led to detailed and prolonged fieldwork in situ consisting of more than a year spent living in three different locations. The primary method used to record all this information was note-taking and diary making. The result is seven diaries with rich information on issues such as organized crime, informal street-level economy, relations and groupings based on ethnicity, race, or religion, the local political and economic processes, the different discourses employed, and visions of the situation in the town, ways of perceiving diversity, social movements, and ways to engage with the town, information concerning the ideological and material foundations of the 'new far right', the historical development of the spatial ordering in town, and the everyday spatial dynamics and practices and the different policies and projects implemented. Throughout the book, I will refer to these diary notes and observations. Sometimes these references have been paraphrased; at other times, I quote my diary, explicitly stressing the day (dd/mm/yyyy), the number of the diary, and the page numbers.

Participant Observation

Apart from living in several places in the town, which entailed intensive participant observations across ethnic groups in the intimate space of the homes, I participated in an extensive range of social activities and took part in the daily life of the neighbourhood, going to different cafeterias, shopping locally, and so on. This way, I familiarized myself with the neighbourhood in the double sense of the term. I was able to strike up informal chats with the neighbours, flatmates, and 'local experts'.

Apart from living in the neighbourhood and participating in its activities, from September 2011 to June 2012, I played football every week in the local team *Coma-Cros*, where I met residents from different neighbourhoods. This way, I integrated into a fundamental social organization of the town—a masculine sector—and often, we would spend some time afterwards socializing in a bar or restaurant. I think this way of bonding with other neighbours and cohabitants has been fundamental to a specific kind of belonging, at least in the eyes of some of those whom I would later meet at festivities, in bars, or even randomly on the street. These were ties that would progressively make possible more profound conversations on different aspects of the social life of the town.

In the same vein of thought and action, I decided to participate in the local *castellers* (a unique sport literally translated as 'human castles') called *Els Marrecs*. I had read some articles and seen several performances in other towns and wanted to discover the particular way of socializing that the sport entailed (Erickson 2011). So, when a friend of mine who had been rehearsing with the local team for some months told me that they needed participants to create a new structure for the local festivities, *Festa Major*, I saw my opportunity (figure 0.8). This way, during July–August and up until the Festa Major, I went to several rehearsals, thus trying out the sport and getting to know the team members. I could observe that the large majority were from Girona and other adjoining towns, and only a few from Salt, and that these were mainly from the Barri Vell; in contrast, only 2 out of 100 were Africans, both sub-Saharan. I managed to get close to some of them and felt integrated into the team, particularly in the days of the Festa Major.

Similarly, I started a Catalan course. My main aim was to meet other people, mainly women, whom I would normally have had difficulty meeting in the typical scenarios and to observe the use of ethnocultural markers in the classroom. We were 17 persons, of whom 11 were women, representing a great variety of nationalities: three women from Spain, four (a girl, a

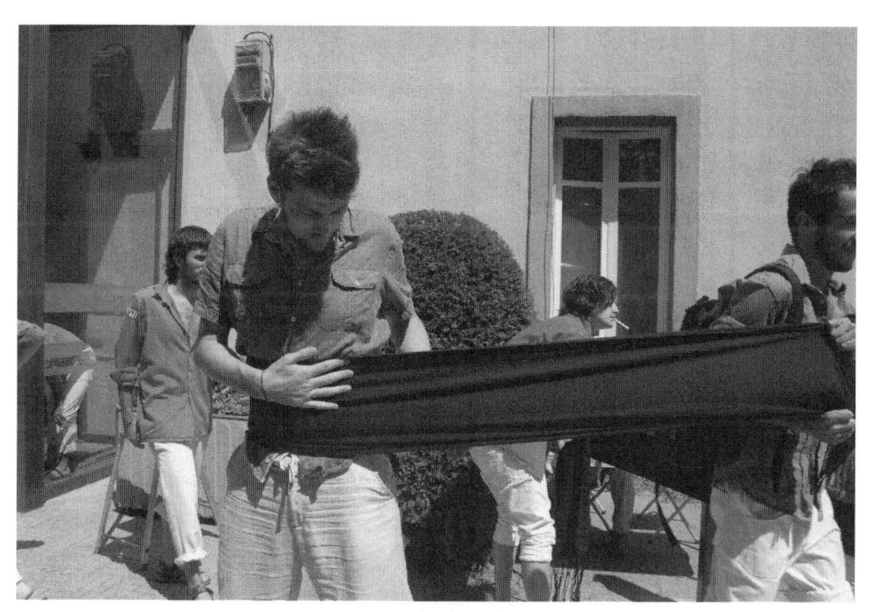

Figure 0.8. Castellers preparing the faixa for action. *Source*: Judit Font.

woman, and two men) from Morocco, three men from Senegal, two (a girl and a woman) from India, a woman from Portugal, another one from Argentina, a girl from Cuba, another one from China, and me. We would meet twice a week for three months, and the classes shaped a space where I could observe the cultural underpinnings of belonging, a theme that I will explore in chapter 2.

During the whole first period of fieldwork, I was a member of a social movement, which facilitated information on local dynamics and history. Many of the members, who had been active in local civil society and sometimes even social workers, would become essential to my way of understanding the social reality of Salt, as well as providing me with a whole network of social relations and contacts that I would be able to explore during the stay. Even in the writing phase, I would often consult different historical events or discuss the interpretations that I was presenting. As a matter of fact, in this sense, I never completely cut off the stream of information.

Interviews

After prior assessment through fieldwork, I got acquainted with the human and geographical-historical context and was thus able to select the most suitable interviewees. In the end, I conducted 52 open-ended and generally loosely structured formal interviews with members of different associations located or working in the town: public officials, police officers, social workers, and inhabitants from the different neighbourhoods.

In particular, I conducted 17 interviews with residents from different migration backgrounds and nationalities (three from South America, three from Morocco, one from Portugal, and 10 from other parts of Spain); two group interviews with presidents of neighbourhood associations of single buildings in the centre (mixed origin); three interviews with representatives of the relevant neighbourhood associations of Barri Vell, Barri Centre, and la Massana; 14 with local associations related to migration; four with representatives of local cultural associations; five with politicians: the former mayor and the former councillor of security (from the Catalan Socialist Party, *Partit dels Socialistes de Catalunya* [PSC]), the former councillor of immigration (from the Republican Left of Catalonia, *Esquerra Republicana de Catalunya* [ERC]), and the councillors of security and community relations/housing (Convergence and Union, *Convergència i Unió* [CiU]); five with practitioners: the head of the local administration in charge of the area of convivencia, a former worker of the self-same administration, the former municipal architect, a worker from the environmental area, and a worker in the *Diputación de Girona* (the county council) in the area of immigration. I conducted seven interviews with social workers from NGOs: two from the *Fundació SER-GI*, two from *Vincle*, two from *Càritas*, and the coordinator of *Jueguem*; and one interview with members of the *PAH-Salt* living in the occupied building.

However, the informants of this research are not limited to these 52 interviews. A large part of these interviews later turned out to be somewhat useless, compared with the information I was able to retrieve through informal conversations with flatmates, bar chats, classes of Catalan, and so on. Often the interviewees would change completely when the interview started, and the exciting part began when I turned off the tape recorder. Similarly, I have had several informal conversations and exchanged emails with a former worker from the *Casal dels Infants* working within the Intercultural Community Intervention Project (ICI) of the bank La Caixa. Any incorrect information in this respect is obviously my fault, and I expect the reader to believe the veracity of these recordings and observations jotted down as soon as possible after the conversations. In this manner, to maintain the sources and not give way to confusion, I shall paraphrase the substance instead of quoting what was said.

In the appendix, I include a section called Dramatis personae, a list and short biographies (depending on the information retrieved) of the different persons I had regular contact with and, thus, often informal conversations. I acknowledge, however, that the list is incomplete regarding all the people with whom I actually often talked.

Secondary Material

I also engaged in archival work. To gather historical information on migration, intergroup relations, and integration patterns, I consulted an extensive range of documents such as newspapers, books on local history, local magazines, and reports from NGOs and the public administration. Most of this secondary material was consulted at either the local library or the local archive or through online newspapers and periodical libraries.

The urban planning documentation has primarily been achieved through the online archive made available by the Departament de Territori i Sostenibilitat (Territorial and Sustainability Department) http://ptop.gencat.cat/rpucportal/inici/es/.

Similarly, a large batch of statistical information and data, the municipal population census, the basis on which I have been able to compose the maps, was made available to me through the local town council. I sincerely thank the staff for their kindness in carrying out this work. Other statistical information, especially that regarding populations, unemployment rates, and so on, has been retrieved from the web pages of the National Statistical Institute of Spain (INE: www.ine.es), the Statistical Institute of Catalonia (IDESCAT: www.idescat.cat), and the European Statistical System (EUROSTAT: http://ec.europa.eu/eurostat), or from other reports on Salt or similar carried out by Càritas, Workers' Commissions (CCOO), the Local Administration (*Projecte Barrido*), Institute of Government and Public Policy (IGOP), and so on. Likewise, the local police department kindly sent me all their annual reports, from which especially the statistics on crime have been retrieved. All the consulted reports and web pages are to be found separately listed in the reference section.

SYNOPSIS OF CHAPTERS

Chapter 1 examines the social setting of Salt, describing both the physical and the social spaces of the town, as well as the social and spatial polarization. It introduces the context of the town, focusing both on the visual setting and the social structures. We see how varied spaces converge, with a vast social diversity in both ethnocultural and socio-economic terms, all of which is epitomized in the spatial configurations of the different neighbourhoods.

The social boundaries and uses of ethnocultural and racial categories are negotiated every day. Although this social differentiation and the social categories might be locally situated, they are also locally-globally constituted by the feeding global factors and discourses and grounding it specifically in local social classifications. Chapter 2 analyses these local-global rationales and power relations of belonging, and it describes the spatial practices and the negotiation of the social groups and categorizations concerning race, ethnicity, and class. We see how because some of the precarious people living in the town cannot pay the community bills, they sometimes use alternative methods of accessing primary resources—all in all, a degraded situation that often generates conflicts in the local neighbourhood communities, mainly but not exclusively, between natives and migrants and foreigners.

In these social spaces, different experiences of conflicts and convivencia take place. Experiences that encourage the emergence of locally situated discourses about space. In chapter 3, we see how concerning the uses of the urban space, many native residents link recent social changes to this high influx of new migrants, speaking of a cultural loss, transgression of civic norms, and a sense of insecurity. We see how different social spaces emerge and enter into conflict. The arrival of new groups of people brings about new social realities. The elder native population tend to feel in the minority, with an unsustainably high percentage of immigrants undermining the social cohesion (cultural order), and hence, problems of coexistence (cultural) arise.

However, in analysing the background of these social conflicts, we see how, rather than being the result of an intensification of cultural diversity, they are the product of growing insecurity, which is in turn the product of the social consequences of the economic crisis.

Another important theme is the management of conflicts and society in general. In recent decades, there seems to have been a shift and convergence in the political interpretations and ways of treating what is perceived as a new phenomenon, migrants from outside the EU. Chapter 4 analyses the different kinds of policies the town has implemented over the last decade to deal with what is increasingly seen as a problem: migration from the Global South. A generalized tendency is observed on the part of the public administration, which perceives that these peoples provoke new demands originating directly from their cultural difference (and not their working-class status). Such demands have, until recently, been handled through social services and only with a minimum of differentiation. This way of managing the 'new social question' has changed in recent years, and the assignment and, with it, the responsibility is increasingly relegated to the third sector, who address their interventions towards selected groups of the population instead of a universal service—a management of inequalities with culture at its core, which I have thus named policies of culture. This new management of inequalities goes together with repressive policies, seemingly universal but profoundly discriminatory, which I call policies of quieting, that is, policies that are implemented to control the increasingly dispossessed and despairing populations, perceived as disturbing and potentially dangerous. At the same time, these policies create calm, thus allaying the growing insecurity and uncertainty (both social and labour related), the social effects of the ongoing economic-political restructuring.

In terms of urban policies, we see on the one hand how certain hygienic discourses of overcrowding of people (urban overcrowding) and, specifically, migrants (social-mix theory) are perceived as bad conditions for the convivencia. On the other, we see how the previous problem, in connection with the social problems in town, is used as a platform to drive gentrification strategies and embellishment campaigns (sometimes directly connected) on the part of a section of the residents (mainly the local-regional bourgeoisie), under the pretext of showing another image of Salt—that of a cultural (high-class) town—and how this tendency is eradicating the working-class history and culture of Salt. Chapter 5 thus brings forth an analysis of these urban policies to scrutinize the relations among the socio-urban developments, the urban planning, the economic-political projects inherent, and the policies mentioned above. It shows how these processes form part of local attempts to change the economy towards a service sector. There is clear support for the arts and culture and, with it, the expectation of future gentrification of the town—seeds that we see flowering in the Barri Vell, where an increasing number of young, alternative and middle-class people from Girona and Barcelona are settling. They move into old houses that they renovate or help to renovate. In this way, they live out a neo-rural fantasy without losing their urban roots, and more importantly, they preserve and reinvigorate a hereditary and historic-cultural capital invested in these buildings and the neighbourhood at large, achieved through the work and consumption that they invest in them. As such, they seem to incarnate and constitute the avant-garde of the desired gentrification, who contribute an added value to the neighbourhood and houses through the symbolic value that they incarnate, hence changing the human composition of the neighbourhood (or simply repossessing it) and in this way creating a surplus value that will be earned when the houses are sold as has happened so often in other studied cases of gentrification in the larger cities.

Finally, this leads to chapter 6, a closing reflection on whether we are seeing the burgeoning of a new kind of management of the poor and the Other in contemporary society and what role the third sector and the State play in this. This includes an analysis and discussion of the political-economic foundation of the State and its management of the poor and 'surplus' populations. We see how although social conflicts are varied in their nature and origin, yet in the hegemonic interpretations in today's societies of the Global North, they are represented as instances of a global cultural conflict and clash. This interpretation is based on the sole factor of the cultural difference, thus leaving out questions of power inequalities, differentiation concerning access to resources, and the territories and convivencias originating from them. The State and the third sector play an essential role in this, assisting in the (re)production of the conditions that favour exploitation and obstruct a radical social mobilization through repressive policing and social reform policies mainly focused on sociocultural recognition and ignoring the redistribution. In a similar line of argument, I hold that the horizontal grassroots movements and new left-wing parties tend to obviate existing inequalities based on race and ethnicity and gender and, by doing this, are bound to reproduce them, thus leaving the terrain for right-wing lectures but, above all, hindering a radical social change favouring a more egalitarian society.

INTRODUCTION NOTES

1. And Bacchi continues: 'A problematization is always "a kind of creation"', Foucault tells us, but "a creation in the sense that, given a certain situation, you cannot infer that this kind of problematization will follow" (Foucault, 1985a). There is

nothing inevitable about it. That is, there are always exigencies that affect how developments take place, putting emphasis on the politics, the contestation, the strategic relations involved in those developments. By studying problematizations therefore it is possible *to demonstrate how things which appear most evident are in fact fragile and that they rest upon particular circumstances, and are often attributable to historical conjunctures which have nothing necessary or definitive about them* (Foucault in Mort & Peters, 2005: p. 19).' (Bacchi 2012, 2)

2. All translations are the authors.

3. *Plataforma per Catalunya* [Platform for Catalonia] is an extreme right-wing party like Front Nationale in France.

4. *Movimiento Social Republicano* [Social Republican Movement] is a Spanish neo-Nazi party.

5. *Partido Popular* [Popular Party] is the biggest right-wing party in Spain of liberal-conservative orientation.

6. *Gent per Salt* [People for Salt] is a local coalition with supposedly ideologically neutral but with clear right-wing stands on migration.

7. I here rely on a total of 41 articles related to Ca n'Anglada from the period, a survey that was complemented by Moreras's analysis (2004).

8. The first part of the citation is the actual words of the city councillor, the second part is the journalist's own words.

9. I follow the interpretations of Martínez Veiga (2001) and Zino Torraza (2006).

10. The public figures always appear with their real names, whereas the rest of the people interviewed or who appear throughout the ethnography carry fictitious names.

Chapter One

The Setting: Salt in the 21st Century

> Salt City like Brooklyn, in the streets you see a lot of *bling-bling*, in the square a lot of *bla-bla*.
>
> —Rams and Lay, hip-hoppers from Salt

I reckon that my first impressions of Salt would likely not differ radically from any other person: a semi-rural town with a high proportion of ethnic minorities and cultural diversity. It is undoubtedly paradigmatic of the geographical developments that Catalonia experienced since 2000 concerning migratory movements and, to a certain degree, later migratory movements towards small towns (Goebel 2011; Berg and Sigona 2013; Rogaly and Qureshi 2013). Before even visiting the town, many people in Spain have a clear idea of what to expect.

This collective imagining has been forged over the last decade primarily through the media, something we will look into in the following chapters. Now the initial reason I chose to do fieldwork in Salt was because of what I had read and seen in the media, such as in the documentary made by TV3: *Salt. An essay in* convivencia. Due to the media representation and what other people had told me, I expected to find a deteriorated social space like any French *banlieue* of Paris. So, I was pretty surprised to discover a small town with lively bars and sociable streets. Indeed, some of the buildings were old and tall, but the town consisted mainly of small buildings and houses, and the streets were wide and spacious.

Moreover, contrary to the typical descriptions of the American ghetto and the French banlieues (Wacquant 2008a), in Salt, one finds a lot of commercial activity and State institutions that are present and visible and not only limited to the schools and the police. However, these superficial observations hide a reality much more complex than what one sees at first glance. The social interactions and the scene within which they take place, and the imaginary that explains this in sociocultural terms are part of a complex web of local-global processes that are both constituted and constitutes the social world in which we live. Describing this in clear theoretical terms would constitute an entirely different book, and any attempt here would be simplified. Instead, I invite the reader to discover how these different layers and their interconnected and dynamic nature are always present throughout the book. In this sense, this chapter is intended to be as naturalistic and realistic as possible (Herzfeld 2018). It introduces the setting necessary to any comprehensive understanding of the theme at stake.

A SNAPSHOT

Salt's Barri Centre is undoubtedly the most densely urban area of the town. Blocks of buildings with more than five floors prevail. The largest is a building known locally as the skyscraper that has 13. The buildings generally have a degraded appearance, blackened by smog, pollution, and dust, with the paint falling off. At the same time, we also find one-storey buildings, new builds, and empty lots (see figures 0.7 and 1.1). The backbone of this neighbourhood is the streets of Ángel Guimerà and Torras i Bages. The neighbourhood is delimited by the streets Major, Santiago Ramón y Cajal and Esteve Vila and the Passeig dels Països Catalans, thus creating a kind of urban islet in the middle of the town (figures 1.1 and 1.1-2).

In this neighbourhood, following the delimitation perceived by the majority of the inhabitants, often referred to as either 'the ghetto' or simply a conflict zone, one finds a great variety of food stores offering products from as far as Latin America and Africa, as well as butchers (including halal), supermarkets (Mercadona, Dia, Suma and Bonpreu), grocery stores, bakeries, and cake shops—a lively local commerce. The area is primarily pedestrian; the traffic is limited mainly to residents and a few visitors.

The many food establishments predominate the urban landscape of the neighbourhood. One finds a great variety of bars and cafes, restaurants (e.g., an Indian-Pakistani and a Moroccan), and many fast-food establishments, especially kebab houses. Other establishments or small businesses found in the area are travel agencies, hardware stores, bazaars, grocery stores, clothing stores, electronic stores, hairdressers, and barbershops (run mainly by Moroccans and, to a lesser extent, Ghanaians). Although one can find a few stores for sale, the small and local businesses are very much alive. This contrasts starkly with other peripheral areas or neighbourhoods such as the French

Figure 1.1. Typical Urban Fabric of Barri Centre. *Source*: Martin Lundsteen.

Figure 1.1-2. Typical Urban Fabric Barri Vell. *Source*: Martin Lundsteen.

banlieues, with which it is often compared and, instead, resembles much more with areas such as Peckham Rye in London (Hall 2015).

On an average day, a visitor would be surprised by the large number of people one meets on the street or in the terraces. In this neighbourhood, the vast majority of the town's inhabitants and visitors gather. It is a leisure area. These daily meetings are concentrated in key points such as squares or areas with benches. For example, in the most emblematic squares (e.g., Llibertat, Guifré i Pelós, Convivència, Colors, Lluís Companys and the squares adjacent to Mercat de Salt and those of Grup Verge Maria), it is customary to see children playing soccer and groups of young people, or older adults gathered on the benches. The youngsters might be smoking cigarettes or joints, flirting out of sight of the adults, or just hanging out. While the elders watch the children play, they discuss current affairs or important news. In this way, these places are momentary spatial-temporal crystallizations of the human flows of inhabitants and people from outside the town. Due to the lack of more formal meeting spaces such as community centres, these spaces are the primary places of sociability, and almost all of them are located in Barri Centre. In these important places of recreation, men mainly drink coffee or beer, play cards, greet passers-by, or even flirt with the girls working the bars. Some simply hang out outside their home, reading the newspapers, watching the world, and reflecting.

Some of the streets are fuller than others. For instance, the central streets of the Barri Centre, Àngel Guimerà and Torras i Bages are usually full of passers-by all year round. One will find groups of children of various ages strolling the streets, often without their parents. They may be on the lookout for ice cream or goodies or on the way to a square to play. Similarly, many people gather on Doctor Ferran Street. Groups of sub-Saharan men gather right outside a Gambian import food store or in front of El Petit Africà (The Small African in Catalan). Strolling the neighbourhood thus often constitutes a social experience that can reproduce relational ties, and through which one accumulates social capital and finds out about a neighbour or the goings-on in a particular building, as the following excerpt from my diary shows:

> When I leave my building, I find myself in one of the town's central streets, the one that everyone knows and everyone curses: Àngel Guimerà. It is full of passers-by. In fact, this street is rather a space of transit than a place to stop up. That is unless you meet someone. Today, and I feel that this is happening to me more and more often now that I live in the middle of everything; the latter is my case. Going towards the bar El Raïm, and after passing the cafe-restaurant Al-Madina, I heard somebody calling from across the street: "Hey, Tintin!". It was Abdul who was walking with a girl and a boy I do not know. We greeted each other, and he introduced me to Diana and Kevin, a Colombian friend of his,

> and her boy. We talked briefly about how we are doing, when I noticed a desire to recognise her being from Colombia and ask her from where exactly. Cali. When I told him that I had not been there but that I had been in Barranquilla and Bogotá, she got surprised and somehow seemed to rejoice at the same time. Apparently, she had only recently arrived in Salt and had difficulties finding a job. She came for her ex-boyfriend, the father of her son. Kevin immediately connected with me, and we played while I was talking to Abdul and Diana. Finally, I would kiss Diana goodbye, and Kevin kissed me on my cheeks too. (02/05/2012, Diary 4, 77)

Besides these public spaces,[1] Barri Centre also has privately owned spaces for public use, such as community squares. They are often open only for a certain period and controlled by the residents. For example, Plaça de la Convivència, where, especially in summer, one will often see a group of older men in front of the access point, either sitting in chairs or standing at the gate. While they take advantage of the breeze and the shade of the building to cool off, they also use this place to control access and ensure that everything is as they want it to be. As one of the community presidents, Josep, says:

> What happened? Well, these fourteen to sixteen-year-old children were coming and . . . but they were not even from here, they came from Santa Eugènia and Sant Narcís. Boys of that age do a little mischief or vandalism every once and again, and some of them were already smoking weed. Of course, we said "no, no, we can't allow that", and that's why we close in the afternoons. And we tell them to try not do not damage or play ball aggressively

There are also several places of worship, including two parishes (in Barri Vell and Veïnat), four places of Muslim worship (two in the Plaça Catalunya area, one in Barri Centre, and another in La Massana), two evangelical places of worship (both in Barri Centre), and a place of worship for the Sikhs (in Barri Centre).

Once it gets dark, the social activities in the neighbourhood change drastically. Especially in summer, people returning from work coincides with others having coffee or beer in one of the bars and cafeterias. Thus, the noise rises in the neighbourhood. At certain times of year in particular areas, the noise intensifies due to the activities of the youth in the squares and streets, often to the point of conflict.

Although life in the neighbourhood is generally quiet, certain events can alter the daily routine. I would sometimes meet a crowd of people watching some extraordinary event, such as when a neighbour fell from a building and had to be rescued by firefighters and taken to the hospital. Such events later become the focus of conversations, and versions of what happened often vary.

Comments on the danger of the neighbourhood or the excessive frequency of such events are common.

There are also weekly or annual events that alter the social order of activities and how people relate. Among the weekly events, the municipal market is held every Wednesday in the Passeig de la Ciutat de Girona and Friday in the Guilleries Street. These events create genuinely diverse spaces in terms of ethnicity, age, and gender—although women, children, the elderly and their caregivers predominate. Secondly, among the annual events, there are local festivities (such as Festa Major, Fira del Cistell, Festa de Sant Antoni, Fira de la Flor i el Planter, Fira Textil del Veïnat) and religious ones (such as Ramadan, Aid al-Adha, the Romería del Rocío, the Cavalcade of the Three Kings, the Carnival).

The distinguishing feature of Salt is its dual rural and urban character. It has many recreational green spaces, some of which are also for agricultural use. For instance, besides the Barri Vell, one will find a park adjacent to the canal Rec Monar and Les Deveses, alongside several hectares of private and public gardens, such as Les Hortes del Mig, Els Comuns, and Les Hortes de les Guixeres. These spaces are all used for recreation and cultivation, an uncommon feature in big cities, at least in those close by. It is common to see inhabitants walking, running, cycling, or picnicking on the weekends and holidays or simply when the town's urban life becomes too much, and one wants a change of scene.

Although public spaces tend to be dominated by children, young people and the elderly, semi-public spaces are dominated mainly by young men and women. Among these, the busiest are the bars, cafes, and shops. There have always been many bars in Salt (La Farga 1981a, 9), but in recent decades, the offerings have been diversified with the settlement of foreign nationals. In these places, men predominate and, depending on the place, either an ethnic group dominates, or it is more of a mixed setting.

For instance, there are what one might classify as 'Spanish' recreational spaces, which bear well-marked cultural symbols, such as the Nou Tertulià (Torras i Bagés St). In these spaces, Spanish-speaking men can often be found sitting, playing cards, and drinking beer, coffee, or cocktails. Another example is El Raïm (Doctor Ferran St), a historic site in the neighbourhood and a prime example of the cultural encounter of Andalusian migrants who settled in the 1960s and 1970s. The blend resulting from this phenomenon can be observed through certain symbols, such as scarves from Atlético de Madrid and the Spanish national team, and references to flamenco music, with everything written in Catalan. Some places are also proudly 'Catalan', such as Can Serrallonga (Major St in front of Plaça Guifré i Pelós). An openly

Catalanist bar that, apart from bearing the name of the famous bandit Joan Sala i Ferrer, also known as Serrallonga, exhibits the Catalan independence flag the *Estelada* and Sankt George's cross from its balcony. Moreover, in addition to other Catalan symbols, in the bar, there is a reproduction of the painting by Pau Bejar, *Guifré i de Barcelona, el Pilós* (ca. 1892) that portrays the moment when, according to the legend Guifré I, drew the four bars of the *senyera* with his blood.

There are also predominantly 'African' bars, such as Fouta, the name of a region of the Republic of Guinea where the owner is from (Torres i Bages St, just opposite the housing estate La Sagrada Familia). Usually, sub-Saharan men gather here to play checkers at a table, while others are at the bar drinking coffee or beer while watching television, which often broadcasts news from Africa via a Senegalese channel. It is relatively small, but there are always at least five people, and it reaches its maximum of 35 when there is a football match on. Though sub-Saharan men frequent the bar, Spanish-nationals and Moroccans often stop by as well. It is generally a place to have a coffee or a beer, but the waitress, Fatima, also serves food. Another similar place is El Petit Africà, a bar owned by a Cameroonian. Much more alcohol is consumed here, and they make traditional Cameroonian dishes. The people who frequent the bar are primarily sub-Saharan, although, as in the case of Fouta, it is also visited by the occasional Spaniard and Moroccan. They also broadcast news from Africa.

Indalo is another kind of bar. It is a Spanish-style bar/cafeteria run by Rosa (her adopted Spanish name), her husband, and her two children, all from China. On a typical day, one may see several groups of Moroccans smoking cigarettes and drinking coffee and a mixture of Spaniards, sub-Saharans, and Portuguese drinking beer and smoking cigarettes. A division that, according to some of the clients with whom I spoke, has changed over time. Before, it had been run by an older Spanish man, and the terraces had been strongly segregated between 'Latins' and 'Blacks' on one side and 'Moors' and 'Spaniards' on the other (23/05/2012, Diary 4, 104).

As well as bars and cafes, there are other places for informal socializing that are often linked to retail. An example would be a place that I will call La Granja for the sake of anonymity. It is a food store where one can secretly consume alcohol and eat food, and deposit stolen objects:

> We passed La Granja, which Demba wanted to show me. It was a big place, a shop where you could also have a drink, and the place usually closes around 22:00. We bought a bottle of beer, and the owner gave us some plastic glasses. There he introduced me to several people, Nigerians, Moroccans, Senegalese, Gambians, Guinean. They were having a drink while some music was playing. Demba pointed to a door that led to a back room where he told me people were

> leaving things they had stolen. There were sofas and so on. I didn't see the room; the truth is, I was a little scared of the atmosphere. (16/01/2012, Diary 2, 67–68)

Hairdressers are another place for informal gatherings and often serve as meeting places. One of these is a barbershop that Daniel and some colleagues from Ghana recently opened on Torras i Bages St, in front of the Housing Unit Sant Jaume.

> Then we went with the nephew to the hairdresser to cut his hair. The hairdresser located in Torras i Bages, was the new one at the end of the street, close to where I lived [Josep Irla]. This place had recently opened, about two months ago. At first, it caught my attention because there were many people inside and almost no furniture. In fact, at the beginning, it looked more like a garage, but now I saw that they developed it much more, and now it looked much more like a hairdresser saloon. They had brought in more furniture, especially chairs and sofas. We sat there for a while. It was much more than a barbershop, a meeting place, where people came in and out all the time, sat down, listened to music and talked a lot. In general, there were a minimum of 4 people around, plus those who were cutting hair, and a guy came in trying to sell some second-hand or stolen sneakers. (19/05/2012, Diary 4, 96–97)

Among similar places, there are bakeries and coffee shops. These are different from the bars and cafes because they are predominantly feminine (mostly Spanish nationals, though). Here, women often meet to talk about life in the neighbourhood, the building, the situation in the town, or particular events. I observed this in Cal Enric, where three women and the shopkeeper gathered, all speaking in Catalan. They discussed a series of robberies that had taken place in the neighbourhood. In fact, small establishments in general, such as butcher shops, are generally spaces of this type, where most of the customers are older Spanish women, accompanied by either their daughter, son or caregiver.

At the other end of the private-public spectrum, are the residential or neighbourhood private community spaces; often limited to the shared use of neighbours. Although men dominate the public spaces of the squares and the streets, these semi-private spaces are dominated by women. In these spaces, one may encounter one's neighbour, and generally, the type of interaction maintained is rather formal yet friendly. However, people often have conversations with some neighbours more than others. In fact, though people who live in Barri Centre are confronted and coexist with a wide variety of ethnicities and nationalities; additionally, in their community space, they tend to gather according to ethnic, linguistic, and other affinities.

The conversations taking place in the landings of staircases, the entrances to buildings, or at the door of one's home often revolve around community issues. People talk about neighbours, but they also exchange views on events in the neighbourhood and town. Favours and services are exchanged in these residential spaces, such as leaving sugar or an egg for a neighbour.

But above all, it is in these places where, due to more significant obligations, it is necessary to reach agreements regarding ordinary expenses related to electricity etc. Such expenses often generate conflict, as we will see in chapter 2. In these spaces, personal decisions (e.g., not paying community expenses) can harm the shared community space, especially if the community has debts and the indebted companies decide to cut various services. These spaces are often fruitful places to observe the daily negotiation of living together. It is, therefore, all the more surprising just how little attention they have received from social scientists.

Through my personal experience of living in three different places in town, I have observed different forms of living. The organization of communities has a lot to do with this, as does the number of people living in the community and their relationship with one another. That is, the social determinants of the community have a significant influence on how well it works and how cohesive it is. It is undoubtedly not the same to live with eight people in a 60-square-meter apartment in the middle of the Barri Centre, as I did during Ramadan 2012, as it is to live two people in an 80-square-meter duplex apartment in Barri Vell. Generally, the migrants I have known in Barri Centre live with other close colleagues or relatives. In these cases, at least three people usually live together, and often those in more precarious situations and with fewer social networks live with people of other nationalities. I shall explain with an example.

One day I visited the apartment of a friend and classmate from the Catalan language course. He had lived in Salt for three years with his cousin and his family, including his wife, children, and siblings—a total of seven people—and he shared a 5-square-meter bedroom with his two cousins. A similar case, equally typical, was that of a Senegalese man, a friend of my main informant. He had been living in the town for decades and had even worked as a bricklayer in the company of the former mayor's father. However, he had been unemployed for some years and had become firmly addicted to tobacco and alcohol. He had no relatives, no children, and no wife, lived in a small room in Àngel Guimerà, which he rented from a Nigerian couple. In the flat, he lived with two Senegalese friends and a Nigerian couple who had a newborn child when I visited him. They were six people, not relatives, living together in an apartment of about 70 square meters.

This might explain why, when the private-community space is reduced, it often results in much more intensive use of public or semi-private spaces in the town. In fact, if we want to analyse the encounters, misunderstandings, and conflicts taking place in the staircase, buildings, or public spaces in general, I argue that this is of utmost importance. We must keep in mind that, as several authors have argued (Fraser 1990; Calhoun 2002), an encounter between equals in an unequal world is an ideological fantasy of liberalism. Therefore, simply analysing their encounter or the discourses surrounding it, without considering the material base and the existing social inequalities, amounts to an analytical bedazzlement and ideological displacement and, in this case, culturalizing the conflicts. Therefore, I will describe the different inequalities and divisions in the town that fundamentally influence the social relations between the inhabitants, and then, I will analyse their interpretations.

SOCIAL DIVISIONS

The continuous changes in the economic-political system and its intrinsic human mobilities have resulted in a diversification of the national and ethnocultural origin of the inhabitants of the town. According to the latest statistical data from the town council, there are people of around 84 different nationalities living in Salt (municipal census). To this diversity of nationalities, we must add important divisions alongside the categories of ethnocultural, socio-economic, legal status, age, social networks, socio-labour insertion, and gender. All these sociocultural dimensions can be condensed into the category of 'super-diversity' (Vertovec 2007).

In this sense, it is worth noting the predominance of men among the sub-Saharan African communities and the predominance of women among the Honduran community, the latter primarily due to the social networks of domestic workers, as Martínez Veiga (2004) demonstrated in the case of female workers of the Dominican Republic in Madrid. On the other hand, many of the other communities dwelling in Salt, including Spanish nationals, are roughly equally distributed in gender. But when it comes to age, the Spanish residents are essentially older, whereas the foreign nationals are usually relatively young.

At the educational level, we see crucial social segregation. According to a report carried out by the Síndic de Greuges (the Catalan Ombudsman) in 2008, titled "The School Segregation in Catalonia", Salt is the Catalan municipality with the eighth-most school segregation. There is a strong division between the 'foreign' students (many of which are actually of Spanish nationality), who are often more enrolled in public primary and secondary education schools, and the 'native' students, who usually study at privately run schools funded by the state. One of the primary education schools is in second place in Catalonia in terms of the percentage of foreign students with

79.9%, a percentage that today is around 90%, while another secondary education school is in the first place with 75.3%. On the other hand, we also find that the schools that are privately run but funded by the state usually have a low percentage of foreign students in comparison to that of the municipality, three in primary education (–46.7%, –46.3%, and –31.1%, respectively) and one in secondary (–26.3%).

These differences point to a socio-economic polarization between older and newer residents (i.e., a division within the working classes), something other reports confirm (Departament d'Integració i Covivència, Ajuntament de Salt 2011; Badosa 2011; Cruz 2014). First, let us detail how the divisions express themselves at a neighbourhood level and their social consequences.

Socio-Economic Polarization: Labour Market and the Informal Sector in Salt

Spain suffered tremendously during the so-called economic crisis at a European level, reaching a record high of up to 6,200,000 unemployed in 2013, corresponding to 26.2% of the active population (EUROSTAT). Within this bleak picture, Salt was one of the most affected cities in Catalonia, with an unemployment rate above the territorial and state average. In fact, the number of people registered as unemployed reached 3,758 in March 2012, corresponding to a 24.56% relative unemployment, much above the 10% in early 2008 (Comisiones Obreras [CCOO] 2011; Observatori d'Empresa i Occupació). However, 5,020 people were registered as jobseekers, out of 16,102 active people (31.11%) to which we should add the people in an irregular situation (IDESCAT; Observatori d'Empresa i Occupació).

Most of the employed people are workers in the service sector, with a small number of employed in the industry sector and a minimum in agriculture. Thus, the vast majority of the men I met during fieldwork either worked in the construction sector or one of the many slaughterhouses in the area. Other possible workplaces are in the Nestlé coffee factory, where they produce the Dolce Gusto capsules for the European market, the Haribo factory, a printing company for magazines and books (Impremta Pagès), and the feed factory (La Gironina). The women primarily work in the service sector in Salt and Girona, mainly cleaning hotels, staircases and hospitals and caring for the ageing population (figure 1.2). Many of these do not count in the official statistics because they are often hired irregularly. Among the more stable jobs, we find both men and women working in education and training in one of several NGOs operating in the areas, social workers, or civil servants. To this, we should add a few who work in agriculture, be that industrialized, cooperative, or smaller-scale agriculture.

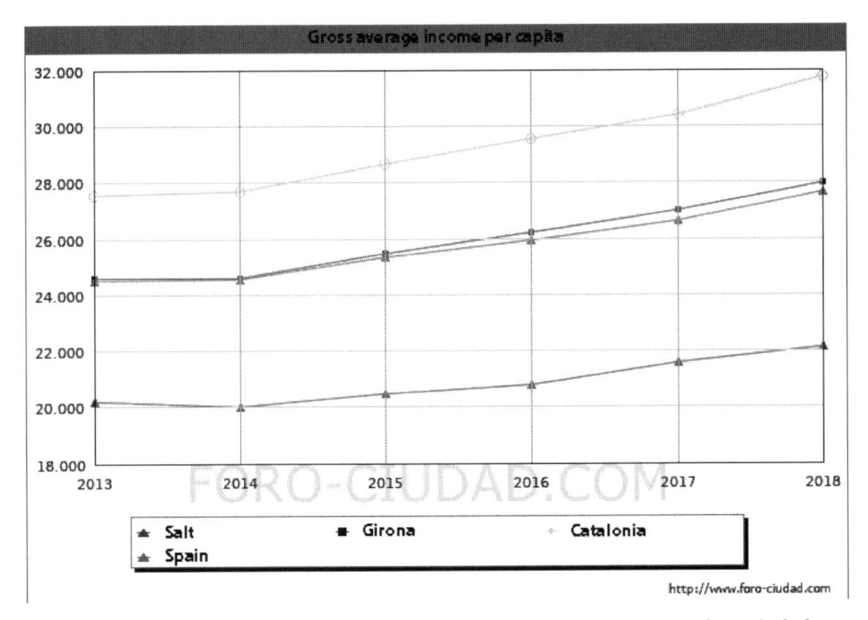

Figure 1.2. Gross average income per capita. 2013–2018. *Source*: www.foro-ciudad.com

The complicated socio-economic situation has had a powerful impact among the weakest sectors and in cities such as Salt, one of the municipalities with the lowest per capita income in Catalonia (Europa Press 2011b). Thus, through a study carried out by the Àrea d'Integració i Convivència of the Salt Town Council in 2011 (Departament d'Integració i Covivència, Ajuntament de Salt 2011) to review the socio-economic conditions of the residents in Barri Centre, we see that the unemployment in this area is quite significant (figure 1.3): Only 20.81% were working, 14.08% unemployed, 20.66% retired, and 26.76% were neither studying nor working. This explains the more intense social activity observed in the town. Moreover, 144 out of 639 say they have no income, whereas 352 depend on social allowances (unemployment or retirement). It has not affected everyone equally. The already existing levels of inequality exploded with the economic crisis, and migrants were among the most affected by this (Colectivo IOÉ 2012, 35; Mahía and de Arce 2014, 146).

The demise of the formal economy led to a proliferation of informal activities. As Gallino (1983, 7) argues, there is a direct correlation among informal activities (whether criminal or illegal) and unemployment, expectations for the future, and the feeling of belonging (in sociocultural terms):

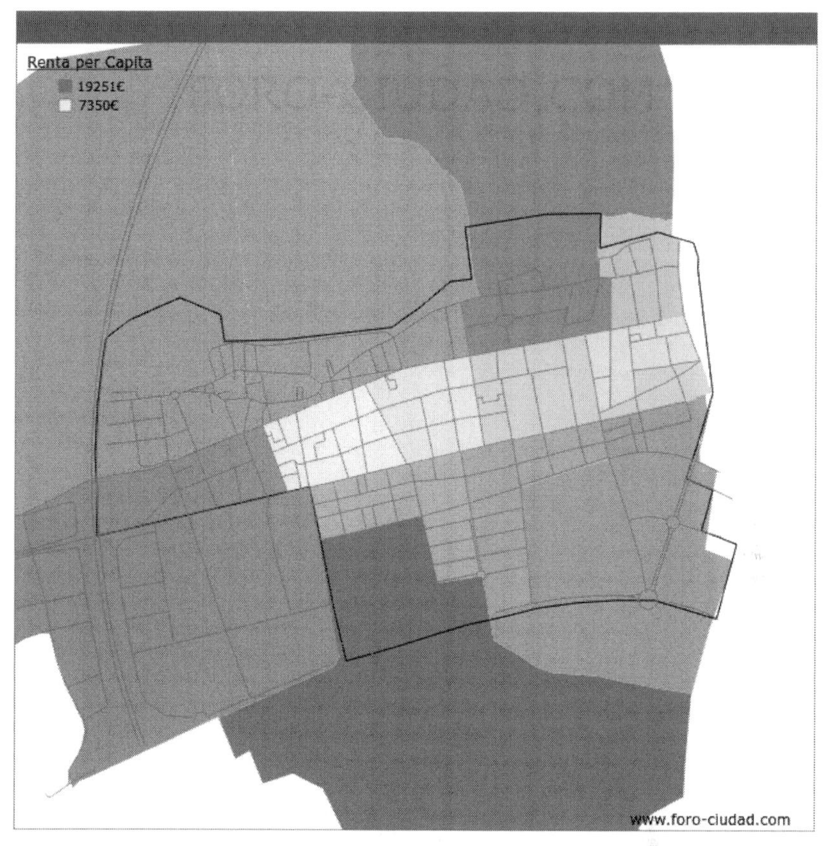

Figure 1.3. Gross average income per capita according to neighbourhood. 2017. *Source*: www.foro-ciudad.com

> informal activities can be seen simultaneously as a) an inevitable result of the development of the economy of late capitalism; b) a free choice and creator of social innovation; c) a set of survival tools; and d) a return to pre-modern social relations with the support of modern technologies. (quoted in Hurtado Jordá 1996, 47).

THE ASPECTS AND SOCIAL RELATIONS OF THE INFORMAL SECTOR

Hence, it should come as no surprise that a large part of the population of Salt is forced to resort to precarious economic practices. They seek other ways to reproduce or access necessary resources. The informal sector seeks to offer ways to satisfy needs not covered by the formal sector. In fact, contrary to formal-informal dualism, these two sectors are part of a single economic system, although articulated differently in different socio-economies (Martínez Veiga 1989, 11). Moreover, to comprehend 'the underground economy today implies contextualising it in the process of restructuring and recomposing of the capitalism that has developed in the last two decades. . . . [T]he underground economy becomes a central element in the restructuring of capitalism' (Ybarra, Hurtado Jordá, and San Miguel del Hoyo 2002, 269).

Hence, in Salt, as in many other marginalized neighbourhoods worldwide, we find an extensive network of informal labour activities (always involving production, labour relations, and distribution) linked to consumption. In fact, following the conceptualization of 'social reproduction' proposed by Narotzky (1997), we can confirm that the continuity of the precarious populations (primarily immigrants) is mainly due to this economic chain of production, exchange, and consumption. According to Narotzky, one can generally denote three aspects of the so-called informal sector: (a) unregulated salaried labour relations, (b) illegal (criminal) activities, and (c) communal, self-help, and domestic activities (1997, 292).

Among the informal, unregulated, paid activities, the many female domestic workers stand out. They either serve as caregivers for the elderly and primarily Spanish population (who can thus access a scarce and expensive resource, care) or cleaners (often in the more affluent neighbourhoods of Girona). These economic networks are explained in the following way.

On the one hand, the Spanish population is ageing; hence, many older people need care. As it is now, there are two options to satisfy this need: get a place in a residential centre or take care of them at home, either through family networks or by accessing that service through the informal sector. Due to a combination of factors, including lower incomes and greater cultural acceptance, many families hire a domestic worker, often a Honduran or, less often, a Spanish or Moroccan woman. There is also a generalized need for cleaners in the community spaces of the buildings and private homes (especially among the wealthier families), work that is often carried out by Spanish women (former migrants) and Moroccans. These can be working independently, often without a contract, or through a large company, such as the multinational company ISS.

Another current practice is that of renting employment contracts. This usually happens between people who are regular and irregular, legally speaking. The irregular workers need the official papers to work on a contract; thus, they rent these papers from another person in exchange for a percentage or a fixed monthly payment. This was the case for one of my roommates, Bouba, who did not have a residence permit and, therefore, worked in a slaughterhouse under someone else's name. According to Bouba, the businessman knew the situation, but when Bouba told him that he wanted to regularize his situation, the manager was surprised and refused to help him. However, Bouba continued to work there, and they did not sign a new contract until he had married a Spanish woman and obtained Spanish nationality.

Criminal activity is also widespread in Salt and a constitutive part of the informal economy. Such activity often complements primary social benefits and low income, and occasionally it constitutes one's sole source of income. Despite its precariousness, it also constitutes a fast way to access and satisfy basic necessities or to access large sums in little time, which can then be invested as a means to regularize. For instance, one of my informants needed cash to bring his wife and daughter to the country (an economic-legal requisite that many workers have a hard time fulfilling), on top of lending financial support to his ageing father and siblings. Although he had a stable job, an obvious solution was transporting drugs to Germany by aeroplane, gaining around €2,000 per trip. If he had had access to a loan, maybe this would not have seemed so obvious to him, but he risked his life and ended up in jail for two years.

Among the communal, self-help, and domestic activities, we find the domestic work (manual, and reproduction, cleaning, to name a few) and, for example, collective gardens, whereby a plot of land is rented collectively—a plot of land, which is either subdivided into individual units or shared both in terms of work and usufruct. On the contrary to stereotypical views, it is common to hear stories of mutual aid between Spaniards and migrants. Thus, for example, an 89-year-old older woman told me that her neighbours from Morocco had brought her many things when they returned from vacation and that they generally took good care of her. Likewise, Carmen, a Spanish woman from Valladolid in her late 40s, remembers how in her neighbourhood, Grup Verge de Maria, in Barri Centre, fellow neighbours sometimes left a bag of food at her door:

> It was a neighbourhood full of Andalusian people. A very cosy place, in the sense of, well, people got a little into your life . . . it was like, you'd go out, and when you came back you would find a bag of tomatoes, or sausages at your doorstep . . . we never lacked anything.

We also find several collaborative financing practices; in a tontine-like fashion, each person pays an amount of money to a common fund allocated to a person in the group monthly, either through a draw or based on special needs. This serves as a kind of savings fund while also bringing people together. Other examples are group loans and community kitchens (Cruz 2014, 18–23).

In precarious times and situations, people resort to risky ways of accessing resources. Therefore, the reasons for obtaining and claiming resources are diversified and cover areas ranging from the intimacy of kinship to arguments based on civil rights or even entrepreneurial criteria. Thus, for instance, sometimes they are based on relationships of solidarity and exchange through social networks that ensure access to essential resources necessary for survival. In Salt, scarce resources also circulate among people through social networks, which can be transnational, just like the lives of the people involved and their social ties—similar indeed to the case described in Carol Stack's ethnography of black communities in the southern United States in the 1970s:

> The most important form of distribution and exchange of the limited resources available to the poor in The Flats is by means of trading, or what people call 'swapping.' As people swap, the limited supply of finished material goods in the community is perpetually redistributed among networks of kinsmen and throughout the community. The resources, possessions, and services exchanged between individuals residing in The Flats are intricately interwoven. People exchange various objects generously: new things, treasured items, furniture, cars, goods that are perishable, and services which are exchanged for child care, residence, or shared meals. (Stack 1975, 33–34)

On top of this, there is a large second-hand market built on the existing informal relationships (friends or family) and formal ones (second-hand products stores). Another extreme but illustrative example is people who buy second-hand cars in Catalonia and then sell them in an African country (in the sub-Saharan area, especially). An informant of mine had done this twice.

We also see high residential mobility. For instance, in one year, from 2012 to 2013, my main informant, Demba, had changed houses five times. In the meantime, his friend Barry changed twice. No doubt, this was often due to conflicts between the residents, but I also learned how some people had been kicked out because they had not paid their rent for months. Thus, on several occasions, I met flatmates who would fight over money issues or conflicts at home, in the street, or in a bar. In general, once you know some people around the town, and therefore, have access to the informal market, you can easily find a room in Barri Centre at a price (verified several times) of between €125 and €150, expenses included.

Apart from the aforementioned informal practices, one must not forget that resources can be found through the public administration via a minimum income to those who meet the increasingly restrictive requirements and, on the other, the work and services offered by the third sector, be that the NGOs operating in the area, the local private associations, or the charitable organizations linked to religious institutions (such as Caritas, the most important Catholic charity organization in Spain).

Amid this, particular social ties emerge and sometimes are required by these production and consumption practices. Hence, in the case of the rented contracts, one of the direct consequences is more people receive a small amount of money and, in addition, a situation of dependency and possible exploitation develops, all due to the existing immigration laws and a lack of regulation. However, for the migrants without papers, the rental of an employment contract also means: not having to wait three years to attain a regular income; not having to resort to other informal practices often stigmatized; aspiring to regularize their situation much quicker; and earn enough money that can be invested in remittances, luxuries, and so on.

In short, despite the precarious conditions in which they work, this practice allows them to live a decent life, thus fulfilling their original aspirations. At the same time, the person who has the contract and rents it with the agreement has a vital complement, which depending on the agreement, might suffice. However, most of them will certainly have to supplement their income through other informal activities.

So, let us not romanticize the informal sector; in it, we see the generalization and radicalization of a depredatory mercantilist logic (Martínez Veiga 1989, 67) because everything becomes a possible source of income or a way of acquiring a new object, which in the end leads to an extreme internalization of the logics of the market or, in other words, the commodification of social relations, as the following extract from my field diary shows:

> In the afternoon, I had an appointment with Houri to fix his computer, which, according to him, was very slow. It was around 3 pm. Demba knew it, and I already knew that he would want to take advantage of the situation, as he normally did. He's always in the loop to know whether he can take advantage (money) of it (service or work of another person), or if you have any money, which he might later ask from you ("do you have 5 or 10 euros?"). He is a broker, the one putting people in contact, for instance, which in the end is the social capital that he has been accumulating, which at some point can be 'commercialised'. (22/08/2012, Diary 5, 133)

In a similar yet distinct manner, a professionalized relationship has also arisen in the third sector. The workers maintain a professional relationship with the inhabitants and their problems and, in the end, establish unequal power relations, a patron-client relationship. On the one hand, there is a vast group of social workers, providers in charge of economic and cultural resources (public and private), while exercising functions of control, although often unaware of it, and on the other hand, there are the potential clients, mostly working migrants. In times of crisis and scarce resources (i.e., a shortage of income through work and public resources), the demands are often delegated to the third sector, which operates in a group-based instead of universalist manner. Consequently, the group members are forced to fight each other for scarce resources, and as a result, a classification is made according to the urgency and justification of the claim, sometimes following criteria such as nationality, age, or sex. I will deal with this further in chapter 6.

SOCIO-SPATIAL SEGREGATION

Let's analyse the data of the 'Population study for zones 2012' (Àrea de Integració i Covivència, Ajuntament de Salt 2012). We can detect strong segregation of the inhabitants in the town in the different neighbourhoods according to the migrant background and their socio-economic situation. We see a higher concentration of residents with a migration background and low income in the Barri Centre (figure 1.4). By contrast, Barri Vell and La Massana are much more ethnically homogeneous neighbourhoods, and the inhabitants have often lived there for more than five years, own their residence, and generally present a better socio-economic situation. This spatial expression of the social inequalities and their cultural interpretation is what this section deals with.

During my fieldwork, I had the chance to live in different parts of the town, which allowed me to observe the different ways of living and identify with the neighbourhood and the town. Much like some of the people who come from the neighbouring towns to participate in the social life of the town, visit a friend or two, or return to their old place of residence, others live in Salt but tend to avoid any social life outside of their own homes or who limit their relationships to when they play sports or other such activities. For instance, when I was looking at apartments in August 2011, I met some Spanish men in their 30s. The three lived in an old house with a garden on Miguel Cervantes St, only a few blocks from Barri Centre. They told me that they avoided any social life in the town, or at least in the centre, which one referred to as 'the mess over there'. They lived comfortably and far away enough not to feel forced to participate in the social life of the neighbourhood.

Other people who did not even live in Barri Centre showed similar traits of avoiding the neighbourhood. Although they would often participate in the social life of their neighbourhood whenever they had to go around the town, they would avoid crossing or go to the Barri Centre. So, I observed how many people living in Barri Vell, La Massana, or Veïnat tended to live in a separate world, a comfortable bubble far from any problem affecting the town. Hence, the perception of Salt is not the same for everyone. Ultimately, it depends on where someone lives, income, and attitude.

Figure 1.4. Foreign nationals according to neighbourhood. 2019. *Source*: www.foro-ciudad.com

The resulting steep social and urban segregation finds its opposite poles in the neighbourhoods of Barri Vell and Barri Centre. In the words of two former councillors living in Barri Vell:

> 1. Well, we have an old part of which goes from Barri Vell to Veïnat which is an attractive area . . .
>
> 2. Yes, the problem is the streets in the middle . . .
>
> 1. You say, 'fuck, am I in the same town?', and yes, you are. Maybe in other towns or other cities, this conflictive part is located in an outer area, so you don't notice. Nevertheless, the thing is that here that part is in the centre, and that is what it is. So you see, we have to fix that.

This obvious opposition, the inherent inequalities and the disdain on the part of some neighbours towards another neighbourhood and its inhabitants and, also just because I was granted the opportunity to live in both, meant that a large part of my ethnographic focus had been put on these two neighbourhoods to compare the social life and vision of the neighbourhood and town in both.

The social distinction between the neighbourhoods has been stimulated by a series of socio-economic and political factors that I will deal with much more in chapters 3 and 5; Barri Centre de Salt became the migrant neighbourhood or the ghetto. Although the migrants could hardly find a residence in any other area, except for Can Gibert i Plà and other peripheral neighbourhoods of Girona, often worse in terms of conditions, location, equipment, and public space, in Barri Centre, migrants could acquire flats in poor condition but at a price much above the 'real value', through the sub-prime mortgages. Later, however, many would be evicted. In this sense, the socio-spatial segregation occurring before the crisis would only increase with it, and the neighbourhood began to see more and more cases of overcrowding and the occupation of flats.

In fact, in 2008, when the local *Pla local d'habitatge de la Vila de Salt 2009–2015* (GMG Plans i Projectes, SLP 2009) was published, the data was worrying. The report makes a diagnosis of the urban and housing situation in Salt. The authors are particularly worried about the Sector Centre,[2] where the main problems detected were: a high density of foreign population, a high unemployment rate of residents (almost 25%), precarious and fragile economic conditions that lead to defaults of the community and mortgage fees, overcrowding, many empty flats, a significant level of degradation in the residential sector, and a lack of green spaces, collective amenities, and parking lots.

In a similar vein, that same year Càritas Salt published a report in collaboration with the University of Girona and EINA (a local community association) (2008). It portrayed the complex social situation of Barri Centre. It was based on the study of a block of houses located at the heart of Barri Centre, more specifically the one in between the streets Àngel Guimerà, Doctor Ferran, Torras i Bages, and Ramon Sambola. In this area, the report observed an array of different socio-economic situations. The origin of the inhabitants was as follows: 32.08% Spanish nationality, 49.20% from Africa, 14.44% from Central and South America, and 2.89% and 1.39% from Asia and Europe, respectively. More closely, we see that, in the blocks studied of between 16 and 22 flats, the number of coexisting nationalities ranges from five to nine.

When talking about the type of tenure of the primary occupant, 76.45% are owners, and 23.55% are tenants. Among the owners, the vast majority of the Spanish nationals have already paid their mortgage, whereas the rest of the residents who have owned the apartment for more than seven years pay around €500. Similarly, those who have owned the flat for less than three years pay between €750 (the oldest) and €1,300 (the most recent) per month. On a side note, I observed that the Spanish nationals usually live in the attics or sub-attics of buildings with an elevator, thus enjoying good views and terraces and more private space.

'Barrido Project' also provides some interesting data on the material conditions of the residence in the neighbourhood, and it gives us some clues about the evolution since the beginning of the crisis (Departament d'Integració i Covivència, Ajuntament de Salt 2011). For instance, we see that many inhabitants continue to own their apartments (about 42.76%), while a minority are tenants (19.25%). However, something has changed regarding mortgages because they no longer exceed €900 per month (the vast majority are between €300 and €600 per month). If we add to this the fact that 17 of the flats are illegally occupied, and 60 are from a bank, we can conclude that many residents must have been unable to renegotiate mortgages and, therefore, have been evicted. In addition, 66 people (32.04%) say they have difficulties with the mortgage payment, and 53 (27.89%) plan to leave the apartment due to the poor quality of the home (18.87%) or to stay in a cheaper apartment (28.30%). We also see how the residents are highly mobile compared with other neighbourhoods in the town, and many people say they have lived in more than one flat during the last seven years.

In the other social extreme, we find Barri Vell and its inhabitants. Although Barri Centre was often described as the ghetto, Barri Vell, on the contrary, was perceived as 'un petit Empordà' (i.e., a small town from the old and beautiful area of Empordà, or a town full of 'saltencs de tota la vida', [i.e., people originally and always from Salt]) as Marta a resident in the neighbourhood since childhood said:

> Barri Vell is a small village [laughing]. I think the people who live here are the people who have always been here. I feel very comfortable here, I mean . . . people. You also always see the same faces. You have the bakery here, which is like a second home [laughing]. It's very quiet. I have even heard that a local police officer told a friend that this was like Beverly Hills in Salt, like privileged. I don't know if it's true or not, but I live very well and peacefully here.

The fact is that today Barri Vell serves as a refuge for a minority, the bourgeoisie, and middle class in terms of cultural capital, who can live a quiet life, far away from the problems affecting the rest of the town; in the words of Pere, a resident in the Barri Centre:

> See, in Barri Vell, there were always four families around, and then little by little, well, they began to fix it, and people started moving in, bringing people in from outside, who were not from Salt either. It's a neighbourhood a bit closed for them; I mean by an elite who are thought to feel superior. I can't complain because I can go there, I can go around.

So, they see only a few migrants, which is apparently fundamental when explaining the good atmosphere and sense of neighbourhood that exists, according to the president of the neighbourhood association, Jordi:

> In Barri Vell, life is good because there is no, there is hardly any migration, of this African. I mean, there might be some South American parts . . . and some Maghreb, but very few and the truth is, very well adapted, I mean, another kind of mentality, they even interact with the neighbours.

Thus, all indications are that many of its inhabitants do not establish relations with the 'migrant' neighbours. In this sense, I remember how one day when I gave a class at the University of Girona to students of social work, I met some girls from Barri Vell. According to them, there were no problems in Salt, or at least they had not experienced them, and at most, they had learned about them through the media. This opinion coincides largely with that of other residents of the neighbourhood whom I have been able to meet and is actually a quite extended opinion even among people from other areas of Salt, as we see from Verónica, who lives in La Massana, only 400 metres from Barri Centre:

> I heard it from the news more than anything [laughing]. Because, of course, the things happen in the area over there, thank goodness, right? I'm here in the new area, and not much happens here. That is, nothing has happened for now [laughing]. And then, of course, through the media, I see that there are a lot of conflicts there.

Barri Vell is similar to Barri Centre in that until the end of the 20th century, both were still in a rather degraded state. However, despite the similarities in degradation, Barri Vell has some characteristics that make it singular. First, as previously mentioned, this is the old town, the original nucleus of the town, so the degraded state refers mainly to the antiquity of the houses and a certain abandonment by the owners. Second, the urban morphology is that of an old town. Although there are some multi-storey buildings, the low-rise houses predominate (ground floor plus two more at most). Third, few people live in these buildings, and people who own homes have usually inherited them. Therefore, the inhabitants are mostly Spanish nationals, Catalan-speaking, and middle class. Fourth, the neighbourhood structure separated as it is from the rest of the town and closed makes it work as a village on its own. Fifth, its particular location on the edge of the allotments, vegetable gardens, and Les Deveses, in addition to its appearance as a village of Empordà, and the history accumulated in the houses and squares (the so-called diffuse architectural heritage or 'urban atmosphere'), makes it a particularly attractive place for the Catalan middle classes with a high cultural capital, who seek refuge from modern urban life, the charm of the town, and proximity with the city of Girona.

Generally, the middle classes avoid the Barri Centre. The arguments typically used refer to the large number of people and amount of noise or dirt that they think is there, quite the opposite to what they are looking for and which they usually find in Barri Vell, as Veronica says:

> In Barri Vell, however, some areas are already more conditioned and are, I think, charming, very good to live, quiet, peaceful. In contrast to the area here where the town hall is, it has much migration. And I don't know; it seems very noisy to me. I wouldn't live there. I wouldn't live there, and it's not that I don't like integration, it's that the people who live there are very noisy. And one is looking for a little more rest, tranquillity.

This socio-spatial segregation, as seen in the introduction, results from complex historical and spatial processes, migrations, and the functioning of the real estate market and urban planning (urban transformation). And the truth is that it has fundamental consequences for the possible convivencia, the sociability that the different inhabitants engage in and how the inhabitants understand the disputes and, in fact, the different discursive devices and the different groupings that occur in the different spaces of the town, as we will see in the following. As Ivan, a resident in Veïnat, states, 'Salt indeed has borders. It is a pity that there are people who do not want to cross them or at least want to see them.'

APPROPRIATION OF SPACE

As Pierre Bourdieu (1990) demonstrated in his famous study of the Kabyle people in Algeria, spatial practices are directly related to the daily social organization in various economic and non-economic (recreational and social reproduction) ways. In the same way, the social space of the street and the squares in Salt are continuously appropriated by different uses and users in a temporary variation.

These daily appropriations of space are constantly negotiated, and yet, seen in the long run, the users recognize a certain continuity. This is clearly seen in some squares such as Catalonia, La Massana, and Llibertat, where groups of men or women (sometimes based on nationality and sometimes mixed) and young people, in general, are used to meet. At the same time, during these times of appropriations, other individuals or entire groups exclude themselves from these spaces or simply avoid them, adducing that they are 'privatized'. So, we see that the social space of the neighbourhood indeed has several space temporalities in the words of Toñi, the 50-year-old president of the neighbourhood association AVV Barri Centre:

> If you look at this neighbourhood, it's a neighbourhood with a social structure during the day at seven in the afternoon, and in early hours another. The older people, well, they have chosen depending on what time they won't go to the street any more. You see, probably nothing is going on, but seeing a group of people on the corner gives them the feeling that 'uff if I pass by there, they will rob me.' . . . From around 19 or 20, and if you look around the neighbourhood, you see squares where groups of different ethnicities gather, and you have corners, different corners. There's no communication between them; each group has its plot, and depending on what time you go there, you will find one or another, and it is very typical of this town.

In the case of bars, the appropriation is different mainly by the role of the owner and the workers as doorkeepers and managers of the cultural logic in place. Certain ways of being are dominant, and others might not be tolerated. This became clear to me from an experience I had at the Can Serrallonga:

> We were sitting inside chatting while some 'Black' children were grouping outside, playing and then when the game had started, they went to the window to see it from the outside. Among them were very young children and older children. Then, when the game was about to end, a young guy with tattoos and two dogs came in. It was obvious that he wasn't welcome, and the waiter didn't want to serve him. He got angry and started yelling and insulting him. Among other things, he said, 'why can these Blacks see the game while I can't?' and 'Is it because I'm not a *moro*?' He also said that they did not want to serve him the other day. I noticed that he had a swastika tattooed on his arm and another with Hitler on his chest. As he was leaving, he kept making a fuss, resorting over and over again to the alleged 'commonality' or rather shared nationality that he and the waiter had, and then immediately after insulted them for being 'red' and said that they could stuff their *estelada* up their asses. (19/05/2012, Diary 4, 99)

In this sense, I believe it is constructive to perceive the different spaces as small sociocultural worlds, where the membership and distinctions of the members are continuously negotiated and reproduced; local cultures are constructed and reproduced in relation to global issues.

In this sense, I have observed how some bars and cafes tend to be more monocultural (i.e., they usually bring together people of particular ethnicities). In contrast, others are rather semi-heterogeneous (i.e., the difference is tolerated, but an ethnicity or culture predominates) or mixed spaces (i.e., very heterogeneous). For example, while one can see a wide variety of ways of beings in Índalo, on the contrary, in Can Serrallonga, the social space is dominated by the cultural logics of Catalan-ness. In this way, we see how the space is sometimes managed more strictly, and the entrance is negotiated according to cultural capital, belonging in cultural terms, and economic capital.

In the inhabitants' social imagination, these spaces are connoted as the places of certain people in terms of nationality, ethnicity, or race. For example, my main informant, Demba, always had an opinion regarding the places I suggested going to. He would often agree to enter while jokingly calling them 'white places', 'black places', or something similar. Sometimes he didn't even want to go to a place because, according to him, it was a 'Moroccan place'. Although it should not be taken as a generalizable truth but rather as a subjective interpretation, it shows that there is indeed a negotiation of presence in certain places in ethnocultural terms. This does not necessarily imply exclusions but rather a negotiation when entering for the first time (Monnet 2002, 114–15). For example, when one day I entered Mana, a cafe where Moroccan men are often playing cards, I had to endure the intrigued gazes of almost everyone present. It was clear that I had done something unusual, though not necessarily bad. In fact, I used to have this kind of experience in other spaces the first time I visited them; in time, however, they would gradually position me. In this sense, the frequency with which one visits a site largely determines the degree of belonging to the place. Thus, for example, you get to know other customers and workers of a bar through daily and continuous interactions, contact, and reunion in this or that place. Although many people circulated in bars and cafes like me, some limited themselves to frequenting only a single bar or cafe. In this sense, space is the physical environment enabling sociability and possible intergroup encounters; thus, any possible constraints become extremely important.

As for the daily appropriations of the squares and streets, I have made a similar observation. In some squares, such as Catalunya and Massana, there is a tendency towards segregation regarding the use and appropriation of space, depending on social groups along ethnic lines. Thus, in the first case, the native population avoids much of the square because some of them perceive it as 'invaded' by migrants, especially Moroccans; instead, they appropriate and use the area around Mas Mota, where two cafes-bars are located. In the Massana square near the bar La Moreneta, on the other hand, the native population are exclusively conglomerated, and on several occasions, I had seen some disapproving glances when a group of Moroccan women entered the children's play area. Meanwhile, heterogeneity reigned in the other part of the square, mainly composed by migrants.

Of course, these divisions are not static or homogeneous but should rather be seen as tendencies; entry and appropriations are negotiated continuously, and any pre-existing order might be altered, especially when there is an act or festival. For example, during the local festivities, I observed an event organized by various native associations of the neighbourhood La Massana and Barri Center, who had appropriated the usually heterogeneous area of the Massana Square, fencing in an area. They had organized a collective dinner with music by a local musician. There were tables for dinner, a stage, and a small dance floor in the enclosure they had created. Of the few migrants who participated, all were curious children, most of whom had to stay on the other side of the fence. A sub-Saharan-looking girl who had dared to enter the compound was quickly thrown away with the words: 'Where is your mother? Well, you should be with her.'

As for the shared space of buildings and stairs, similar dynamics of membership negotiation occur. The negotiation does not end with the residence in this or that apartment building. For example, in the three different places where I stayed during fieldwork, at one point or another, I would be able to witness a group of Spanish women gathered at the bottom of the stairs in the entrance of the building discussing news and stories while indiscreetly also checking and controlling who entered the building and who lived where and with whom:

> Throughout the day, I have encountered two Spanish women at the entrance to the building. Each time I opened the door for them, and they were both equally surprised that I was living in the building, they weren't familiarised with me yet. One of them even asked me how and where I lived. When I told her that I was living in the mezzanine, she responded, 'but, with the Brown[3] ones?' (24/05/2012, Diary 4, 110)

This kind of social control of the community relates to the aforementioned field of belonging: These practices of filtering influence the feelings of belonging that the neighbours experience and establish borders between those who are in and those who are out, those who belong and those who do not; they indeed constitute practices of everyday bordering in the local communities (Yuval-Davis, Wemyss, and Cassidy 2017).

A friend of mine experienced another example of bordering practices. Some months after a Senegalese friend, Demba, had moved in to live with him, he told me he was having problems with his landlord. It turns out that when he had called the landlord to get them to fix the water heater, his wife had blurted, 'oh, but you're the one who rents out a room to some Black guys?' Moreover, he told me, since Demba had moved in, some of the neighbours had stopped greeting him. A fact I had myself been able to confirm, enduring strange looks when I would visit Demba or go out with him. One might argue that this was an example of an everyday bordering practice of a local space of the town located in an area in dispute at the margins of both the stigmatized central neighbourhood and the old middle-class neighbourhood. And indeed, it is. However, if we observe some other examples from much more stigmatized and therefore non-conflictual areas in that sense, we can see more clearly how this relates to sociocultural dynamics beyond the mere local space.

Similarly, certain emblematic buildings or activities might be rejected, such as establishing places of worship. An occurrence that happened on several occasions in the Barri Centre. A premise used as a place of prayer in Guifré el Pelós Square had to close in 2009 due to pressure from some neighbours and, above all, the AVV of the Barri Centre. In the words of the former mayor, Iolanda Pineda:

> Q: In Guifré el Pelós, there was a mosque, wasn't there?
>
> A: Yes, but that's another story. They asked for a license for a cultural association, and then it wasn't only a cultural association. And there was also pressure because every time someone went to the place, the neighbours went to see what was going on. Of course, I couldn't say if it was a cultural place or not, but if they go there to pray and it was approved that they weren't going to pray . . .

So far, the social space of Salt in general and Barri Centre and the Barri Vell, in particular, has been described. At the same time, we have seen how conflicts emerge between the different social actors around the production and use of the space and that access to this process is not equal for everybody. In the following chapter, I will describe the actors involved and how the different social groupings are negotiated.

CHAPTER 1 NOTES

1. In recent decades, research has proliferated on public space from such disparate disciplines as geography, sociology, and anthropology. Such is the attention that some scholars have questioned the usefulness of the concept itself. Certainly, I think there has been a tendency to study only public spaces, ignoring the importance of semipublic and private spaces, or even fetishizing it (Delgado 2012). Nonetheless, here I will use it while adopting the following heuristic separation: public spaces (squares,

streets, parks, etc.), semi-public spaces (bars, restaurants, cafes, shops, hairdressers, phone booths, etc.), and private spaces (stairs, floors, etc.).

2. Remember that Sector Centre is the administrative name used by the town council, which largely coincides with Barri Centre, the predominant perception of the neighbourhood and name among the inhabitants.

3. Brown, as opposed to Black, is often used as a more politically correct way of referring to people who are dark-skinned.

Chapter Two

Social Conflicts

Negotiating Borders and Boundaries

What migration means as a social phenomenon and what it means to be a migrant or non-immigrant has indeed been changing over time and is, at the same time, locally situated. However, surely there is an inherent problem to migration studies when still many studies adopt what has come to be called a 'methodological nationalist' approach (Wimmer and Schiller 2003), one which presumes the neutrality of the existing ethnic and national categorizations. According to this, a person who moves in from a town in the same region is not considered a migrant when one might argue that, demographically speaking, a migrant is anyone who has moved from one location to another. Accordingly, one might state the obvious, insofar that they are all different kinds of mobilities, the relevant question should be: At what point does one mobility gain importance and in what way? Hence, the relevant question is how these mobilities are understood socially.

Clearly, these questions relate to the dominant social understandings of territory, culture, ethnicity, in local society and beyond—essentially political issues. For example, the territory that determines a state, a town, or a neighbourhood for that sake is not a natural entity, nor does it correspond to a homogeneous cultural reality. Instead, we are dealing with a political delimitation that often encompasses multiple ethnic groups, cultures, and nations. Moreover, these notions are continuously produced and contested at different scales in a complex process of cultural negotiation of the social relations and group boundaries (Barth 1969), often closely related to differentiated access to economic and political power and resources (Wolf 2001). Albeit not essential, these social categories become socially relevant in the everyday lives of people over time. They are both used to reproduce the existing power relations between groups and question them. Therefore, they are heuristically relevant as part of a social classification that makes sense of the world, and through them, people make sense of the social changes.

Social conflicts are indeed tense moments during which normality is lost for a certain period. However, although many different conflicts occur every day, the majority do not transcend the local scale, yet they are equally important, if not more, to the inhabitants involved. However, one should remember that the divisions and social groupings involved in these conflicts are mobilized in a certain way. They are framed within the hegemonic narrative of opposition between migrants and natives, known as conflicts of convivencia or intercultural conflicts.

Therefore, when describing and analyzing the social categories, we should instead focus on the processes in which they are involved, the negotiation of the boundaries and borders. And here, it is crucial to remember that they are in local-global processes that sometimes cross state borders, and other times they only make sense from a local point of view. In this chapter, following the ideas of Fredrik Barth (1969), Anthony Cohen (1985), and Southerton (2002), I will study the continuous negotiation of social groups from a daily point of view and in a relational sense. This implies analyzing the symbolic and discursive markers that sustain them in the daily social space of the town of Salt, in particular Barri Centre.

NATIVE AND MIGRANTS

> Imagine a town like this, a small town with only a few inhabitants, where conflicts between families over pieces of land were the standard, receiving this amalgam of different people. People who have come from everywhere, but here. . . . I mean, very few people are real natives of several generations. This does not mean Catalans, because I can talk about my mother-in-law who was born here in Rocacorba, and her whole family were from around here and so on. But she came to Salt at the age of 3, and I only know a few people who are more Catalan than her. But she is not a native of Salt, and like her, many families here have parents who weren't born here either. *Pere*

These initial reflections show how fragile and undefined the idea of native or nationals is. It is complicated if not impossible to answer who is and is not native when one has lived in the town for many years. It is crucial to analyse the subjects considered native and foreigners, the relevant attributes, and who defines them. For instance, why is Carolina, who has been living in Salt for 36 years and has Spanish nationality, is still considered Peruvian when most likely she feels culturally distant from Peru? Although she might be more native than Francesc, who has just arrived from Mataró, many do not perceive it this way. There is no questioning this perception is grounded in dominant ideas of ethnicity, but it also seems to hide latent racism evident at the level of society; implicit ideas about what it means to be native on a national scale (not necessarily the State) are projected onto the local scale. Francesc, it seems, is native because he is and looks Spanish/Catalan.

Currently, the category 'native' (*autóctonos* in Spanish) includes all people who consider themselves Spanish or Catalans. Internally, however, there are particular relevant distinctions. Previously, differences were established between the then native Catalans and those from other parts of Spain. In time the distinctions have become more muddled. The grandfathers of Catalanism, Jordi Pujol and Heribert Barrera, would ascertain deep and incommensurable cultural differences between Catalans and Spaniards, or more concretely, people from Andalusia, Galicia, or Murcia (Alberch and Portella 1987, 393; Maluquer i Sostres 1963). Nowadays, these ideas are far more complex and would take an entire thesis to explain well. Here I will only explain them superficially, and throughout the rest of the book, distinctions are made only when they become ethnographically relevant.

Spaniards refer to a person from another part of Spain than Catalonia. It is important to note that people of a Spanish background (i.e., they were born in another part of Spain other than Catalonia) seem to have assimilated into the category of Catalans. Though one can speak Spanish, it does not exclude one from 'feeling Catalan'; in fact, many children of Spaniards speak both but may prefer to speak one over the other. This is where the primary distinction lies between Spaniards and Catalans, the preference in the use of one language over another, although, in recent years, it has also come to refer to the adherence of a person to Catalan independence or sometimes simply a cultural project (Clua i Fainé 2011). Similarities can be drawn here with the category *gitano* (Roma), which seemed to lack importance during fieldwork, though historically, it has been relevant.

In Salt, although this distinction is not homogeneous, it is predominant among the Catalan middle classes of the town and among parts of the Spanish-speaking communities, especially the right-wing parties that have tried to mobilize the Spanish working classes against the Catalan civil servants and bourgeoisie.

A small group of people often go unnoticed within this grouping: 'the invisible migrants.' These are people who have arrived from other parts of the Catalan territory. Socially, they are not perceived as newcomers, nor do they consider themselves migrants, and hence, they fall into the category of native and Catalans. However, sometimes I have noticed the use of the word *xava*, a derogatory term that refers to people coming mainly from the metropolitan area of Barcelona.

On the other pole of the tension, there are the migrants. Although they might obtain Spanish nationality, they will remain in this group; as other authors have astutely shown (Titley and Lentin 2008; Hage 2000), citizenship has an ethnocultural or even racial matrix, and the migrant condition cannot be as quickly erased as some would have it. The social understanding of citizenship is part of a continuous negotiation located in a specific territory and social reality and relates to ideas of belonging and the values and moral projects associated with the social space involved (Back 2009). In the following section, we will be looking further into the complex social categorizations.

SOCIAL CATEGORIZATIONS

The truth is that being or becoming part of one community or another is a complex process, which I will simplify in the following way: Although the negotiation of the borders between the different groups is continuous and never finished, when it comes to demarcating the symbolic boundaries of the inhabitants of Salt, specific markers are used that generally follow the lines of more global social categories based on sociocultural factors, such as physiognomy, gender, language, religion, ethnicity, and class. Thus, we can distinguish various ideal types of migrants in the town.

First, we should distinguish between *estranger* or *guiri*, which refers to migrants coming from the Global North, such as the occasional French student from Escola Universitària de la Salut i l'Esport (EUSES), tourists, or someone like me, for example, and *immigrant*, which refers to people from the Global South. These two categories have other ethnocultural distinctions depending on the speaker and on the relationship established with the listener. Thus, either notion is linked to existing power imbalances and the perception of the other. Migrants are indeed the ones who occupy the subordinate positions of the social structure (Delgado 1997, 11). In this sense, three characteristics define the migrant: foreignness, hailing from the Global South and being a low-income worker (Ribas Mateos 2004, 184).

Thus, *marroquí* (Moroccan) is the most accepted form among the community of people with Moroccan nationality, whereas *moro*, another frequently used term, carries pejorative connotations and could also include people of other nationalities. *Arabs*, which has no pejorative meaning, is seldom heard and would, first and foremost, be used to distinguish between Arabs and *Berbers* or *Amazigs*. For this reason, it requires particular historical and geographical knowledge that is often only found among the Moroccans themselves. This is because most Moroccans who live in Salt are from the Rif area, where the Amazigh ethnic group has a significant presence.

Due to geopolitical, historical, and colonial reasons studied elsewhere (Lundsteen 2018), the distinction between moro and Spaniards in terms of physiognomy is highly unstable and sometimes directly unsustainable. For this reason, the typical and hegemonic system of distinction is what has been called *casticism* (Staellert 1998), an ethnocultural distinction based on a religious distinction and, above all, the visible social markers of this. Thus, both the (Arabic) language and the clothing are used as exo-descriptors, to the point of arousing a certain suspicion among natives. This phenomenon increases during the month of Ramadan (both the visibility of the Muslim religion and the suspicion that it raises).

However, a certain suspicion is also common among other migrants, neither Moroccan nor Arab. They reiterate the same discourses used by some natives. For example, my Bengali flatmate, Toqueer, told me that, 'they are different, they can take things, on the other hand, well with Blacks, Hondurans, and so on, there's no problem, but you cannot live with Moroccans.' Another example was Camila, the Romanian partner of my roommate Bouba, who told me that all '*moros* are bad, they receive all kinds of aid, and they steal.'

As for Blacks, sub-Saharan Africans, Browns, or Africans, these are categories that generally refer to the group of people from the sub-Saharan region of Africa. However, the primary distinction is related to the black phenotype of the people. The perception is of a poor person, poorly cultivated' and savage, as in the following quote by Ángel: 'the Blacks are very dirty, but they are not as harmful as the Moroccans', and sometimes they are described using the diminutive hence giving them a childish character. Therefore, certain racist ideas continue to reign both in the eyes of the natives and among the migrants themselves, as shown in the following story by Conchita: 'In terms of education. I do not know if it is the strata that has come, but it isn't very easy to find an educated Black guy, I have met an educated *moro* . . . I have worked with some Brown . . . and you don't realise that they are Brown.'

Rather than a simple historical continuation since colonial times, the reason for the prevalence of this social classification can be found in a complex conjunction of local-global processes, among which the main factors at play are the place that this social group occupies in the socio-economic structure, performing manual and low-skilled jobs, existing neocolonial relations between the Global North and the Global South, the symbolism of the poor Black who arrives on the Spanish coasts in boats or trying to cross the fences in Ceuta and Melilla (which, in turn, is the result of unequal global relations, as well as in the countries of departure, such as Morocco), the experiences of NGO workers, and the image transmitted by these same organizations (to attract resources they sell stereotypical images).

In any case, the use of these categories by the natives largely depends on the level of study. Thus, the most politically correct categories—*marroquí,* árabe, or *moreno*—are often and above all used by middle-class Catalan speakers. On the other hand, moro and Black are predominant among the working classes. Most middle-class residents, Catalan speakers, are aware of this difference in discourse to the point that they often use it to distinguish themselves from Spanish-speaking immigrants in a pejorative way. As Pau, resident of the Barri Vell, says: 'It is contradictory that those who felt threatened and ended up leaving the town were the Spaniards; we have a situation here.'

However, these broader differentiations contrasts with the lived reality, where contacts frequently occur between people of different origins, regardless of their origin. In the following subsection, we will analyse how these different categorizations and groupings have become mediated and consolidated through social events and crises in the town and later through the everyday encounters in the community and shared spaces.

CONFLICTS IN SALT: NEGOTIATING THE SOCIAL BOUNDARIES

As classic studies in political anthropology show (Swartz, Turner, and Tuden 1972), the agents of economic and political mobilizations are elites that try to win favour for their activities by combining claims to economic resources with appeals for political support. Appeals for political support, in turn, require the development of the appropriate symbols and codes of behaviour that can elicit a positive response from potential partisans. Contending elites, therefore, not only compete for resources and power but also vie with one another in the elaboration of symbolic systems that can 'win the hearts and minds of the people'. Moreover, these symbols and codes of behaviour must form part of an ideology that defines the goals to which economic allocations and political support are to be put. Competition between elites for resources, allies and followers, and symbols create a political-ecological system of relationships that depends for its very existence on its ability to manipulate micro-ecological adaptations. Therefore, if we are to understand what happens in villages within complex systems, we need not only a better understanding of the political economy, of the processes of economic funding of power capabilities, but also one of political ecology, of the system of relationships between groups possessed of differential access to resources, power, and symbols (Cole and Wolf 1999, 286).

Instances of Insecurity and Crime

In 2009, according to Andreu Bover, head of the *Àrea de Convivència i Integració* (Area of Convivencia and Integration), an administrative department of the town council, two significant conflicts took place. The first was from 24 to 25 August 2009, when a group of young Moroccans apparently tried to steal potatoes from a shop run by a Pakistani couple in Francesc Macià, located in the Barri Centre neighbourhood. According to reports, they insulted and attacked the shopkeeper's wife and stole €280, but the police intervened and arrested them (Barrera 2009a). Later, after being released with charges, they returned to the shop, and a fight started with the shopkeeper. This incident led to a brawl between friends and families of the two groups. Following this, a group of shopkeepers of Indian and Pakistani descent arranged a meeting with the deputy mayor and others demanding a solution to what they referred to as a problem of convivencia (CCMA, TV3 2010b). They referred to a kind of convivencia that does not imply specific cultural values, but rather specific 'civic norms', and above all emphasizes the problem that petty crime creates for the shopkeepers in general. Similar incidents occurred between 'young Moroccans' and 'Pakistani shopkeepers'.

The second incident took place on 25 December 2009, in the street of Doctor Ferran, when, for reasons unknown, a fight broke out between 'ten or fifteen people of black race and Maghrebs who beat each other up with sticks, belts and bottles' (Barrera 2009b). The police issued a warning shot to scatter the fighting parties. This fight was one of several similar incidents in the following days.

Tensions were rising between different groups, but what was interesting was how the media treated these stories. Although the problem of convivencia in one case had nothing to do with that of the other, they were conflated to enhance an imagined community of foreigners as inassimilable cultural others, explicitly drawing on latent social imageries that regard Moroccans as potentially conflictive (see Martín Corrales 2002; Staellert 1998; Mateo Dieste 1997; Lundsteen 2017).

Nonetheless, instead of taking these statements for granted, we should rather aim at critically examining their words, images, representations, and descriptions conveyed. As a matter of fact, here, the media is considered yet another social actor in the field, and taking this seriously calls for scrutiny when treating the information gathered to describe and analyse the social situations historically. To this end, and to attain an overall vision as realistic as possible (Herzfeld 2018), I draw on different sources such as: (a) interviews with important actors in the social situations described, (b) archives, including documents from the local archive of Salt, Arxiu Municipal de Salt, the online archive of *La Farga*, the newspaper libraries of *El Punt/AVUI*, *La*

Vanguardia, *El País*, *La Razón*, *El Mundo*, *El Periódico*, *ABC*, *Diari de Girona*, and the news collection provided by the municipal library of Salt, (c) videos available from the YouTube accounts 'Antonio Martinez Caceres', 'Isabel Pallares TvSalt', and 'InformatiuSaltenc', and (d) reports, and (e) council minutes (2008-2013).

Tense Moments

On 22 February 2010, a 'spontaneous demonstration' of around 200–300 people took place in front of the Salt town hall at the same time as a municipal plenary was being held (Barrera 2010e). The participants entered the hall noisily and insulted some of the politicians who were present (Nadal and Barrera 2010). The mayor asked for a spokesperson to step forward, but the group had none. After a quick meeting with the whole town council, the administration decided to postpone the plenary to Thursday 25 February—a first in the history of Salt.

The aim of the demonstration was, in words of the participants, to draw attention to a growing feeling of insecurity and impunity, as one of the slogans repeated during these incidents—'enough burglaries, more security'—stated. The demonstration was, therefore, related to developments in the town at that time, such as the rising media attention to specific crime incidents (Barrera 2010b, 2010c), some of which seemed to have had significant symbolic value, as with the case of a violent robbery of a bar run by an elderly couple (Barrera 2010d).

Although the mayor and the local police chief repeatedly stated that there had not been any significant rise in the amount of crime committed in Salt, they also acknowledged a change in the manner of crimes committed during the previous months and that the local police had already caught some of the perpetrators (Pinilla 2010). Furthermore, on the same day of the plenary, the budget for the coming year was to be discussed and approved, which already included an increase in the local police force, instalment of CCTV, and similar investments. Moreover, the autonomous police, *els Mossos d'Esquadra*, had changed their actions, an essential fact that the young migrants had experienced in person (CCMA, TV3 2010b).

Among the chief promoters of this demonstration, we found a group of middle-class and mainly Catalan-speaking residents from the Barri Vell neighbourhood, following the words of Alim:

> Many residents in Barri Vell had begun talking, and this place [Can Serrallonga] was crucial in the preparation, the insecurity theme, and so on. People met up here, talked about the topic, "what do we do?" and so on, and "I've had my bike stolen" and so on . . . and around five or ten persons promoted some kind

> of campaign, although not very explicitly, that we are being invaded, and now we are even suffering in our own lives . . . and obviously there were concrete incidents that, well now that we are talking about a small town, and we are talking about a part of that town which is tiny which is this part, Barri Vell, people entered their garage and although part of which is undoubtedly true, there have been lies as well, some people who said they had suffered burglaries when they had not, sometimes people make up things.

An observation that David Estevez, the former councillor of security, backed this up: 'the insecurity demonstration was led by . . . let's not say that it was the neighbourhood association [of Barri Vell] who organised the demonstration, but neighbours of Barri Vell definitely organised it.' In fact, from the information gathered by the local politicians and police officers, it is clear that during the preceding period, a rise and a change in the composition of the type of crimes had taken place. Criminals were now targeting people with possessions, principally in parked vehicles or the theft of bicycles in garages and the like (Barrera 2010b). Moreover, above all, it affected the neighbourhoods of Barri Vell and La Massana, which are middle-class and Spanish working-class neighbourhoods. Thus, this sudden rise in insecurity occurred just when the type of crime changed and the people who were hit by it constituted the more powerful parts of the local society, who would then start a campaign to protect their interests. These campaigns would ripple out to the rest of the local society and implicate the local and regional media.

This promoted an apparently neutral discourse on the insupportable situation of insecurity and crime in the town through a support campaign with banners and posters tagged with the slogan, 'I've been robbed' ('a mi m'han robat') in local shops (Carreras 2010). Again, nobody knew who had made and distributed these banners. The agency was entirely obscured; the real agents (who had been meeting in Can Serrallonga and were most probably from Barri Vell) never stood out, and instead, they started a conflict that other agents took over and led (is this not a classic example of middle-class racism?). Thus, it seems that they were able to mobilize a 'jumping scale'[1] (Smith 1993), including the Spanish working-class, 'old migrants' from the Spanish State and mainly Castilian-speaking residents from the Barri Centre and La Massana, and a lot of media coverage, which helped to produce a 'tense environment'—fertile ground for the plenary on 25 February, when another demonstration took place.

This time the plenary did not get cancelled. Instead, the virulent protesters were expelled from the meeting, and outside it came down to verbal clashes in front of TV cameras when the protesters faced migrants and other residents. The result was a scene of violent verbal confrontation, in which people with explicit racist ideologies got their '15 minutes of fame' by directing abuse towards some of the Moroccans gathered. Because the adolescents were in school, mostly adults were at the scene to respond to the accusations, and it was striking that few sub-Saharan Africans were present. Although 'new migrants' could have been perceived as victims of the rise in crime as well, they were not (Oller 2010).

Thus, lines were drawn between the groups, and although the protests initially were against the local government and did not explicitly name any groups, the ultimate opposition between 'native people' and 'Moroccans' was grounded within the main themes of petty crime and insecurity.

Later that evening, a group of around 200 young residents, mainly of Moroccan origin, gathered in front of the city council to protest against what they perceived as police harassment: On the one hand, they claimed to be subjected to an increasing number of random police controls due to their physical appearance and, on the other, the portrayal of their criminalization in media and local civil society. They described a feeling of uneasiness when walking on the streets where they were in danger of being subjected to arbitrary treatment and symbolic violence (Cosculluela 2010). This feeling was confirmed by some of the social workers working in the neighbourhood of Barri Centre:

> It was continuous, and the youngsters protested because they felt very harassed. After all, it really was exaggerated, VERY exaggerated, some people, even I experienced this, I believe that once I experienced being asked stopped and asked for my papers two times in one day with only a two to three hours difference. *Alim*

Similarly, an unpublished report carried out by a team of researchers at the University of Girona collected interesting statements from a young migrant who clearly showed disproportionate and discriminatory behaviour by the police. Furthermore, even a local police officer confirmed to me that they had sometimes done some pressing in terms of identification that might not have been the most appropriate because it created a sensation of discomfort among the migrants.

Two days later, a meeting was held between different 'Moroccan' associations and people of Moroccan origin on how to deal with the situation, and it became clear that internal conflicts existed (Carranco 2010). Many youngsters seemed to be opposed to the more conservative parts of the 'Moroccan community'. Mohammed At-taouil, a charismatic 'cultural broker' and leader of the cultural/religious association *Al-Hilal*, had a good relationship with the local administration and asked for the meeting to be held in the municipal pavilion. At first, a group of youngsters were gathered outside and refused to enter, but after a brief conversation, At-taouil convinced them that the best way to tackle the situation was when all entities showed a united front. In the meeting, representatives from regional associations, such as the Federation of Cultural Entities of Moroccan Origin (FECCOM) and the Union of the Islamic Centres in Catalonia (UCIC) and the Moroccan-born PSC representative of Barcelona, Mohammed Chaib, were present.

The only attendee not of Moroccan descent was Andreu Bover, the head of the *Àrea de Convivència i Integració*. The administration had been worried about the social tension created and thus tried to calm the youngsters and their sympathizers (such as 28-year-old Ismael or Morad El-Hassani). The fear of a social breakdown or unrest was manifest, and one might speculate whether the more conservative parts of the Moroccan community—including At-taouil—had made a prior arrangement with Bover to try and reduce the tension. It would have been in their best interest because they might have been worried about the future mosque construction project they had invested in, an argument that the administration had used in other events. What seems clear is that the conflict and its management ended up mapping a specific power field, where both At-taouil and Andreu Bover seem to have gained a certain legitimacy and influential positions, both politically and economically.

Finally, an agreement was reached. They would refrain from protesting and organizing any further demonstrations until a scheduled meeting with the mayor on 1 March had been held, and a commission was set up in agreement for the meeting with the mayor, Iolanda Pineda. This commission was mainly composed of representatives from each entity and association operating in the region, leaving young people a minority. The members were Mohammed At-taouil (*al-hilal*), Mohammed Abderraman (spokesperson for the new young people's entity *Joves per Salt*), Mohammed Chaib (*PSC*[2]), Younes Oussaid (*al-mohajirim al-maghriba*), Mohammed Houri (*CODENAF*), Morad El-hassani, and a representative from the other religious Islamic association of Salt, *Magrebins per la pau* (also invested in the project of building a mosque). This way, it stood clear that before the meeting with the mayor, the dominant attitude among the commission members was pragmatic rather than critical.

The meeting took place in the town hall with Andreu Bover and Iolanda Pineda and representatives from the local police department and the autonomous police (els Mossos). Although the commission informed on the young people's complaints regarding the pressure put on them, there was no change on that point when considering the outcomes of the meeting. Instead, it was decided that the police would continue their 'strong presence' until the end of June, and the youngsters accepted this publicly, only shyly requesting 'a little respect'.

It ended with a famous photo and the announcement of the creation of a *Taula de Convivència* (Nadal 2010), followed by a public statement by Mohammed At-taouil, saying: 'I am happy [that] today we have reached an agreement that we are citizens here in Salt and we want to live peacefully, *convivencia* and integrate.' A statement that Mohammed Abderraman backed: 'All the young ones here in Salt will contribute to having a cleaner town and a good image, and that the immigration will bear a lot of advantages and good stuff from now onwards' (see CCMA, TV3 2010a).

In the town, the photo of the mayor and the commission soon came to confirm the initial suspicions concerning who had been to blame for the social situations and conflicts: the ones who felt targeted by the criminalization. In this way, despite the rhetoric, it seemed that the Moroccans and the police were the only parts involved in a dispute that had earlier been described as a problem of crime and convivencia. Thus, I think it fair to say that the social effect of this social conflict, though maybe only implicitly, was that the problem had been one between the Moroccan youth (and not young migrants in general) and the local society—a reading, which in the eyes of the more sceptical parts of the local society, had been latent the whole time:

> Yes, it became explicit. The mayor didn't say it, but there were comments like 'you know what youngsters we are referring to' and then they would say youngsters of Moroccan origin . . . and well sometimes reality speaks for itself. The people who demonstrated used this as an argument, 'we went to the town council to complain, and the ones who reacted were the ones who felt targeted, which means that they are the ones doing it' words of the owner of Can Serrallonga. *Alim*

Although a variety of opinions were held, most people—such as the local neighbourhood and shopkeepers' associations who were planning a demonstration for the upcoming weekend on insecurity—presented the problem mainly as one of crime or insecurity. Even among the 'Moroccans', there were people who felt embarrassed by the situation, as Alim recalls: "'[S]ee what these scoundrels have made to us' talking about the youngsters, and there were others who said 'look we have come here to work, we have come here to make a living, but what the heck are these people doing? They must be sent back to Morocco.'"

However, a different kind of mobilization not founded in ethnocultural lines could have been possible because some migrant shopkeepers and citizens were saying they had been robbed, and some 'migrant' residents had even attended the demonstration (Quesada and Carranco 2010; El Periódico 2010). Nevertheless, this representation was cancelled. So, despite similar opinions, the latent interpretations became manifest. This way, the imagined communities of 'us' and 'them' and their symbolic borders went from being abstract ideas and loosely bounded to becoming materialized and reinforced in the everyday practices during these social conflicts. One side accused the other of being responsible and felt they were victims and reacted collectively, thus reinforcing the us and them opposition, as we see in the following quote: 'Another girl with headscarf explains to two others in perfect Catalan that this is the second time today that she has been told that the "moros are the ones to blame"' (Playà Maset 2010a).

In the aftermath of the demonstration, Salt received much attention from journalists looking for stories, most of whom emphasized the size of the migrant population living in the town and the continuing tension between residents, distinguished by their nationalities, due to a rise in crime. For instance, a small and seemingly insignificant incident, a simple discussion between two residents over a parking lot, turned into a fight, which was described in several newspapers as representative of the unprecedented situation that the town was experiencing.

The media also played an essential role in making a further jump in scale possible by conveying an image or representation of chaos and a sense of insecurity primarily through Spanish and Catalan television channels, such as *Cuatro*, *Antena 3*, *la Sexta*, and *TV3*. Thus, it reached the point at which Salt became infamous at the State level. As Marta recalls: '[S]ometimes I talk to friends of mine from Barcelona and even from Madrid who says «wow, Salt your town, how dodgy!»' The depictions are mainly negative, sensationalist, and alarmist, with headings such as 'Salt, a steamer—A report: The laboratory of hate', and 'Salt: A Trial of Convivencia' (see also Antena 3 2011; Libertad Digital 2011; RTVE 2011a, 2011b, 2011c).

Convivencia: Frictions and Fusions

Against static descriptions, the inhabitants negotiate the endo and exo descriptors daily through their encounters and relationships. Some already know each other, but the distance is greater with others. In the spaces of the cafeterias or bars, frequented above all by local and Moroccan workers, there are talks between several of the clients and owners that are often based on the daily experiences of coexistence, as we see in the following extract from my diary:

> Today in Mari Carmen's bar, I met an elder lady called Josefa; she was 89 years old and Mari Carmen's mother-in-law. Both were originally from Andalusia. When I entered the bar with Mostafa, they talked together while a Moroccan-looking guy read the newspaper at one of the tables. Mostafa said 'Hi' to the ladies and greeted the guy shaking his hand and then putting it to the heart. We then sat down with the guy at the table and ordered a coffee, when suddenly the 'grandmother' started to talk to us. She said that she wasn't feeling well and had had a hard time getting out, which is why she hadn't gone dancing. And then she

> added that she is old. Mostafa then told her that she's not old. The ones who are old are permanently in their beds. She said she doesn't want to be like that. She then continued saying that her neighbours take care of her, they worry about her. 'They're moros, but they're good people'. Mostafa laughed while replying, 'oh, despite being moros, eh!?' Afterwards, Josefa told us how the last time they had been to Morocco, they had brought her tons of gifts and that they really treat her very well. They've grown quite attached. However, the whole time she referred to them as 'moros'. Later, she told us that the other day she had to knock on her neighbours' door and scold them. Apparently, they were celebrating a birth, and they were dancing and making much noise, 'boom, boom, boom, just like the black people do it.' (24/09/2011, Diary 1, 35–37)

The first thing to notice in this case is how the categories are used more descriptively as a simple statement of the facts with no clear negative undertone or pejorative implication. Indeed, as symbolic interactionism explains, the attribution to one group or another depends to a certain degree on the person who enounces and the symbolic, cultural, and economic capital at their disposal (i.e., the intertwined power relations) to be considered socially effective or valid. An agentic approach that must be paired with a view on the more structural aspects, in a more Althusserian approach perhaps: What are the symbolic representations offered via the media, culture, and the State in general? Pierre Bourdieu articulated this tension quite successfully via his notions of the *field* and *habitus*. The field is the socially constructed possibilities of action and enunciation in their interplay and tensions, observable via the sociological and discursive analysis. The habitus is the sum of possibilities that a specific individual have within these structuring structures (Bourdieu 1977). Let us have a look at another example.

During my fieldwork, I took part in Catalan language classes. Although one of the main reasons for doing so was to meet potentially new informants, during the lessons, I was able to observe the negotiation of belonging and bordering practices regarding the aforementioned sociocultural logics. During the classes, students were encouraged to present 'culture' in a static way and, more specifically, as bound to the territory where we 'come from'. We would then talk about 'what we do there' (i.e., the country we are from) while the teacher would explain 'what we [Catalans] do here'. In this way, cultural boundaries were clearly established, relegating a territory for each culture, defining what is 'normal' in each national context, and what would be considered 'native' or 'appropriate'.

Given the insights from research in social sciences that point out how culture is a never-finished and relational product of local-global processes, we might consider the habits practised by the students as new and hybrid; after all, they live in Salt and Catalonia and not in Morocco or India. However, in the classes, each would be considered and, to a certain degree, presented themselves as the representative of each their origin. This way, they strengthened the hegemonic ideas regarding what is considered normal cultural expressions in the town, Catalonia, and Spain. There is no doubt that the predominance of a celebratory multicultural pedagogy in Catalan language classes—resulting from what Sahlins called the 'Culture of cultures' (Sahlins 1993, 19)—has undoubtedly influenced the prevalence of this classroom dynamic. However, why did the students not question this and instead reproduce the categories that would exclude themselves from any claim to belonging and establish boundaries? To explain this, one would have to bear in mind the field in which the interactions took place and the social agents at play.

The ideas of the Lebanese-Australian anthropologist Ghassan Hage are of much use here. Following his theoretical-analytical proposal (2000), one may understand the classroom as a field constituted by cultural and symbolic capital that situate the social agents in social positions and unequal power relations. In the national field, the ones who have more capital are placed in positions whereby they have more legitimacy to decide what belongs and what does not in terms of cultural practices and, therefore, 'the power to position others in it' (Hage 2000, 55). Hence, the teacher is dominant, followed closely by those who have Spanish nationality and comply with the expected ethno-racial characteristics; they are the ones who define the sociocultural dynamics and eventually how they can be presented and in what order. This conceptualization of the logic at play reveals a close and fundamental relation between bordering practices, belonging and space.

Although truly ethnocultural identification is a mundane yet complex phenomenon—indeed multidirectional in that it can be appropriated and put in force by anyone—the process is not void of power relations. Although any normative identification implied in the communication taking place in an apparently egalitarian public sphere has been widely criticized (see, e.g., Fraser 1990; Calhoun 2010), the critique could as easily be transferred to any kind of racialized communication because racism is indeed exercised from a powerful position,; otherwise we would not be talking about racism (Miles and Brown 2003; Lentin and Titley 2011). Therefore, when analysing the use of labels, discourses, or in this case, bordering practices, one must always bear in mind the locus of enunciation as well as the immediate and more global context surrounding the speech act.

Both during language classes and in the street, I saw how migrants with a whiter skin colour and middle class (high cultural capital, but often working in precarious conditions) positioned themselves differently to other migrants, often either Africans or American migrants of darker skin colour. Veronica is particularly representative in this regard. Originally from Portugal, although she had lived several years in both Switzerland and Venezuela, she had a bachelor's degree in biochemistry and lived in the more recently created neighbourhood La Massana for the previous three years. During our conversations, she regretted having few interactions with her fellow neighbours. According to her, the neighbourhood was exempt from any social life. At that time, she was unemployed but would attend language classes, including the introductory course to Catalan, where we had met. When talking about the central neighbourhood where she had been working doing interviews for a social survey, she would refer to the migration and instantly distinguish between her and them, often using the African migrants as points of reference. Somewhat like another, Conchita, a 53-year-old Argentinian woman, resident in the area surrounding the Catalunya square, with whom I was also studying Catalan, told me:

> I've had a hard time familiarizing myself with the fact that there are Blacks and moros here . . . and I'm a migrant, eh . . . but in Argentina, if you see a Black guy he'd often be a football player . . . and a moro is very unusual [to see], you'd see them dancing belly-dance . . . but the girls dressed like nuns you'd see them in the nun's school . . . so, obviously, it's a bit of a shock . . . Moreover, the perception that we have of the women who are dressed that way . . . . Sometimes when I see one of them in the street passing me by, and you can only see their eyes, I think to myself 'what has that women done, to be obliged to walk the street dressed like that?' [laughing] . . . I think of it and laugh because then I think, 'how can I think this way if she dresses like this it must be because she wants to' . . . I don't know honestly, that's what I understand now. . . . What's more, in the building where I live there are many people, it's multi-ethnic ok, I get along much better with the ones from here maybe because we're much more alike.

Some are more used to diversity than others, a fact which Wessendorf (2013) has called 'commonplace diversity'. In this sense, it is significant that, already in origin, many sub-Saharan Africans are accustomed to high levels of diversity in terms of ethnicity and languages. Thus, for example, many of the people I met knew at least three languages and used several on a normal day, thus coinciding with the observations of Heil (2014).

Many natives use one ascription or another in addition to the various qualifications linked to social groups, influenced mainly by the media and daily encounters and experiences. In this sense, the following conversation between Ángel and Pilar is revealing. They are a Spanish couple born in the late 1950s and originally from Andalusia. In 2012, when I interviewed them, they had been living in Plaça Catalunya for 37 years, 13 in their penthouse where they received me.

A: When I see reports, for example from Casablanca, Marrakech . . . I don't see people like that

P: But in the touristy cities they can't give an example . . . of dirt

A: If they leave a town and go to a place outside the capital

P: They live the same way as they do here in town

A: Of course, they live in a small village because those in cities and communities do not live as they do.

P: Yeah?

A: The Blacks do, but the Moroccans in their country do not do what they do here, and I doubt that they will, I have not been to Morocco, but I've seen reports, and I work with people . . . Because work in many places, and my relationship is with them. . . . Because they are often either bricklayers, painter, etc. and I live with them and work with them, and they tell me that in their country they do not do what they do here, that's what they tell me. . . . Then why do they do it here?

In a similar vein, a symbolic community is created among Spanish speakers. In this sense, people from Latin American countries are in a more favourable position than those from African countries or Asia and who do not speak Spanish as their main language. In a sense, they share a certain annoyance about mastering Catalan with many Spanish speakers. Not mastering the Catalan language can relegate them to a lower position than others who master it.

There are also visions in which belonging to one religion or another becomes essential. The strong contrast that some perceive between the Christian Catholic community and the Muslim community (which is often equated with Arab) is exemplary. The visibility generated by some practices related to Islam, especially during Ramadan or the celebration of the ritual sacrifice festival (Aid al-Adha), makes the socio-religious more visible and thus gains more significant importance in the day-to-day life of the inhabitants (both Muslim and non-Muslim). During the month of Ramadan, Muslim people dress differently, and due to fasting, *sawm*, their practices in the social space of the town also change significantly. Those who do not work go from being in the terraces to being primarily at home or in the squares or parks (thus avoiding terraces). Therefore, because a great majority of the migrants are from countries where Islam is the main religion, activity in public spaces during the day is less than at other times. Furthermore, to avoid the social control exercised in the community, non-practitioners frequent other places on the margins. At night during Ramadan, human activity increases significantly compared with other months. Thus, for example, it is common to find people walking towards the mosque to pray at night in addition to celebrating a significant collective prayer on Fridays at the soccer field Coma-Cros.

Faced with the growing visibility of Islam, a latent hostility becomes apparent, a phenomenon some call *Islamophobia* (Allen 2010; Esposito and Kalin 2011). In this sense, the following anecdote is exemplary. One day in Catalan class, a colleague told us that until three years ago, she had not been wearing a veil and that when she put it on, her neighbours and work colleagues treated her differently. She was continually questioned, and she lost her job because her colleagues could not accept her wearing it, even though she did not wear the veil when she worked. She also said that she was fed up with having to explain herself to her Spanish friends and that people perceived her as a victim when she had chosen to put it on of her own free will; it seemed paradoxical to her that people imagined an imposition when they could not accept her will.

Although I largely agree with some authors' critiques of Islamophobia (Cesari 2006; Halliday 1999), it is often challenging to distinguish Islamophobia from racism (anti-Muslim or anti-Maghreb). I believe that there is an essential aspect of Muslim anti-religiosity in these expressions that racism per se would not be able to account for. However, as racism and anti-religiosity often overlap and are confused, I would advocate for a relational understanding of this; they might be two sides of the same coin, and of course, the importance of relating them with other factors, especially those of a (geo)political-economic nature (Lundsteen 2020a).

We can also observe important internal divisions within the migrants. For instance, what could be a grand Muslim, pan-Islamic community, shows internal contradictions and hierarchies. Demba, for example, generally did not like Moroccans. He wanted to avoid 'their sites', and they annoyed him because 'they always spoke to him about issues of Islam.' This might indeed draw on pre-existing socio-historical relationships between groupings and ideas of race, according to which Sub-Saharan Muslims are perceived as less illustrated and do not dominate or know Islam well because of the continuation of animistic and mystical practices. Something similar is said about the Amazig populations, as Nadia points out:

> [Speaking of the 'Moroccan community' of Salt] Is quite united when dealing with associations and so . . . However, there are also separations like between the Catalans and the Spanish, because in Morocco you also have Amazighs, Berbers. . . . We are from the west, and there are Arabs, and in fact there is discrimination.

Although it is not the object of the present research, it seems relevant to me in that it shows how social divisions based mainly on ideas of human evolution, often the product of socio-historically unequal relationships (Mateo Dieste 1997), have become globalized, creating hierarchies among the populations of the Global South as well. Something that the Peruvian sociologist Aníbal Quijano (2000) called 'the coloniality of power'. This division permeates the entire global society and confers on some people more symbolic-cultural power, according to their position in said economic-political structuring, based on ethnic-cultural, gender. and class factors.

Nevertheless, how can we explain that some inhabitants have more symbolic power and establish what is considered normal or even original? What practices and which subjects belong to the social space of the neighbourhood?

'AT HOME': URBAN BORDERING PRACTICES

> Familiarity is essential for a sense of community, but the latter also requires a sense of shared symbolic forms and the existence of support networks of friends and relatives (Hage 2000, 40)

Influenced by Ghassan Hage (2000), I will here take my point of departure from the idea of a 'field of national belonging'—an idea that stresses that although certain cultural differences might be tolerated in one country or territory, some cultural practices considered original or native tend to dominate over others. Hage argues that the natives (i.e., people from the hegemonic socio-cultural group) employ what he calls 'nationalist practices' via a spatial/territorial discursive projection. This conceptualization explains very well how ideas such as 'home' and 'nation' are closely linked and why they have such a symbolic power: They are all based on some kind of territoriality, one which the ethnography is full. In fact, the following quotation from an interview with Pilar, a 58-year-old woman who lived in the area of the Catalunya square, is a good example of this:

> What I can't stand . . . is that they don't know how to live with us . . . that is, I'm not supposed to adapt to them, I'm sorry but . . . I'm at home you know . . . Carolina [a Peruvian woman living in the town for almost 30 years] explained it very well the other day. . . . It's as if I was at home and somebody from outside came and dictated some norms that I'd have to follow, right? That is if somebody comes from outside the normal thing would be to follow the existing rules and norms of living together in that country...one can't just come here and try to change everything. . . . I'm against that

So, we see how the idea of 'home'—in sociocultural terms and implying a territorial identification—serves to justify some cultural practices over others. Some practices are presented to belong more to one territory than to another.

It is a move that justifies a more privileged position of some people over others and the right to discursively manage others, including any symbolical and material inclusion and exclusion:

> The discourse of 'home' is one of the most pervasive and well-known elements of nationalist practices. Strangely enough, however, it has become part of an anti-racist common sense to consider 'go home' statements as mere 'racism'. Yet, surely, the expressed wish to send undesirable others to their 'home' is as clear a nationalist desire as can be, even if it involves a racial categorisation of those one wishes to see 'go home'. In the desire to send the other 'home', subjects express implicitly their own desire to be at home. . . . Furthermore, because 'home' refers more to a structure of feelings than a physical, house-like construct, it is fragmentary images, rather than explicit formulations, of what the homely nation ought to be like that we obtain by listening to people's comments. Together, however, these fragments show the national home to be structured like many other images of homely life, around the key themes of familiarity, security and community. (Hage 2000, 39–40)

Although a minority, there alternative views of the social, people who resort to class or neighbour as when referring to the social groups in town. In fact, in some local settings in Catalonia, where social conflicts, often dubbed cultural conflicts, have taken place, such as Salt, we see recent attempts to bridge solidarity across an increasing plurality of identity markers, often perceived as something negative to social cohesion. Hence, we see a proliferation of the use of the category of 'neighbours', as an alternative marker, a categorization especially promoted by activists and NGOs, to create an alternative and local community of belonging. It renders residency and implication in the neighbourhood or the town more relevant than ethnocultural aspects, gender, or citizenship. It allows for equal inclusion of people of other nationalities and minorities in general and creates an egalitarian sense of belonging. However, I argue that there is a catch and possibly a risk with this reading of the social reality. By ignoring the existing structural inequalities, one projects an illusion of equality that might finally reproduce or naturalize these inequalities, accordingly responsibilizing the individual for their position.

The slogan, 'we are all neighbours', as a social worker expressed it in a documentary by TV3 (CCMA, TV3 2010b), visualizes an idealized horizon in which everybody who lives in the neighbourhood is content with one another. Nonetheless, this apparently neutral idea runs into problems because it neglects pre-existing inequalities. The mere reliance that some of these actions have on 'public space' as an adequate arena for meaningful and egalitarian intercultural communication or dialogue is simply too naïve. Although Fraser (1990) pointed to many of the problems with this belief in her critique of the public *sphere*, other authors have shed similar critiques regarding public *space* (Staeheli and Thompson 1997; Di Masso and Dixon 2015). Some residents can manage the cultural codes, symbols, and so on better than others. The entrance and belonging to an imagined community are always negotiable and negotiated, boundaries and borders are (re)created and crossed, and the same thing goes for the social category of 'neighbour.' As we see in the following extract:

> I entered a bar that I'd categorized as 'Spanish' due to its regulars and ordered a small beer I'd drink in the bar. Many people were outside the bar or in the doorway [observing a police raid]. After a few sips, I would join them outside. It wouldn't take a minute before two of them would ask me if I was a journalist (a young guy around my age and an elder one). They said 'that, or secret police' when I refuted such a claim. I told them that 'I'm from the neighbourhood' and laughed at the secret police claim. The younger guy said they were just kidding and told the others to 'leave Bojan [a Catalan football player of Croatian descent] alone'. Meanwhile, the other insisted on me being a journalist, and said 'you're from the neighbourhood? But I've never seen you here, you're not from the neighbourhood', talking to the others and drawing attention to my [foreign] presence. (14/10/2011, Diary 1, 52–53)

The symbolic community of neighbours at first seems like an open and inclusive category, which depends on neither nationality nor ethnicity. However, in practice, it is wedded to implicit ideas regarding who belongs and what neighbourhood and neighbourliness are, which all transcend the initially civic and inclusive notion.

One logical conclusion from Tim Edensor's work (2004, 2006) on the asymbolic aspects of nationhood is that unremarkable material aspect such as house styles, leisure facilities, urban design in general, and subtler aspects such as 'soundscapes' and 'smellscapes' 'contribute making the nation a visible, tangible presence in people's routine experience of space' (Antonsich 2015, 302). It was the famous Spanish writer Goytisolo (1985) who often referred to this when talking about his sensory experiences with the plurality of cultures, cuisines, and people in places such as Paris, New York, and Berlin. Hence, we can deduce that concerning a specific space such as the nation-state's territory and that of a neighbourhood, some forms of being and belonging, smells, and sounds (language) might be rendered more natural than others. Similarly, some subjects might be perceived as more 'indigenous' in racial and ethnic terms than others, and some cultural expressions are more genuine than others. A phenomenon that Hage (2000) has named a homely imaginary, that is, 'an idealized image of what this national spatial background ought to be like' (Hage 2000, 39).

In practice, this would explain why residents more often resort to a unique and privileged position in terms of the moral, cultural, and ethnic aspects of belonging, as the ones we have seen in the previous, and to a lesser extent to an abstract urban belonging to the neighbourhood or the town; their relative privilege might be at stake. The neighbourhood is truly 'a politically charged category that gives symbolic meaning to the social space: it can promote forms of exclusionary belonging reproducing class inequalities . . . or challenge them' (Palomera 2013, 11). Therefore, we would have to study the relationship between the social space and the symbolic communities arising and how these communities are composed: What are the national or ethnocultural ideas about belonging, what does it mean to be a neighbour, and what contending visions of the neighbourhood are present? The obvious deduction is that conflicts might arise around contending conceptualizations of living in space and with each other and to whom the shared space belongs.

Often, people who feel and are perceived as native refer to the insolent and contingent appropriations of space by those perceived as foreigners (in their eyes) as 'invasions' and 'occupations'. These discourses often take the shape of moral judgements regarding the belonging or not of specific values and social practices. To this end, they resort to a greater legitimacy based on their moral-cultural-ethnic belonging and, to a much lesser degree, citizenship status. They define and decide which practices are acceptable and which are not, projecting the latent logic of the nation-state on the scale of the neighbourhood. All in all, the product of a nationalist-culturalist reading of the social world and space, which is hegemonic in the social field, according to which a Muslim is considered less of a national or 'from here' in Salt, despite being born in the country or even in the town. The same can be said for a Black person (due to skin colour) or an Arabic speaker. So, instead of creating a symbolic community of neighbours, certain symbols such as the veil or phenotypes are considered the contours of incommensurable cultural borders. In this way, the culturalist readings are self-fulfilling and end up naturalizing the divisions created, as well as the cultural conflicts emerging from the space:

> Social life here is fine as long as you meet with people from here . . . and they gather on their own. That's it, each lives their own life. . . . *Pilar*

> Everyone lives in their world, I think. Although people talk about conviviality, and that we understand each other well here, and so on. By the end of the day, everyone gathers with their group of equals. They look for each other and are there for each other. The people of Africa have a culture, a tradition, and for this culture to endure and grow, of course, people have to stick together, right? It may be more difficult if you go with a Catalan or with a . . . *Nadia*

The atmosphere engendered in the town, especially since the tense moments of 2010–2011, has cut ties between migrants and natives. An interesting case was that of Nadia. Born in Calonge, her parents are Moroccan. She was 19 years old and studying psychology. In her youth, she had always had many relationships with natives, but as she had grown older, she discovered certain differences that, according to her, made it more normal and comfortable to be with people alike (in ethnocultural or religious terms). An experience that had intensified after her decision to wear a veil (when I met her, she had only been wearing the scarf for half a year). In the case of my Catalan classmate, the experience of wearing the veil had been somewhat traumatic for her, above all because of the reactions of many of her native acquaintances. Nadia's reaction to these experiences seems to be a good example of what I would call an *essentialist defence*, often observable among descendants of migrants, and it also shows to what extent the negotiations of the groups are not unidirectional. According to her, there is an incompatibility between her cultural logics and the hegemonic ones of society, and this tension creates an identity crisis that she expressed as follows:

> Q: Do you believe there is any inconsistency between being Catalan and Muslim?
>
> A: No, you can be, if you feel that way, you can be both, and I know, I have a friend who is Muslim and feels Catalan, who was also born here. Yes, indeed you can be, but I don't, I'm sorry, I don't feel Catalan
>
> Q: Then what do you feel?
>
> A: Well, that's another thing. . . . It would take me a long time to explain this. I don't know what I am. Because when I was in Morocco, I also thought that it was my place, but when I was there, I realized that it was not. Neither is my place. I don't feel here or there. I'm from the world [laughing]. I do not know; I do not know. Well, I have lived here all my life, and I'm used to this, so. But do I feel Catalan, feel like a Catalan from here? No, I don't.

Instead of seeing the internal heterogeneity of the national field, of which she was part, and the unequal power relations that compose it, she surrendered to what we can call the fantasy of cultural hegemony of the dominant classes. Instead of struggling for a more diverse and heterogeneous composition, she reproduced the symbolic boundaries between social groups that present themselves as natural and, therefore, falls into the same essentialist trap as many natives.

However, the negotiation of the boundaries is continuous, and they are reproduced or transformed daily. One day, when I was going to Catalan class, a group of Moroccan women approached a crossroad with their children. As a car was approaching, a girl of about three ran across the street. The driver of the vehicle, a native woman, managed to divert the car enough and stop, thus avoiding an accident. Later, she left the vehicle visibly frightened while the girl's mother lay down on the ground due to the fright, and another woman tried to comfort her, saying 'everything is fine, nothing has happened.' The woman in the car approached some other native women and a man, and I heard one of them say, 'they run loose, they run loose. That's what they're used to.' The other Moroccan women comforted and helped the woman whose child had nearly been hit, while none of the natives, including the car driver, approached the Moroccan woman.

Two important things happened here. First is the remark that the girl is 'used to it', as if the little girl had been raised in the wilderness. It showed that the interlocutor assumed that even though the girl was young, she was used to 'another culture', that of her parents. In this way, she established a direct link between the culture of a specific place and the innate culture of the girl. The second was the symbolic division created. There was no contact or words between women built on and reproduced an already existing division. In the end, the course of the event ended up reinforcing the borders of the imagined communities and the links between their members.

Another event occurred one night when I was at El Tinell, the only bar in Salt that closed late. Demba, my main informant, and I had decided to go for a beer. He was unhinged and talking about leaving town. Suddenly, a dark-skinned man who had been at the bar began to vomit on the floor. Consequently, the waitress came over and dumped coffee on the floor where he had vomited. The man appeared drunk and ill, and the woman asked him calmly why he had not gone to the bathroom. A Spanish-speaking boy then spoke to Demba. Demba had not listened and asked what he said. Another man said, 'Don't look at me!' Demba then asked him why he said that. Then the first boy asked him, 'Is this your friend?' referring to the man vomiting at the bar. And Demba said, 'no, what's that got to do with it, cousin?' To which the other man replied, 'I'm not your cousin; don't look at me.' Thus, a brawl began. In the end, Demba wanted to approach him calmly to clarify what happened, but he could not do so because when we tried to separate them, more people were involved. There were some Moroccan boys whom Demba had greeted and spoken with, and there was also a small group of Spaniards, people with whom Demba got along well, such as Pere and another younger guy. However, an older man with them also got close to Demba and said something that made Demba furious, to the point that he started threatening him. Demba told him that he would aim a 9-mm pistol at him if necessary. When he said this, the man got angry. In the end, the owner of the premise intervened and reprimanded Demba. In an angry tone, he told him to stay away from the others, sit and calm down, or leave.

In this chapter, we have reviewed the social categories and categorizations in the making. Following this line of enquiry, the next chapter will deal with the spatiality of the conflicts and, more importantly, how these conflicts over and in space relate to the social groupings and, in chapters 4 and 5, how they justify both urban and social policy measures.

CHAPTER 2 NOTES

1. Neil Smith (1992) and other radical geographers introduced this concept to describe a political strategy to circumvent and challenge the present entrenched structure of scale. Groups at a disadvantage at one scale will pursue their aims at a different scale, hoping to turn the balance of power to their advantage.
2. *Partit dels Socialistes de Catalunya* [The Catalan Socialist Party] is a regional branch of the Spanish Socialist Party, PSOE (Social Democrats).

Chapter Three

Spaces of Conflict, Conflicts over Space

> Socio-political contradictions are realized spatially. The contradictions of space thus make the contradictions of social relations operative. In other words, spatial contradictions 'express' conflicts between socio-political interests and forces; it is only *in* space that such conflicts come effectively into play, and in so doing they become contradictions *of* space (Lefebvre 1991, 365)

What we have seen so far shows us that the daily life of the town is both full of simple cohabitation (i.e., simple living side by side) and confrontations and conflicts, the meaning of which is in dispute. Likewise, we have seen how social markers are used both by natives and migrants, although from unequal positions, to make sense of this. This chapter will show how social inequalities among residents foster internal divisions expressed through or in a competition over space, which any critical analysis on the topic must address.

Among the civil society of Salt, there is a generalized perception that it is a 'welcoming town', in the sense that it is made up of various and continuous migration processes (Catalan society has a similar perception of itself). However, this generalized meaning collides with the social reality lived in Barri Centre. Here we see that a large majority of the Spanish nationals express a divide between 'those from outside' and 'the ones from here', divisions that could easily cross the symbolic boundaries of ethnicity and culture, mainly referring to the temporal settlement of the inhabitants. However, in this case, they coincide with a grouping of the former migrants from other parts of Spain and the Catalans, in distinction to the migrants.

In the hegemonic vision of the social space of the town, these 'foreigners' are continuously blamed for the negative changes perceived in the town. Supposedly, the arrival of the foreign nationals made a large group of Spanish nationals leave town and, more specifically, the Barri Centre, with the subsequent deterioration of the social and physical space. However, adopting the widely accepted idea that there is a dialectical relation between space and social relations (Lefebvre, 1991), I argue that these changes should be understood in relation to changes in the real estate market in the region and specifically the neighbourhood and the labour market—in sum, the production of space and the economy. The liberalization of the real estate market late in the 1990s created a new situation, fostered speculation, and above all, led to critical urban transformations and disinvestments in the neighbourhood in question. A process that implied, and simultaneously produced, specific kinds of mobility and immobility (people who would move in and out, and others who could do neither), in which the foreigners played an essential role.

The arrival of this new contingent of people brought a new super-diverse social reality as opposed to an imagined cultural homogeneity and previous social cohesion. Faced with this new scenario, the native population felt that they were in the minority: They perceived an excessively high percentage of migrants, an increasing cultural diversity that undermined the social cohesion (cultural order), from which problems of convivencia (cultural) arise. Certain attitudes are continually ascribed to newcomers, not perceived as belonging to the original social fabric. 'Outsiders' are perceived as transgressors of civic-cultural norms and invaders due to their appropriation of collective spaces. Consequently, there is a sense of cultural loss and insecurity. In this way, convivencia is shown at the ethnographic level above all as a cultural-moral issue.

When analysing the background of these social conflicts, we see that, rather than being the result of an intensification of cultural diversity, they are the product of a growing precariousness, which in turn is the product of the social consequences of the economic crisis.

HOUSING BOOM AND 'NATIVE FLIGHT'

> What happened? First one came, then another, and so many young ones left. Those people from across the street left, then these others came, those who lived right under my house, and they also left, they sold the apartment, which is when they all started to sell flats, the housing boom, which the banks benefitted from later. *Carmen*

At the beginning of the 21st century, many Spanish residents in Barri Centre moved to other neighbourhoods, such as the recently built La Massana or other towns such as Taialà. As Concepción says:

> Many people moved to Taialà or other places close by to Caldes de Malavella. Yeah, they bought apartments, houses and left back then. Yeah, many people live in Taialà. I know three or four whom I knew from living here together, and now when I go up to see my son, I meet them, and we have a chat and about this, and they live there and have lived there for many years.

In their place, new inhabitants moved in, most of them migrants of non-European nationality—a mobility promoted by various socio-economic factors and agents. For instance, according to one of the former residents and a member of the neighbourhood association Can Mericana Seca AVV, one of the main reasons people moved out was the desire to improve their living conditions given the progressive degradation of the neighbourhood and the impassivity of the town hall. However, according to many of the remaining native residents and some social analysts, the reason for what some call a 'native flight' lies in the arrival of migrants. According to this argument, they were the trigger:

> Yes, many people went to La Massana, and they left because the others came. That's the reality . . . Why? Because they're a different culture, a different way of living, and people thought, "oh, no, I'll be leaving." Moreover, since there were cheap loans, they left. *Pilar*

This process of concentration of the migrant population in one area of the town has led to the departure of many of the old residents of the neighbourhood. This continuous trickle of former residents leaving Salt, this flight effect, is even more worrying for municipal officials than the call effect. According to data from the Salt Town Council, from 2004 to the present, some 1,500 people of Spanish nationality who resided in the municipality have gone to live in another city (Sandoval 2007b).

In this way, the degradation of the neighbourhood is presented as a result, and not the primary condition, of the arrival of the new contingent of inhabitants they call 'migrants'. Thus, the socio-economic factors of this population change are entirely ignored. Let us see how it happened.

When analysing the data more closely, five stages become apparent.

Stage 1 (the 1960s–1970s). This was an era marked by the socio-economic effects of the Spanish Civil War. Some regions of Spain were having severe supply problems, whereas others began to prosper at the industrial level; the industrial bases, founded in the colonial era, were already in place, and in this new stage, more labour force was needed or could be used. These two phenomena generated a socio-spatial and human reconfiguration at the State level. Large groups of people migrated from the rural regions and desolate areas of Spain (often Andalusia, Murcia, and Galicia) to the industrial and tourist zones (Basque Country, Madrid, and Catalonia). A development that, at the level of Salt, being as it was the industrial centre of the area, meant a new socio-spatial configuration with the arrival of migrants from other parts of Spain and, thus, a spectacular increase in inhabitants. With this massive influx of people (around 5,520 in 1950–1970), large parts of the Centre neighbourhood and, more specifically, the Catalunya Square were built with poor materials and barely any infrastructure.

Stage 2 (the 1980s–1990s). During the Transition in the 1980s and the 1990s, through neighbourhood struggles for improvement, areas such as the Catalunya Square experienced a vital improvement process in terms of infrastructure, but often the buildings remained the same and progressively decayed.

Stage 3 (the late 1990s–2000). The liberalization in the laws of land ownership introduced by the changes proposed by the laws 7/1997 and 6/1998 promoted greater commercialization and speculation within the housing sector, of which a significant proportion had until then been semi-public. In this context, many homeowners benefitted from the vast increases in the valuation of their flats (according to the Spanish National Institute of Statistics [INE], the prices increased by 180% in Spain in the period between 1998 and 2007), as Carmen recalls it, 'This flat costed me 4 million pesetas [€24,000 in 1995]. They wanted to buy it from me for 18 million [€108,000] in 2001–2002.' Consequently, many neighbours of Spanish nationality left the neighbourhood, ensuring individual progress moving to newly built housing in other parts of the town (e.g., the neighbourhood of La Maçana) or villages with more 'quality-of-life'. At the same time, this mobility was made possible due to the settlement of people from outside who would envision their social mobility through the acquisition of housing stock (figure 3.1). These would often have been rushed into specific areas, such as Salt, niche sectors often promoted by agencies and made possible by racist practices in the housing market (see Lundsteen and Sabaté 2018 for further details).

As more migrants moved in, however, this fact was forgotten or ignored, something we see reflected in most of the interviewees' narratives. As the following account from Concepción shows:

> Q: Why do you think the first ones moved out?
>
> A: Because of what I just told you, because the migrants were moving in
>
> Q: But why did the first ones move out when there were still no . . . ?
>
> A: No, but that doesn't matter, they might have left because their standard of living made it possible to buy a house in Caldes (Malavella), and so they left, the first ones. . . . of course, at that time, a (real estate) agent would come to you and say, 'You put your flat for sale because now you can acquire a house or a living

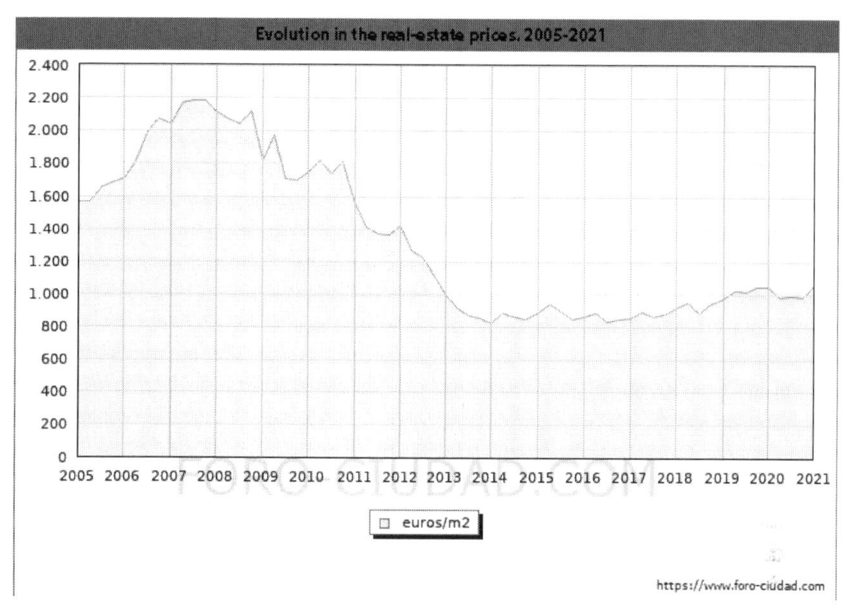

Figure 3.1. Evolution in the real-estate prices. 2005–2021. ***Source*****: www.foro-ciudad.com**

> standard.' 'Great!' So, they started to sell. The real estate agencies started selling flats, and they sold them to the migrants. That's how and why the first ones left.

Stage 4 (2000–2007/2008). In this phase, the patterns mentioned above of mobility continue and intensify. People were beginning to leave because their old neighbours were moving out, and because of the people who were arriving, xenophobia, fear, and racism are important factors in this regard. Although flats were being sold at increasingly high prices (the peak was reached in 2007), at the same time, the town and the area around Catalunya Square were experiencing growing territorial stigmatization. The buyers and, therefore, the residents in the area were mainly 'foreigners', and the increasing numbers seem to have incited some of the remaining neighbours of Spanish nationality to move out as quickly as possible. Obviously this should be considered in part a racist or xenophobic practice, as Carolina shows us.

> Yes, yes, because there was a, a Brown one living here. He was the first brown one to move in. Even I got scared because who knows, maybe I was in a hurry, I found myself leaving the elevator, I will always remember this. I thought that since some Brown ones were already living, they were already living in another building, but none was living here. . . . So, I thought he must've been mistaken, you know, that was the first thing I thought, and I said to him 'what are you doing here walking on the wet floor?' And the man stays like that, paralyzed,

and he said, 'no, I'm sorry, eh, but I live here.' And I responded, 'No way. You must be lying.' And he said 'no, I'm not lying, I bought the flat,' and I kept questioning him. The neighbour downstairs had been listening, and afterwards, she asked me, what did that individual say to you?, And I told her, well he says that he lives here. She responded, what? Has he bought a flat here? Oh no, then we will be leaving because with these. . . no, that can't be!, And the following week I saw an ad that the apartment was for sale, and I said to myself, now they are going to leave me alone, and look, there are only five of us left, those of us who cannot leave, the others have left.

In this way, Mikel Aramburu's (2002) hypothesis, the result of his doctoral research on neighbourhood relations and images on immigration and urban transformation in the Ciutat Vella de Barcelona, seems to be confirmed. His study shows a generally accepted idea that the residential concentration of migrants generates a flight of natives. As Aramburu well points out, the extension of this perception is often due to the interests of real estate developers, banks, and agencies, the ones who end up capitalizing on all these mobilities and (mortgage) transactions (figure 3.2).

Among the inhabitants, we see another equally important reason to move, which resembles a pyramid scheme. Often promoted by the real estate agencies operating in the territory, the idea was that this moment would not go on

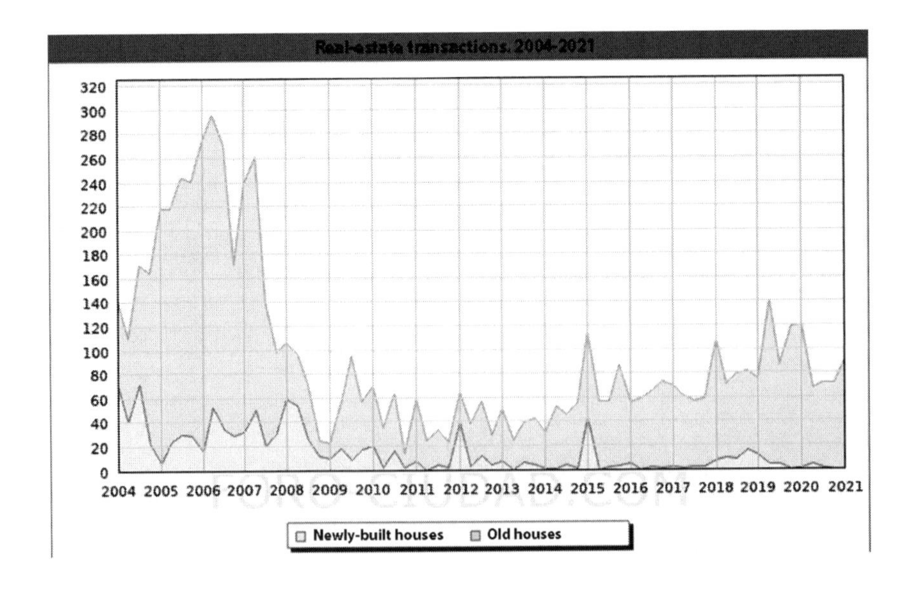

Figure 3.2. Real-estate transactions. 2004–2021. ***Source*****: www.foro-ciudad.com**

for long and that one should take advantage of the situation and earn some money and, most importantly, get out before the flats would lose value and thus be a loser in the game of social mobility. Ironically, these inhabitants had been lured into the scheme already too late and had accepted expensive mortgages that they would later not be able to pay, therefore being forced to move back once the prices had dropped. Meanwhile, the flats were often sold under fraudulent conditions, a practice Dymski (2009) has called 'racial exploitation'. In the real estate sector of Salt, a similar thing took place (Bernat 2014; Lundsteen and Sabaté 2018), where people signed (sub-prime) mortgages despite the agents' knowledge of the signer's incapability or improbability to fulfil the conditions of the agreement.

First of all, access housing and possibly to socially progress, migrants were led to buy a flat (often in 'degraded neighbourhoods') due to segmentation and racism in the housing markets, which kept them from renting both during and after the housing bubble (Leralta Piñán 2005; Palomera 2013; Sabaté 2018; Bernat 2014, 49). In some instances, migrants who found themselves in an irregular situation were encouraged to take out a mortgage by merely showing their passport, while more constraints were imposed on them if they tried to rent an apartment.

Moreover, all the processes involved in the buying and selling of properties, mortgage contracts, and renegotiation are in their essence built on several social encounters and social relations at different levels. In some instances, these imply an actual physical encounter, whereas others do not. Hence the different people involved (such as valuation agents, real estate agents, mortgage brokers) have a certain autonomy of manoeuvre in terms of the decision to be adopted concerning the person(s) they are dealing with. Because these encounters are not neutral, it is essential to acknowledge that different ideas, ideologies, interpretations, stereotypes, and prejudices—racism and classism included—may influence the decision and actions adopted.

We see clearly how working-class migrants comprised a distinct sub-prime market that had been targeted by mortgage brokers operating in decayed neighbourhoods where the housing bubble had a significant impact on real estate prices. Such brokers, using aggressive strategies, were not interested in testing the reliability of customers but, rather, in offering banks the opportunity to operate in this niche market.

In this way, a sales market was created mainly for immigrants while at the same time promoting the idea of flight among native residents. This is confirmed in the following accounts by Pere, a resident of the Barri Centre, and Jordi:

> Agents have to me, to my home, not to force me to sell but saying things like 'man, you have to sell your flat because this will be filled with migrants and

> you will not be able to live here.' To which I've responded, 'well I'm sure they're better people than you. . . . Listen, if the migrants come it's because you sell them the flats, and you're telling the same story to another neighbour, and he believes you.' 'The prices will go down, man,' and I say, 'you are the ones lowering the prices.'

> Of course, imagine in a building that a Moroccan or a Black family moves in. Automatically the value of the property is less, and the people who started seeing this started selling their property. Of course, helped by this housing bubble, this real estate bubble, where everyone could access credit and buy at prices that were not real.

In addition to this, flats were sold under fraudulent conditions. There might have been a sense that there was little time left before the real estate bubble would burst, and therefore, many economic agents sought to maximize their benefit from the investments by signing mortgages knowing that the conditions would hardly be met. In Pere's words, 'Moreover, they deceived the migrants, they told them "If you there you don't have to pay anything, everything is free." Of course, they came here with loans that the Banks knew they couldn't pay.' In this way, there was an appropriation of the little capital accumulated by the migrant workers, to whom impossible dreams are sold (through financialization) to execute evictions later and repossess the properties (Bernat 2014).

Stage 5 (2008–). In the last stage, once the crisis in the real estate sector kicked in, no more inhabitants could move out. Granted that the mortgages were no longer easily given; in fact, often a lot of the real estate agencies and banks in the area had closed, and the prices of the flats had decreased considerably: The average price of a house in downtown Salt fell by half, while in Barri Vell there appears to have been little change.

At the same time, due to the preceding process of stigmatization, many of the remaining Spanish residents had ended up feeling 'trapped in the misery'. As Josep said: 'So, what happened? Well, when the relatives came here, which of it is normal, but that meant that is . . . I do not know if the word is the most correct one, but it became something like a ghetto, and Barri Centre has become like a ghetto, which has a bad effect.'

Simultaneously, the crisis contributed to increasing instability and precarity among the workers (both Spaniards and migrants), who were often forced to turn to informal economic practices to survive and who would no longer be able to fulfil the financial agreements of the neighbourhood communities, thus aggravating the deterioration the neighbourhood had been experiencing since the beginning of the 1990s.

IDEOLOGICAL DISPLACEMENTS

Even though the real estate market played an essential role in the latest transformations of Barri Centre, many of the interviewees ignore the first two phases of (im)mobility and their insertion into the political-economic logic of the market. Instead, they often only focus on the last two. Meanwhile, others also point to widespread working-class racism that, according to them, is the actual logic behind the native flight, as shown by the following reflections by Pau and Joan:

> Here in the 50s, 60s there was the first wave of migration, and people came from Andalusia, Extremadura, all people from Spain, and the Catalans didn't leave. Then when the second wave of migration came, from the Maghreb and the sub-Saharan countries, and all, the Catalans didn't leave. And it's a bit contradictory that those who felt threatened was the Spaniards, and they eventually left.

> Who left? The people who came as migrants left. The migrants who came in the 60s and 70s left. They left because they could not stand to see the migrants moving in. This is the only problem. . . . Either maybe they left because two Black moved in, and they don't like Black people. You tell me, I know many who have left for La Massana who regret leaving.

As I have argued, racism is fundamental to understanding migratory movements. However, if the economic-political factors are ignored, it leads to sociological myopia that might reproduce a classicism, typical of the politically correct middle classes accusing the 'uneducated lower classes' of being racist. Let us remember that the neighbourhood has been undergoing a process of degradation since the end of the 1990s and that the houses in the Barri Centre were generally of poor quality. In addition, the quality of life that the new neighbourhoods such as La Massana offered was visibly better. Therefore, many of the first inhabitants who left the neighbourhood did so to improve their social life, so at first, it had little or nothing to do with the arrival of migrants.

It is also important to acknowledge the absence in their accounts of the fact that the upward mobility of the natives was largely possible thanks to the arrival of migrants. In other words, many of the old inhabitants benefited from the arrival of the new ones because it was thanks to the purchase and sale of flats that they could climb socially, moving to other more affluent neighbourhoods. The interest on the part of some new residents, in this case, the migrants, in buying the flats was one of the necessary conditions to be able to redeem the difference in value that came about due to the so-called real estate bubble and, thus, invest in a new home.

The developments created an internal polarization among the inhabitants in material terms. Thus, two groups of residents of the Barri Centre were formed. There are 'the old ones', who had a comparatively low mortgage (both the price of the house and the mortgage have been acquired in better conditions). They often have the mortgage paid, and, perhaps due to favourable conditions (residing in penthouses, sub-penthouses), they have never left. As Pere said: 'I am very well at home, I have the apartment as I like it . . . I have a view that apartments worth more than 100 million don't have.' And there are 'the new ones', who acquired much more expensive mortgages (sometimes directly fraudulent), for flats in poor condition. For this reason, many of them have been forced to sublet rooms to cover the expenses, or they have faced eviction.

These socio-economic and class distinctions are often read according to their ethnocultural expression. Often the old ones are native, and the new ones are non-Spanish migrants. However, there are also several natives in the last group; the only difference here is that they sold their apartment to take a mortgage and climb socially. However, due to the crisis, they could not afford it and were evicted and so had to returned to the neighbourhood; some even live with their parents or in-laws (i.e., they have experienced a critical setback in their upward mobility). Such an experience is often perceived as a failure because they return to the 'ghetto', the place from which they cursed and ran away. At the same time, many migrants have extensive social networks, so often, they do not have as much difficulty meeting their most basic needs.

A bleak picture has been drawn in the neighbourhood, a neighbourhood in social decline, with an increasing precariousness and an eroding social fabric, in Carolina's words:

> It's only misfortune here now . . . Why? Because nobody can pay their mortgages, their children come home because they cannot pay, they take away their apartment, take away their car, take away everything they have, and they will be poor. . . . It's misfortune. However, not before, it looked good and there was a good *convivencia*.

Faced with this scenario, some inhabitants, especially people who experienced a rise during the first phases and now live in other neighbourhoods, such as La Massana, express a fear of the social decline that it may mean them. This process of degradation, epitomized in the image of a ghetto, has the migrant as a degrading social category, an agent of marginality that drives that change. As stated by Pilar,

> I am not against them being here. Whoever has a job can stay, whoever does not have a job and who is stealing and doing all sorts of things, well what do you

> want me to say. This is not a refugee camp. I understand that in their country, they have nothing, I understand that, but if you arrive here and receive something, enjoy what you have, value what you have, but we lose the quality of life that we had.

I argue that the main antagonism in this field is the one that exists between these groups: natives who see their social advancement in danger or who have already experienced a setback, and the newcomers and migrants who live the precariousness differently and for whom moving to Salt was always upward mobility.

THERE GOES THE NEIGHBOURHOOD

The relationship between space and social relations entails a process, which following Low (1999), can helpfully be distinguished between 'the social production of space', which includes all the factors—social, economic, ideological, and technological—that pretend to construct the material setting physically and 'the social construction of space', which refers to the spatial transformation of space—through the social interactions, conversations, memories, sentiments, imaginations, and uses—into scenes and actions that convey symbolic meaning (Low 2000, 112). Accordingly, the neighbourhood should not merely be understood as a geographical, physical space but also both a social process and collective project—both a practical and sensorial experience and a common-sense—emerging from the everyday experiences of living together (including any more or less conflictual situations) and an experience that translates into a kind of collective conscience, a structure of feelings (Williams 1977).

When I spoke to inhabitants in Salt who had been living in the town for decades, I would hear stories about how nice things were before and how well everything had worked. A tour around the Centre neighbourhood that I would take with a social worker was especially relevant. In one of the buildings in Esteve Vila Street, we met an elder man of around 70 years old, Catalan-speaking, retired worker. He assessed the changes in the building and, with it, the town at large in the following manner. He said that the migrants had eroded the social space of all the native folks, following which he explained that he had been living in the building for the last 15 years and that beforehand it had been a 'working-class haven', according to him, united and in good conditions: 'the door would always be closed, the intercom always worked, the glass would never be broken.' However, the most interesting part is when he explained how they would live together as a community:

> Right here a man called Joan lived. . . . Asunción lived on the second floor, Fina on the third floor. . . . On the first floor, a widow lived together with her two sons, on the third floor everybody was from here, on the fourth floor everybody was from here. . . . The community expenses were paid. . . . And one would only hear two languages spoken in the staircase, Spanish and Catalan. Everybody understood each other. . . . Now nobody does.

Although he hinted at a sense of abandonment, which the broken windows literature would applaud—despite much more well-founded critiques of it (Harcourt 2001)—in his memory of the neighbourhood, we can detect a certain sense of *being in* and *belonging to* a community, which has been lost with the arrival of new inhabitants of other nationalities and cultures. This view of the community, implying a cultural homogeneity fictitious as it may be, and its erosion coincided with that of many other older Spanish residents I spoke with during fieldwork. Although these memories might be a product of recent changes, many people recognized some cultural commonality in their shared histories of migration, often from a rural setting in Andalusia. As the former mayor recounts:

> Barri Centre where most of the migrants arriving in the 60s and 70s settled. . . . Where the majority were homeowners. . . . Well the neighbours more or less knew each other, if they weren't from the same town, often it was from a town close to, in Andalusia, or wherever that was. . . .Thus, Maria, Puri, and Paquita knew each other and lived together more or less peacefully and in harmony.

Not forgetting that, apart from sharing similar histories of migration, they also shared residential and convivial spaces (of social reproduction and leisure) and that a lot of them even worked together in the same factories (such as Coma-Cros, Maret, or Gassol). They were traditional working class, an identity that was also based on experiences of spatial injustice, in opposition to the middle-class Catalan-speaking populations of the Old Neighbourhood (Barri Vell).

Therefore, I believe it is fair to say that the local community shared some set of moral values or 'structures of feelings', as Williams (1977) would have it, emerging from the everyday experiences—of both conflict and peace—in the social space of the neighbourhood—a habitus of place or neighbourhood conscience, similar to the working-class conscience in the sense that Thompson (1968) conferred to it. The Catalunya square is exemplary in this regard.

Through several accounts of the old-timers of the area, I have been able to recount how certain feelings of belonging and community developed in the neighbourhood. A particular memory of the place has been produced, which is often in stark contrast to the younger generations. However, these feelings, never clearly defined, coexist alongside a romantic vision of cultural homogeneity, as we have seen. It is a memory of a united neighbourhood, a unified and unifying identity that opposes those coming from outside, be they young or old. In the narratives of the elder and younger middle-class residents of other neighbourhoods, the outsiders are often perceived and portrayed as moral-cultural transgressors, responsible for the erosion of the neighbourhood community or simply the social conflicts taking place in the town (Lundsteen 2020b).

CATALUNYA SQUARE: MEMORIES OF A PLACE

During the 1980s, due to the progressive construction of the neighbourhood, some of the residents gathered to prepare parties or other social activities. These collective activities culminated in mid-1984, with the formation of a neighbourhood association called AVV Can Mericana Seca. Their main objective was to reclaim the urbanization of the site around Can Pou and Mas Mota. Until then, it had been a lot, which had served as a landfill, generating complaints from the neighbours who complained that the local administration did not help; they could not act due to economic scarcity. For years, the neighbours fought against the town council, which at first did not pay much attention to them and later wanted them to make them pay part of the work costs. The association organized parties and cultural events to raise funds and, at the same time, energize the social and associative life of the neighbourhood (figures 3.3-1 and 3.3-2). Among these acts, the bonfire of San Juan was crucial, as Pilar recalls:

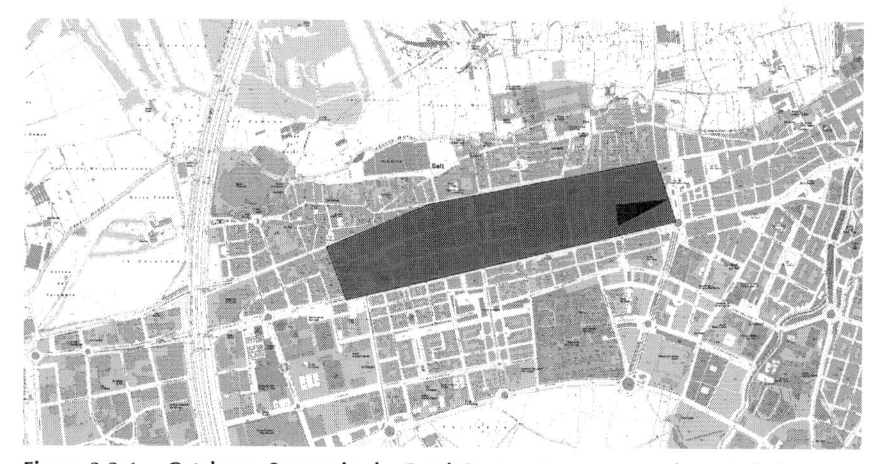

Figure 3.3-1. Catalunya Square in the Barri Centre. *Source*: www.foro-ciudad.com

Figure 3.3-2. An areal view of the square. *Source*: Google Maps

> We made the bonfire of San Juan a week before the children took everything, and there in the middle of the square, we made the bonfire, and we went down. It was more like a village back then.

After several years of dispute, with interruptions of plenary sessions and protests with hanging sheets with writings draped from windows, the pressures finally paid off when an agreement was reached, and the square was officially inaugurated in 1991. Both the protest actions and the festive events created a sense of belonging among the area's residents (according to newspaper articles from 1987, there were around 400 residents). As Concepción stated:

> We knew each other, and we all met in the park with the children, and we all got along well, and the children have practically all grown up together here, and there, in the square. That square that all the neighbours went to the town hall to claim the square . . . and there in summer we would all hang out to one or two in the morning, children and mothers, talking, playing . . . all the neighbours together.

Structures of feeling linked to a specific social space, the square, which explains why some of the old inhabitants, such as Concepción, now feel affection and pride with the place and the imagined community of the community of old-timer: 'I'm sad because it was a neighbourhood for which people would give an arm to live in, it was the best neighbourhood in Salt, the best place to live.'

Similar experiences can be detected in other neighbourhoods, such as Barri Vell, and in housing estates such as Grup Sant Jaume, Grup Verge de María, and Grup Sant Cugat, where as a result of the degradation of the buildings, the neighbours would mobilize. They got to know each other and created social ties that would last and give rise to significant social experiences through this. As Carolina recalled, when she arrived at the Barri Centre from Peru in 1976:

> It was very peaceful; this was a bit like my hometown, back everybody would feel at home, and people would greet each other. Instead, now you go out and say hello, and people look at you like you're a freak, and why are you going around saying hello? Shut up.

But if we look at the stories of several migrant residents, such as Carolina and Nadia, we see that there have already been cross-cultural encounters and experiences:

> Before we all helped each other, we were all. . . . I don't know, it was different. . . . Even for Christmas, we drank champagne downstairs, all the neighbours together, and now no longer [laughing]. . . . Now you can't do that. Before we used to go downstairs, one would carry cookies, another something else from a party . . . together. *Carolina*

> Where I grew up there were many natives. Then it started. . . . The migration you know . . . When I was little, we went to the park and well we all played together; there were more native people. *Nadia*

Although a great majority of the old inhabitants sketch a romantic vision of the past, some also remember existing divisions and conflicts. They point to the social problems linked to economic crises, drug addiction, and the social consequences. In David Estévez's opinion:

> Many things happened back then; many of the things have always been here in Salt. Here in Salt as everywhere there was the issue of drugs in the 80s, here it was a hotbed. . . . I have been here for thirty-one years, and I have lived all this… We shouldn't forget that it is a town that has received many people, many people from outside, but at that time, people from outside came from the rest of Spain and they, like the people from here, had their vices.

We also see a cultural and class confrontation between migrants (from Andalusia and *gitanos* from the Montjuïc barracks in Girona), the vast majority of whom lived in Barri Centre, and middle-class Catalans, residents in Barri Vell. These confrontations were linked to the symbolic communities described in the previous chapter but were also related to neighbourhood and class identities. Before, the confrontation was between the inhabitants (workers and migrants at the time, too) of Veïnat and those of Vila de Salt (back then perceived as separate towns). In the 1970s and 1980s, the conflicts were primarily between those living in Barri Centre and the rest of the town (Veïnat and Barri Vell). The following is an excerpt from a conversation with some of the community managers, women and men between the ages of 30 and 60 who occupied the role of president or secretary of the building, conducted at the Local Offices d'Habitatge-Salt 70:

> Woman 1: Many people came from Andalusia, they came here to work, and we have always had those who came from Font de Pólvora.
>
> Man 1: Gitanos . . .
>
> Woman 1: Gitanos . . . I remember that they were between Torras and Bagès and Àngel Guimerà, that was their neighbourhood if you wanted to go and see there were many good ones, and some that weren't so, but there were some good ones
>
> Man 1: Maybe it was different because the language was the same, Spanish
>
> Woman 1: Well yes . . . Of course, I remember that I had friends who were also Andalusians in school, and when I came home, my grandmother always told me "those Castilians", and I thought, why Castilians? They were my friends. . . . Of course, she saw as conflictive something that wasn't there, which I guess the kids nowadays experience something similar. They don't experience any . . .

Thus, the neighbourhood identity of the past was based both on shared migratory and cultural experiences, as well as on a class reading against an unequal production of space, which relegated them to a neighbourhood with deficient and undervalued infrastructure.

In the 1990s, however, important socio-economic changes took place that would lay the foundation for the future changes to the neighbourhood and the town. The increasing improvement in the labour conditions, social mobility, consumerism, and individual prosperity of some, seem to have induced a need for upward mobility in terms of housing and living. Alternatively, a specific idea of progress was promoted in Spain, especially through homeownership (Palomera 2013), eventually leading to the first rupture of social ties.

Because the neighbourhood was in decline, new attractive zones were built, and values were increasing, the dream of a better life seemed to become a reality. For instance, according to some of the neighbours who moved, one of the reasons they left was the deteriorating state of the old neighbourhood, whereas the neighbourhood to which they moved was utterly new. Hence, in the past, the deteriorated state of the neighbourhood had been the reason to put in collective efforts and mobilizations, but now each inhabitant would seek out his or her fortune individually. In this sense, some of the residents who remained, like Concepción, place some moral responsibility on those who left:

> Of course, it's what we say, it is our fault. Because when we saw the migrants moving in, we sold the flats, sold them to the migrants, so it's bit of a double standard. I had a neighbour who left, and she always said, 'I tell you this, once I sell my apartment, it won't be to any immigrant, not to a moro or a Black or anyone else, it will to be a Spaniard. . . . They offered her 30 million, and she didn't give a god damn whoever bought it, and she sold it to a Black guy. I mean, are we playing at double standards here?

Those who moved out left the neighbourhood in a deteriorating state with broken social ties. As a result of this upward mobility (perhaps illusory), a new social configuration was created in the town. Those who stayed directed their struggle against what they perceived as a socio-urban degradation provoked by their new neighbours. Nonetheless, this symbolic formation, based on a romanticization of the past, pitted the established against the outsiders and complicated creating a new shared social project for the community. Although we can observe an aim for a good life and social justice present in this formation—by, for instance, prioritizing the collective interest of the neighbourhood, improving the social space, over the private interests of speculation—it is also highly exclusive, casting on the social space a specific moral project of belonging-in-space, ignoring that all the neighbours might largely share the aim. Hence, the initial question of socio-spatial inequality has been displaced discursively and vertically; from emphasizing the aspects of the common conditions of neighbours and workers, now the struggle seemed rather be expressed in cultural terms: a social construction of space and community that posed the newcomers, the other neighbours, the migrants, as the degrading agent, an enemy to the community.

LOSS OF COMMUNITY TIES AND A NEIGHBOURHOOD IDENTITY: A CULTURAL IMPOSITION OR INVASION

Today there is an idea that there has been an erosion of that imagined community of neighbours or rather a loss of the sociability associated with it and a generalized decline in community life in the neighbourhood. As we have seen, an 'original' and 'homogeneous' local culture is recalled, which is supposedly now disappearing—an identity linked to the neighbourhood and the street, a feeling of symbolic community with structures of sentiment and concordant cultural practices. There were more recreational activities between equals such as, for example, meals in the squares, streets, and a particular way of doing and feeling the neighbourhood that has been disappearing.

Thus, throughout the fieldwork, I have observed that there are several discourses among the native residents; there is a widespread idea that there has been a loss of identity in the neighbourhood—an idea especially prevalent among the natives of the Barri Centre and La Massana, a phenomenon well reflected in Pilar's words:

> A: We have lost our identity. . . . It's that simple.
>
> Q: And what identity was that?
>
> A: Look, for a starter you didn't see any satellite dishes when walking the street. . . . In all the shops we knew each other well. . . . You'd go to the park and play with the kids, and you wouldn't be afraid of leaving them alone for a while, and now it's not like that, now you don't know anybody. All the shops are [owned by] Moroccan, blacks, and so on. And the square, you won't go there because the only thing you'd find is young people selling drugs... Moreover, the children, none of them are from here. . . . Everything has changed, everything. . . . Before, we all knew each other, and now we don't know anybody.

These developments, which many describe as a breakdown of the original community ties, supposedly took place due to the arrival of outsiders and the departure of inhabitants of those from before. In this view, the neighbourhood's coexistence degraded with the arrival of migrants, as the resulting super-diversity made previously existing social cohesion impossible. Implicitly, it is understood that social cohesion requires cultural homogeneity and that in practice, it requires cultural values and a sense of common identity.

A paradigmatic example is found in the perception that there has been a decline in the 'traditional trade' (by which in reality is meant 'native businesses') produced by the entry of immigrants who bring with them other consuming customs and establish 'their businesses'. In this way, the influence of the 'economic crisis' and the construction of the Espai Gironès shopping centre is completely ignored:

> No, no, no, no, what happened here is that, well, people left, and seeing that the people who came weren't interested. . . . Of course, if you open a store, you want it to prosper. . . . If nobody comes to you . . . in the end you must close because you have more losses than profits. Now the people who have come here have opened their own businesses. The native business does not come here. *Toñi*

> We have the best business here, it's resistant, second generation, third generation. The rest isn't, well yes there are some shops. I mean there are some old [Spanish] bars, such as the Ideal Bar 1926. *Pere*

They minimize the fact that there still are some old businesses running, and if not, these have often closed down because the younger generations have not wanted to continue the business. The great variety of commercial offer that continues to exist in Barri Centre is mainly due to migrants, many of whom also run old-style bars and restaurants. For this reason, it is curious that (as we will see in chapter 5) only 'traditional' businesses are being promoted.

Again, the developments are perceived according to the prism of the established and the outsiders: the native as opposed to the migrant community. Consequently, I often heard there were no longer young people in the neighbourhood, even though there are more young people than ever, and that trade is closing when there is an active commercial activity.

This perception of identity loss was directly linked to the perception that there is an invasion of public space, as well as a decline in the social life of the native:

> This town was different when I came. . . . You would see more people in the street, people were more socially active, people were more talkative, however now. . . . I suppose that because of the atmosphere that has gotten into this town, people have backed down and locked themselves at home. You will see it because you go down the street and you only see foreigners. . . . Countrymen you see four, because they stay at home, that is, they have allowed themselves to be stepped on, eat the land. Well, here they have come. I don't know if they have come to invade, they have had the thing that there were five to twenty of them and then families and families and families have begun to come, then, of course, it has flown over. . . . Here there are practically more migrants than people from the country. *Carmen*

Inappropriate Uses of Space

There is a widespread idea among the natives that the migrants appropriate the space of the town. As the former mayor Iolanda Pineda relates:

> It had happened that people had the feeling that there was a lack of civility in the village, that there was an intensive use of the public space and that this intensive use by some of the public space caused some tensions, it gave the feeling for some that the public space was only occupied by some and that they did not have the right to access this public space.

A phenomenon similar to many other examples of conflicts in public space that have been described and analysed by anthropologists in other parts of the Spanish geography (Moncusí Ferré, Torres Pérez, and Fioravanti Álvarez 2018; Gómez Crespo and Torres Pérez 2020). An illustrative example of this is that of Massana Square. At night, groups of young people meet. This type of activity in a residential area creates problems. As Veronica said:

> But that is not quiet, and one seeks a little more rest, tranquillity, this area is quieter, here where I live is the new area. . . . But of course, the boys, the youth, also come. They come here, and at night it is a little conflictive, conflictive in the sense that, well they start talking here at the benches, it is not that they make brawls or fights, far from it, but well, simply because the youth does not realize it and speaks and it is eleven or midnight. . . . and one who works or who wants to rest cannot.

Often, they are conflicts that are initially presented as intergenerational but that end up being interpreted under an ethnocultural prism:

> You hear them speak in their country and they speak just like that here. They have very developed lungs and speak very loudly [laughing], but they don't realize it, of course, they don't realize that they do it; it is their natural way of speaking.

The arguments used by Verónica are similar to those I heard in Premià de Mar in opposition to the construction of a mosque in the Barri Maresme (Lundsteen 2020a). Activities in public spaces carried out by foreigners are seen as a degradation that collides with the expectations of quality and standard of living ('a calmer life') that they bought. Verónica said that she and her husband now feel trapped. Although she likes the place, he wants to leave:

> Yes, I really liked this site, even though, I don't know. . . . Well Jaume [her husband] doesn't like it. He says that if he could. . . . But of course, once bought, you are not . . . you are tied up, you have the mortgage on top, and you cannot leave. But he says that when he chose it, it was not like this, there was not so much migration. . . . It was much better, but he says that had he been a fortune-teller, he wouldn't have bought it [laughing] even though we're fine here. *Verónica*

When I asked her if the discomfort he experienced was due to the boys, she would list all kinds of causes:

> Well, also now in summer most of all because the neighbours . . . as you have surely noticed, this is a closed area, and all the houses here have their garden, they have their patio with table, so they also have their parties mainly in summer. . . . And well, you hear everything, everything, I don't know why, even if they are only talking, you hear the laughter and things like that . . . [laughing] So it's not just the boys, there are many things here, the dogs barking.

The problems they suffered were made worse by the husband's timetable. He worked in Barcelona and got up between 4:00 and 5:00 a.m. They also have no relations with the neighbours, which creates a feeling of social uprooting. Despite this, they blamed the young migrants for their big lungs' and called the police to expel them from the park. They did not, however, put an end to the annoyances generated by their neighbours:

> Call the town hall for the police to come because Jaume does call. So the times the police come here is because we have called them . . . and they evict, well, the boys, and they say "speak lower", or I don't know what they tell them, but the truth is that they leave.

In the same vein, many of the natives interviewed comment that the squares are invaded, that now 'you only find immigrants':

> You do not see any child, no Spaniard playing in the park, no Spanish child playing. . . . Why? Because let's see, the browns, the children, they are in the street all day, and the truth is that they are bad, they are bad. . . . It's not only the children, if you go there now, it's all full of older people, all migrants, all Moroccans. *Concepción*

This obviates the fact that the greater presence and visibility of migrant children may be because the native young people have left and that the natives who remained are generally older. Instead, the reason given by some inhabitants is that there is a cultural invasion, in which the Other (the migrant) appropriates and degrades the social space and, thus, obliges the native residents to follow its rules. In this sense, certain practices linked to Islam create suspicion among some natives. Omar once told me that he had been surprised and outraged to see that 'the fucking *moros*' had put 'their carpets' on the soccer field to pray after we had finished playing. The culture of the Moroccans is seen as a threat to a perceived homogeneous 'national culture', where the ghost of the 'return of the Moors' seems to resurface, as Concepción said: 'They have always said that Spain is theirs. One day I argued with a *moro* who was saying that Spain belonged to them, and they had come to take it back again.'

It becomes clear that there is indeed a set of hegemonic sociocultural practices that derive from the historical experiences of the dominant ethnic group. This would explain why some feel they have the right to say, 'we've been invaded by them', positioning and signalling the outsiders from the insiders, drawing boundaries, and setting borders, justifying and naturalizing their superior position.

At the same time, through the examples, we see just how much of an ideology the idea of public space is (i.e., in the sense of being an egalitarian and shared space). According to this, in theory, everybody can access and make use of it, but when outsiders do so, they are breaking a moral code and doing it in a way that the established residents see as an invasion or occupation, opposed to the 'normal' or 'correct ways' of doing it. They, therefore, reclaim a privative use of space and resort to discourses of national-cultural belonging, in which they have more right to the space than others, via the use of civic notions (culturally-based as they are) of what activities are correct and which are not. Often this right and the implicit power imbalances are not questioned, either because they share the vision of the native inhabitants in their exclusive right to manage the space or because they want to cater for them due to political interests. Either way, a comprehensive analysis of the actual workings of these bordering practices is much needed.

Hage (2000) invites us to analyse these disputes and conflicts in terms of what he refers to as 'categories of spatial management', as he explains:

> Most humans perceive ants as a different species, and certainly as an inferior species. Yet, just on the basis of this belief, they do not perceive them as 'undesirable' or as 'too many'. They do so only when these ants are seen to have invaded spaces where humans find their presence harmful such as in their houses or on their plates. And it is only in such situations that practices of violence are directed against them. Consequently, categories such as 'too many', while embodying some form of 'racist' belief, are primarily *categories of spatial management*. (Hage 2000, 37–38)

When justifying this *spatial management*, the ones in the position to carry it out often refer to extreme cases of the transgression of civic norms. As we can see from the conversation with Toñi, 50-year-old former president of the neighbourhood community and resident in Barri Centre:

> Well, you see that's what such a culture from other countries brings with it. . . . There are no rules. . . . But well, now they're here, and here we've got another reality. . . . Although you might not understand that . . . But they also have to understand that in the receiving country, you have to comply with the rules that apply. . . . What one cannot tolerate in any case is those kinds of situations that Federic mentions or other kinds of situations we have experienced where people have peed or defecated in the staircases. . . . Well, things are changing . . . But in the beginning that's what we found. . . . And these kinds of situations created a neighbourhood which wasn't well functioning you know. . . . In fact, everybody would isolate and defend their own tiny territory in their home and wouldn't want to know nor share anything with anybody else.

NEIGHBOURHOOD CONFLICTS: PRECARITY AS THE MAIN DRIVER OF 'CULTURAL CONFLICTS'

> I'll give you an example, okay. We have a community of neighbours, okay. All Andalusian people lived here, and a half or three-quarters left. What's left is a

> group of four or five who are the ones who continue managing the community a little bit, and a whole bunch of new people come in, but they don't know each other or know these people. Okay, that's the panorama. Then imagine that of these people who came here, who had started to pay, but because now more than half don't. Because they have lost their jobs, or because they cannot or won't pay, what happens? Coincidentally, those who don't pay are the ones who came last, who are foreigners, and maybe most of them are even from the same country, say Moroccans. What happens? It turns out that they cut off the light in the community because more than half of the residents do not pay the community bill. What happens? Conflict. *Albert*

Undoubtedly, the so-called economic crisis had a destructive impact on Salt, especially in Barri Centre. The global situation of precariousness affects the relations established between neighbours when conflicts based on inequalities arise. As the head of the Area of Coexistence and Integration, Andreu Bover, said, 'In the neighbourhood communities there are conflicts, but they are fundamentally economic conflicts, between people who do not pay to the neighbourhood community, of people who have a flat and cannot pay for the repair . . . and then the neighbour gets angry because he has a filter, a water stains his wall.'

As we will see in this section, the problems are interpreted as 'conflicts of convivencia'—a daily vision that implies a subsequent ethnoculturalization of socio-economic conflicts. It is assumed that it is an encounter between equals; they are all neighbours, but due to the cultural norms of some (they do not pay, they do not get involved in the community, they want to segregate, and so on) that convivencia is 'complicated' or 'impossible', and, therefore, unwanted.

Housing

Housing is a fundamental resource that, in the Spanish case, tends to be accessed increasingly through buying and selling. However, with the political-economic restructuring of the last 10 years, access to this fundamental resource has been forbidden for many inhabitants who cannot assume the expenses of a mortgage or who have directly been victims of fraudulent mortgages and subsequently evicted. This phenomenon at the State level 'has created a real social problem, affecting more than 415,117 flats from 2008 to 2012, according to the General Council of the Judiciary' (Bernat 2014, 37). Although there are no official figures for the number of evictions at the municipal level, through information collected by the same author (not yet published), these are understood to be significant figures compared with other Spanish cities. Among the people affected, many are migrants, thus indicating evidence of structural racism (Lundsteen and Sabaté 2018).

The crisis of the capitalist accumulation system enters a phase that can be understood by resorting to the concept of 'accumulation by dispossession' (Harvey 2003). Seeing that the overinflated prices of the houses were not going to be able to be sustained for much longer, owners, real estate agents, and banks adopted fraudulent methods to continue until the end. When that fleeting moment and the beginning of the crisis ended, the banks and real estate managers dedicated themselves to the repossession of properties because it was evident that many of the buyers could not afford expensive mortgages. Such mortgages sometimes approached €1,600 per month and more if we consider that, for many, the crisis meant the loss of work or income. My roommate from calle Josep Irla 21, Toqueer, a Bengali who had been in Spain for eight years, told me that he had agreed to give up the apartment and the money invested (around €25,000) because the bank told him that he could not renegotiate the mortgage. Another case was that of a Senegalese friend, Abdul, who, after more than 15 years in Salt, had decided to buy a flat with his brother. In the end, they lost it along with the more than four years of invested mortgage (between €50,000 and €90,000).

This promoted a return to informal ways of accessing housing: either by renting a room or through social networks (such as family and friendship). This often led to overcrowding and subletting, where several families or individuals crowded together, thereby reducing the costs of overpriced mortgages or rents (figure 3.4).

Likewise, there has been a proliferation of more precarious ways of accessing housing (e.g., squatting). As a result of the crisis, an increase in squatting has been noticed while the evictions leave empty apartments (and people without homes). As the head of the local police pointed out, 'With this issue of the real estate bubble, the banks have started to have an incredible number of empty flats here that are impossible to control . . . and we started to see some occupied flats.'

According to several of the interviewees, squatting can cause possible cause discomfort and a sense of insecurity that might originate in problems of convivencia in the communities when suddenly there is much mobility of new faces and little interest in the social space of the stairs and the community.

This can hinder the development of good sociability among neighbours and, therefore, aggravate the community, creating a feeling of insecurity. However, it could be argued that the practice of walling up empty houses leads to a sterilization of the space that creates a feeling of abandonment or loneliness.

However, I would argue that the problem is not that they are people from outside the community, which would happen with any newcomer, but how they integrate (both by the community and by newcomers). This is undoubt-

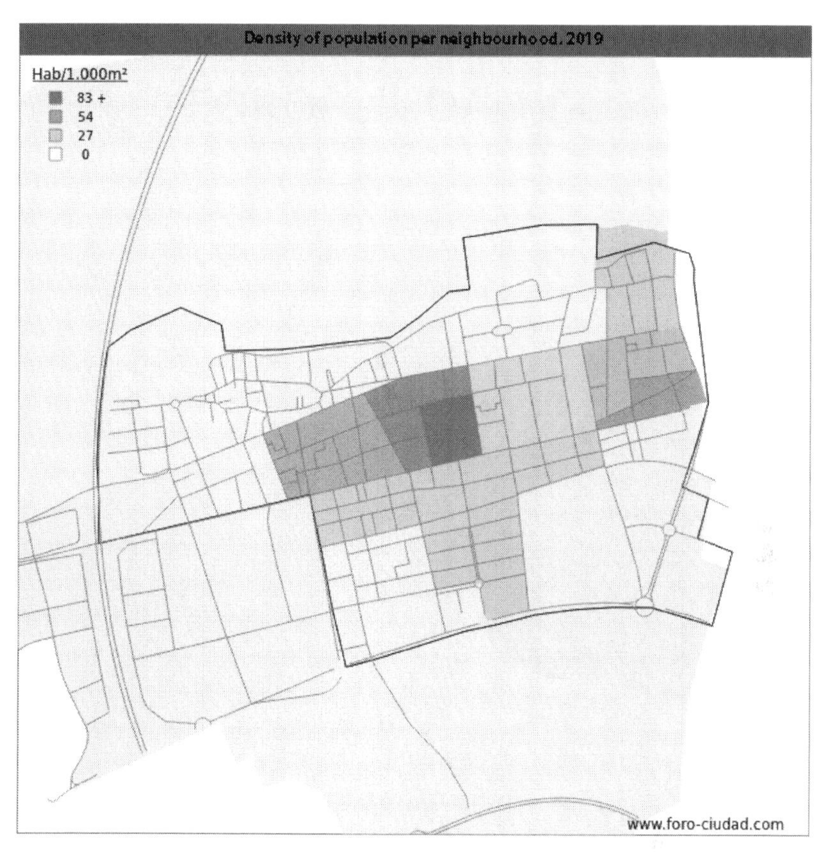

Figure 3.4. Density of population per neighbourhood. 2019 *Source*: www.foro-ciudad.com

edly a sociocultural and economic issue. In this sense, it is essential to note that the category of 'squatters' is often conflated with 'outsiders'. There is no clear causal relationship that determines that the squatter is less interested in the community's well-being. The following account by Carolina shows a greater complexity:

> Look, at first, a 45-year-old entered, with another young man of about 30 something. I thought they had rented them, but no. Look they behaved well, especially the 45-year-old . . . 'You have to clean', and he cleaned it and well, no problem with him. The problem started when he left, and the 35-year-old started letting it out to others. They came, and they didn't want to clean, they put the pretext that "I don't have water" and yet he was stealing water, electricity and not only for himself but giving to another, on the other side, who was also a squatter and so . . . they spent us about 700 and something . . . of electricity

> only, and water well it has made us remove the water from the community, we do not have water for the community.

I argue that the real issue at hand here is not the squatter but the precariousness in which that person lives, both interpersonally and in terms of access to basic resources. As David Estevez related, 'It had happened once that something had ignited, of course when you enter you don't legalise water or light or anything, you make a bridge, a bridge went wrong, and you burned something, you made a joint with it and . . . some fire, some accident and something.'

The issue of community expenses and defaults is undoubtedly important. A worker for the stairs and the mediation service of the town council told me that it was necessary to encourage the involvement of the squatters into the social space of the building and, for example, make them pay community expenses. See, for example, the comment that Ricard gave:

> If the squatter tries to, there are even occupants who clean or those who pay the neighbourhood community bills. . . . Why does this person not deserve to have a key? Because he is having a bad time? Because he was silly, was deceived, or made a bad calculation and went wrong? That's a bit unfair, isn't it?

Defaults and Community Debts

> The community debts are significant, there are many stairs, not here in my community, but there are many buildings where the lift doesn't work, because no one pays the community fees. *Joan*

However, in times of crisis, it is not only the most precarious who are forced to economize on behalf of the community expenses. At the beginning of the crisis (when it still did not seem nonsense to continue paying the mortgage), it became common not to pay community expenses to afford the sometimes increasing mortgages (Palomera 2013). In hard-hit communities, often several households were in this situation, and therefore, the community accumulated debts. Consequently, their electricity or water would be cut off, and sometimes they could not afford to repair broken glass, elevator costs, and so on. The immediate consequence is a degraded shared space, an aggravating factor for sociability between neighbours. The number of cases of community debt that I have come across in Barri Centre was high. All 10 community presidents and secretaries with whom I spoke confirmed that community debt was the biggest problem. Moreover, the town council launched several community aids programs (Europa Press 2011c).

Often, disputes around defaults stem from misunderstandings or inherited debts. There are many cases in which new owners have inherited debt from previous owners or have not been well informed about the mandatory payment of these community expenses. Some presidents have tried to anticipate this type of misinformation:

> We had another setback which didn't help us at all. The real estate agents were selling flats and didn't inform the new owners of anything . . . I only saw a gentleman coming with his things, suitcase or whatever . . . I had my character, and straight away, I told them, 'hey, where are you going? Who is there, how are you, am I the president and what is your name?' This way, I think the gentleman is already. . . . 'Well, I thought I didn't have to pay anything here.' So I told him, 'well, we'll talk about that.' Inform them about the stuff nobody had informed them. *Josep*

It is also important to note that in some cases, community and account management was previously managed by an external agency, so sometimes, the exact origin of the debt is unknown. Joan tells us that when he first started as president of the La Sagrada Familia (largest housing estate in the town), he found that the previous managers, in his case, the president and the secretary living in the community, had not kept the accounts sufficiently, nor had they reported them well. He discovered that 'the community insurance had not been paid for three years, the well had not been maintained for two years, the water had not been paid for four years . . . the electricity had not been paid for two years and they had a total deficit of €150,000.'

Therefore, each neighbour now owed €750, an expense that few people living in the community could afford:

> Do you think that each neighbour has paid the €750? . . . No. You know what part of Salt we're talking about, right? We're talking about . . . neither La Massana nor Barri Vell, but Barri Centre . . . First, do you know how many migrants live there? A 70 or 80 percent . . . . Now, do you know how many of these migrants work? 10 percent . . . We barely pay our quarterly dues, and now you want me to charge the debts? Instead, you should ask, how do they manage to pay at all?

Moreover, in some communities there never was a president or secretary. The organization was non-existent. As Albert, a former EINA community worker, said:

> There were communities . . . that worked well and communities . . . that worked poorly, and of course, this very much depended on whether they were organized or not. For example, communities that worked well or reasonably well, they

> were the ones who had a president . . . who had been president for a long time, with much experience. . . . Very meticulous you know, with the issue of payments. . . . They handled the people well. These communities usually worked fantastically, and the default rate was shallow. On the contrary, the communities that had no tradition of, or that had changed the entire population and had no presidents, for example, of course, some communities didn't even have presidents, they didn't have any meetings. . . . If there was light in the building, it was a coincidence, it was because the light had been cut off, and they all got together and paid the debts. . . . They came together by force so to speak, and paid the electricity bill, but there was no organization you know.

Obviously, poor organization of the community makes it more difficult for newcomers to integrate. However, this problem can also be understood as a field of struggle over meanings. When dealing with a problem of non-payment, it is common for presidents, who are often native, to base their ideas on subjective assessments that have to do with how they understand the problem and what relationship they have with the person in question. Based on these assessments, they can make the task easier or more difficult. In addition, the natives have more tools to manage the neighbourhood conflicts, a greater command of the language and the ability to manage the 'correct' ways of acting and interacting with others, which can make it easier to defend their interests when faced with the manager or president—often another native. If we analyse the cases that appear throughout the fieldwork and in the interviews, we see that bad information or poor communication between the parties often configure the problems. As Pere points out:

> 'Did they tell you that you have to pay for the water, that you have to pay . . . ?' 'Oh, no, they told me I don't have to pay for no water, nor the community,' 'Well, listen, here everybody has to pay the community fees, how do think the lift and light work? And the water you spend, what do you think, that they here by magic?' . . . 'ah, but they told me . . .'

Importantly, this is not limited to the migrant populations, several Spanish nationals do not pay, as Carmen remembered:

> The worst case we've got is the town councillor. . . . That's why I say that sometimes the worst ones are from here because come on, a councilwoman, totally xenophobic because she is from Plataforma per Catalunya [Catalan right-wing party]. . . . According to her, she doesn't deal with *moros* and can't even see them. . . . Yet she buys drugs from them. . . . She buys tobacco from them, she spends all day with them, and she pays neither for the flat nor the community nor electricity.

Although several presidents confirmed that the problem did not only refer to migrants, when the native neighbours narrated the community's existing problems, they pointed to the newcomers, the outsiders, as guilty of creating the malaise within the communities. When a native did something wrong, it was due to irresponsibility, and when a migrant did a similar thing, it was a cultural issue generalized to a specific people. As we can see in the following conversation between Ángel and Pilar:

> A: It is not because they do not pay. . . . If you see that they cannot pay and they have intentions, and they are good people you say, 'they cannot, what can we do, they just can't,' so you get on their side. . . . But if on top of that they say, 'I don't pay because I don't want to, and I don't pay, and I don't pay' . . .
>
> P: It makes you angrier . . . because if I tell then 'Bintu . . . if you can't pay, pay me, but pay something every month,' and they say 'Yes, I will talk to my husband,' and when they talk to their husband, they don't come, and I tell them 'Bintu, why haven't you come?' and she says, 'ah, yes,' and I say, 'don't you remember that you have to come to my place to see me?' 'Yes, yes, I have to go up . . . I'll go, I'll go,' they always tell you that . . . Moreover, I gave the other Bintu a book number, her name, everything so that . . . and I went down 'Bintu, have you gone there yet?' 'I will go on Monday.' . . . 'Bintu, have you paid yet?' 'No, I will go next week' . . . and you get tired.
>
> A: On top of that they're liars, because if you say .no, I don't even have enough to eat.' . . . you say. 'well let's see what we can do,' but if they say 'no, I can't, tomorrow, the day after, the week after,' man they're deceiving you, I don't know . . .
>
> P: Sure, but that is their culture . . . it is that shock that we have, so big, ours and theirs, it is a shock

Following this line of argument, the people in question should be less proud and more pitiful, that is, accept their subordinate position. However, what if it all comes from a misunderstanding or inherited debt? We have seen that, in this case, it was a management entity that had previously kept the accounts, and it was not known exactly how the debt had originated.

Furthermore, the existing economic inequalities are ignored. As shown previously, the development of the real estate market in the last 15 years has given rise to socio-economic differences between the established and the newcomers. Some have already paid their mortgage, and if not, it is probably low, whereas others, the newcomers, often struggle to pay their mortgage—sometimes being forced to resort to subletting rooms, saving community expenses, or other reasons. Thus, two opposing groups are formed in the same community, those who pay (or can pay) and those in default. In Albert's words:

> There's a conflict between those who pay and those who do not pay, and on top of that those who pay are the inhabitants who already lived there, because of course they have got a pension . . . and more or less a minimum income, because it is low-income, but they can deal with these payments, and then on the other side, another population of whom right now many are living in fucking misery.

Given that these symbolic communities are often demarcated by social categories of an ethnocultural nature (Spanish on the one hand and migrants on the other), according to the vast majority of social workers and community mediators with whom I have spoken, these neighbourhood conflicts are generally interpreted as cultural conflicts.

The following reflection by the president of the AVV of the Barri Centre is exemplary:

> Here what we have had is a cultural clash, because we are talking about different cultures, different ways of thinking and proceeding, and they need time to adapt. . . . Now, because things are being understood, because every new process needs its process of adaptation, and we are still in this process because it is not an immediate process. . . . In addition to cultural, it's idiomatic, because we don't understand each other either, because this has created a certain discomfort added to a significant economic crisis, which has damaged the communities due to default.

A default problem, often the result of growing economic precariousness, ends up being presented as a problem of convivencia, based on moral and ethnocultural terms.

CONVIVENCIA

> The conflict now is more related to *convivencia* I think. . . .The problem I see now is more between a migrant, with different cultures, and not well prepared. . . . They are the ones living with us, and it is we who will accept him and live with him, *Man 1, Group interview at Salt 70*

Other conflicts occur due to festivities and celebrations of various kinds in the social space. It is common to hold a festive event after the birth of a child or on the birthday of a relative. Although often these take place in an authorized venue or on a public green space, such as the Rec Monar or Les Deveses, some people decide to celebrate it in their own home due to financial reasons or lack of time to organize the event. This often causes inconvenience to some neighbours, as we see in the case of Pilar:

> They held parties, and we called the police; the police came three times one night. Then they notice who you are . . . and that's it. . . . It's funny that they were the ones who went to the mediators, and not the president nor me [secretary] who let them live in peace... Until three in the morning when they had baptized the child, with Arabic music and I don't know what dance, they do a glo-glo-glo-glo dance. . . . The police came, and when they left, they continued. . . . The police returned, and the same, that is, they didn't pay any attention to the police.

I have observed the same kind of problems with celebrations in public space that were also recriminated. One day a wedding was held in the shawarma bar below my house. Once the bar closed, people went out to the street, where they stayed talking for a while. There might have been about 100 people gathered, and 15 minutes later, the police had arrived.

Likewise, my roommate in Josep Irla St, Mostafa, told me a curious episode with a Moroccan acquaintance. His friend had commissioned a live lamb for a ritual sacrifice (Aid al-Adha). Because he did not speak Spanish well, he had got the wrong date, so he received the lamb a week before and decided to keep it in his apartment. After a few days, the police knocked on his door, alerted by neighbours who were bothered by the crying of the animal. Upon meeting the police and learning the reason for his visit, the man replied: 'ah, a few days of maa-maa-maa [imitating the cry of the lamb] no, but wauw-wauw-wauw [imitating the barking of a dog] every day is okay!?' (Excerpt from Diary 1, October 20, 2011, 64).

The typical argument used by natives when explaining this type of conflict follows an interesting discursive pattern. Some express that living together with specific immigrants is extremely difficult, emphasizing cultural differences as the root of the problem. For instance, in the case of the lamb, we see how some sounds are considered more natural or accepted than others. In the end, the arguments are all related to a normative culture of living together, as Pilar stated:

> I came from Andalusia, and according to many people, I am also a migrant. However, I do not consider myself a migrant, because I am in my own country, in another region, another nationality, in another country as they now call it, okay. . . . But I do not have to apply for a visa or anything. . . . I am in my country. I came, and I abide by the rules that are HERE. . . . What you cannot do is live . . . in a flat, as if you were living in a hut in Africa . . . do make myself clear?

Often, the problems arise from precariousness. In the case of the celebrations, the people often cannot afford to celebrate it in the right places, no matter how much they want to. However, even though deprivation creates certain problems directly related to convivencia, it is the different cultural expression and, not the precariousness, which is considered problematic. Although, as the following excerpt from my diary picks up, not everyone follows this storyline:

> Mari Carmen, who runs the bar, says: 'Before people did it in the restaurants and such, but now because of the crisis they have to do it in their flats' to save money, or rather to be able to continue doing it. . . . Mari Carmen believes it's quite all right to do it every once in a while, and she explained how she had also celebrated something at her house, and the neighbour had complained about it. She told him, 'today I'm going to do this. Normally we don't do anything, but today we will. I have not complained about your son who plays the flute every day, but it bothers me.' (Excerpt from Diary 1, July 24, 2011, 37–38)

Mari Carmen questions the importance of ethnocultural markers as the explanatory variable and emphasizes 'the normal' in these types of conflicts, turning to her own experience and practice. However, what are these 'norms' that everybody refers to? In some celebrations, appropriations of public space are accepted, and transgressions of civic regulations are tolerated, whereas, in others, they are not.

One day Edgar told me that a neighbour of his had complained that some French students, his neighbours, were having parties with loud music. In this case, the conflicts of convivencia, however, were not understood as cultural but, rather, as intergenerational. These examples of similar conflicts show how there are several ways to approach conflicts, which have to do with group markers. What in one case is understood as a cultural conflict (because they are from Africa), in another is understood as related to a difference of generations (because they are students and young people).

Although the conflicts, due to either default, squatting, celebrations, and others, can be understood as a result of economic marginalization that effectively causes relational and coexistence problems with the rest of the neighbours; eventually, they are read as a problem resulting from cultural customs. The consequence is that the culturalist readings end up self-fulfilling themselves, and the differences are heightened. So, although there are various types of problems and conflicts, in the end, everybody ends up pointing out culture as the core of the problem. Faced with this perception of a degraded and conflictive public space, especially the older native population say they are afraid and feel insecure and, as a consequence, tend to abandon said space to take refuge in the private sphere.

This alleged insecurity in the Barri Centre is a recurring discourse closely linked to a romanticization of the past (recalls drug problems and theft and stories) that serves to draw a dystopic vision of the present. As Pau stated:

> When I was six, seven, eight years old, from my grandparents' house to the club . . . I could go there on foot, be that night, day, or whatever. Now nobody will leave their children cross Àngel Guimerà.

Thus, it is frequent to hear among the native inhabitants that migrants, or certain groups of migrants, cause insecurity. This phenomenon is related, on the one hand, to the intense use of public spaces such as parks and squares because, as we have seen, the use of public space by the migrant populations is often perceived as exclusionary since supposedly they inhibit the use by the native and, on the other hand, with the accusation that these groups commit crimes and mistreat the elder native neighbours. All of this creates greater social unrest and a feeling of abstract insecurity, especially among middle-aged women. More unemployed people often result in greater use of the town's public space by a larger number of people (including people of legal age). This appropriation of space is key to understanding the insecurity that some native inhabitants feel. Thus, there is a tendency to criminalize migrants for the simple fact of meeting in the street, loitering, or simply sitting in the squares. We see that the 'common-sensical idea' of linking migrants with crime is reproduced, and many native inhabitants imagine their activities are illegal. As Carmen recounts, she does not feel safe in her neighbourhood because groups of strangers gather in the square:

> A: Yes, yes, yes, I am afraid, and I have always been a person who has not been afraid . . . but seeing what there is, it gives me, I am afraid of living in the neighbourhood.
>
> Q: And what do you mean (when you say) 'seeing what there is'? In what sense?
>
> A: In the sense that I am afraid of being mugged, of being robbed, I don't know, of a thousand things, because they are so desperate because there is no money, because there is no work, and they are so [hooked] from drugs that they are capable of anything. If they see you with the purse, they know if you carry five euros, ten euros or whatever, they push you, scare you and steal your purse.

However, this feeling of insecurity seems to be the product of the bad sociability that reigns in the neighbourhood, rather than a rise in crime. The new faces, or the unknown and strange ones, result from little sociability between the new and old neighbours, creating a feeling of uncertainty and insecurity. In this sense, (strange) looks are important, as we see from Concepción, 'There is a group that you see them every day, every day, that they are not from here and you see that they are . . . well, selling drugs, smoking it, and it is as if they were there controlling, it gives you the feeling that they are, controlling, seeing when you leave, when you enter.'

We see that the precariousness—a product of the crisis—and its spatial fix—the result of the real estate market—creates a particular geography: with spaces in a state of significant degradation, where a large number of precarious people, old and unemployed, live together in a confronted sociability following ethnocultural markers and where informal economic activities (although not necessarily criminal) proliferate. Because of this socio-spatial configuration, many inhabitants, especially from the region, refer to Salt as a 'ghetto', a territorial stigma that moves horizontally at the scale of the town, towards the Barri Centre, and towards the most precarious and newcomers, the migrants.

In chapter, 5 I will analyse how the different narratives have created a territorial stigmatization that has prompted a series of urban policies aimed at curbing this trend and promoting a different town, but first, let us take a look at the policies dealing with the aforementioned social conflicts.

Chapter Four

An Iron Fist in a Velvet Glove

From Zero-Tolerance to Policies of Quieting and Convivència[1]

The new social situation product of the economic crisis was in Spain, as in so many other countries of Europe, succeeded by the implementation of austerity measures in the public sector and a ferocious labour-market restructuring. Not surprisingly, these institutional and political changes would have an important influence on the livelihood of a large proportion of migrants and those perceived as such, as will be apparent from this chapter. In fact, while as we have seen in the previous chapters, during the economic recession starting in 2007, the situation of many migrant households became increasingly (more) precarious, a change which would force many to resort to informal economic practices, often leading to social conflicts in these spaces. However, despite a clear relation to socio-economic changes on a more global scale, these varied social conflicts were often perceived as mere products of ethnocultural differences and the conflicts arising from these social situations.

In this sense, certain localities with a high percentage of non-EU immigrants often served as social laboratories for experimentation with and implementing new social and integration policies. Salt was such a place. Therefore, in this chapter, I will analyse the different policies implemented in Salt during the last decade to tackle what is considered a "social problem": migration from the Global South. I have been inspired by Carol Bacchi's (2009) 'What's the Problem Represented to be?' (WPR) approach to policy analysis and the considerations and reflections of Cris Shore and Susan Wright (1997), and from this, the following question has emerged: What are the implemented measures, their inherent assumptions, and their (possible) social consequences? The aim is to discern and analyse the abovementioned institutional and political changes within a critical and integral framework. It shows how although these policies were in their essence a continuation of earlier trends, they constitute a double movement in the field of the management of the poor, racialized, urban populations, operating both in the social domain, with policies aimed at strengthening the 'social cohesion', and the repressive one, through policing and zero-tolerance policies aimed at calming discontent and unrest.

CRIME AND INSECURITY: ORDERING THE SOCIAL SPACE IN A TOWN PLAGUED BY THE 'CRISIS'

During the last decade, the idea that there is a problem of insecurity and *convivencia* caused by a high level of crime has become hegemonic, an issue often linked to a high level of immigration. Until 2009 the majority of the problems mentioned had, to a large extent, dealt with the incidence of migration for social resources; after that, another element of concern was added: crime (see for instance ACN 2009, Barrera 2009a, and El Periódico 2009).

The central concept articulating this was *citizen insecurity*, which basically refers to a perception of a lack of security, especially in the public space. However, as might be clear, this perception is subjective and socially constructed and, therefore, essentially political. On the other hand, if we review its use in the academic field, we see that it covers disciplines such as criminology, politics, sociology or law and that it entails specific ideas of how civil society, democracy, and social order work.

Indeed, although crimes or misdemeanours—building occupations, buying and selling drugs, and theft—are part of the social reality of the neighbourhood and the town, the issue of 'citizen insecurity' is not such a recent problem, as some political commentators and actors argue (see also Zuloaga 2014 and García and Ávila 2016). At the level of the Spanish State, the concept was used with force from the Transition, especially at the end of the 70s, reaching its zenith in 1984, as shown by a cover of the newspaper ABC on the 2nd of March 1984. According to the newspaper, shopkeepers of Barcelona closed their establishments in protest against rising insecurity. In the opinion of the conservative newspaper, this was due to a relaxation in the criminal laws and the release of prisoners under the then Minister of Justice, Fernando Ledesma Bartret (ABC 1984).

Through a review of the news published since the 1980s in municipal or regional newspapers and magazines, I have been able to order information regarding the phenomenon of insecurity in this town. We see that already it is related to growing conflict and immigration—which at that time is dominated by 'internal immigration':

> After the moments of initial euphoria, after the municipal elections, the truth is that the everyday reality has presented the serious problems that the new municipalities have, especially Salt, which, due to its census, now approaching

> 25,000 inhabitants, its social structure, a dormitory town, a high unemployment rate, and a strong presence of immigration, is the scene of frequent cases of citizen insecurity, with complaints and confrontations, in the face of which the scarcity of the Municipal Police do little and the economic difficulties of the municipal budget don't allow short-term solutions. Precisely, in those aspects in which services of all kinds are coordinated with the Girona City Council, a better and higher level of services should correspond. (Onyar 1984)

The first time that there was a demonstration concerning the issue was in July 2004 when a demonstration "against citizen insecurity" took place (López 2004). This incident was almost identical to the demonstration that took place in 2010. "Officially, the neighbourhood mobilization was spontaneous, improvised, and was convened the same day through word-of-mouth. Nothing could be further from the truth: in fact, neighbourhood groups have been aware for several weeks that 'something big' was going to happen" (López 2004). The only difference was that, on this occasion, it did not get the same media attention. The issue at hand, a concern on the part of some of the residents of Salt regarding the 'migratory fact' and its correlative assumption of insecurity, was therefore recurrent and not at all something particular to the year 2010, 2004, nor to the 'new immigration'.

Even so, from the first demonstrations and until the extraordinary period of 2010–2011, a discursive change around the town's problems can be discerned, which is evident in the newspaper clippings, especially since 2009. At a general level, the media began to echo an alleged growing conflict in the municipality, which has to do, on the one hand, with the high percentage of 'migrants' mentioned above and, on the other, with citizen insecurity linked to an alleged increase in crime rates. It is difficult to establish whether this discursive change is the cause or the effect of a change in perception in civil society, but I have been able to verify that it only partially corresponds to the feelings of the inhabitants with whom I have spoken. Instead, most of them identified Barri Centre as a conflictual area.

By reviewing the statistical data of the Local Police of Salt, a general trend towards an increase in petty crimes, such as theft and robbery, can be detected (see figure 4.1). The index rises in 2006, especially with the outbreak of 'the crisis', reached its maximum in 2009. However, it is relevant that this increase ran parallel with a significant population increase (37.64 percent, IDESCAT) and that this phenomenon was repeated in other towns in the Girona region, such as Figueres, at the regional level. At the county level, recorded theft incidents increased from 1,775 (2008) to 2,138 (2009) (EUROSTAT). At the level of Catalonia, the interannual variation 2008–2009 was a ratio of 2.43 in the case of crimes against property and 1.79 in the case of offences against property (Home Office, Generalitat de Catalunya 2010).

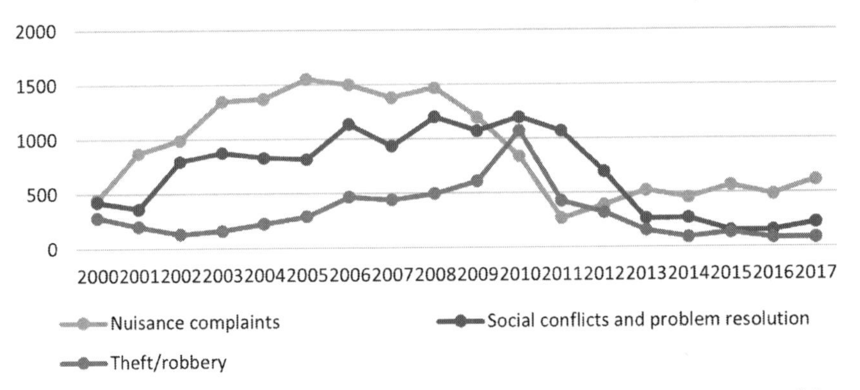

Figure 4.1. Evolution in the police interventions in Salt. 2000–2017. ***Source*****: Elaborated by the author from police figures provided by the Local Police Department.**

It is interesting to note that the municipal government and local police had already noticed a change in the type and frequency of crimes a few months before (Barrera 2010a), although, in their opinion, this did not represent a worrying situation compared to other towns. According to the testimonies of the former security councillor, David Estévez, the former head of the local police and the former mayor, Iolanda Pineda, there was a previous phase in which there was an increase in robberies at homes (in brand bicycles stolen from garages) and inside vehicles (Barrera 2010b). A type of crime directed more towards the inhabitants with possessions, the middle class, and specifically, the inhabitants of the neighbourhoods Barri Vell and La Massana. It is significant that the moment the middle class began to be affected by crimes and misdemeanours, there was a *jumping scale* (Smith 1993). They mobilize their capital and start a campaign involving the local and regional media and promoting a supposedly neutral discourse on how unbearable the State of insecurity has become due to crime.

At the same time, other types of minor crimes intensified, such as robbery with force and violence. These crimes stood out for their visibility—since they were often committed in public spaces and daylight—and for their physically violent nature. In 2009, robberies with violence increased by 173 percent, robberies with force 157 percent—compared to 2008—while robberies inside vehicles increased by 159 percent. On the other hand, in 2010 more or less the same levels were maintained, and in 2011 they fell significantly. These mainly affected the inhabitants and users of the public space of Barri Centre and had, of course, a more immediate effect on the perception of security in the neighbourhood. These are essential facts when it comes to understanding one of the reasons for the social mobilization of February 2010. They serve as the base for the construction of a hegemonic narrative (in the Gramscian sense) regarding the problems the town suffers. At the media level, the idea spread that the victims were generally defenceless older people who had their jewels stolen, which had come to symbolize the fruit of the effort of a life of work. Another significant media impact was the occupation of flats in the Barri Centre (see ACN 2010 and Barrera 2010c). What stands out from this news is the point of view that was applied, they are all spectacular cases, and the treatment was rather sensational (see, for example, RTVE 2011b).

There are several news items related to both topics, especially bicycle thefts, occupations of flats and, to a lesser extent, theft and violent crimes (Barrera 2010b and 2010d). News and reports that echoed the subjective insecurity of some inhabitants created a specific social alarm that would eventually settle among many inhabitants of the town (Pinilla 2010). Common crime served as the basis for a generalized criminalization of all informal economic activities and thus their deep embedding in the capitalist (formal) economic market. In this sense, a series of articles published in La Vanguardia September 9, 2011 (La Vanguardia 2011, Vivir 1–3) is paradigmatic.

Here the problem of multiple recidivists is dealt with in an alarming depiction of daily conflicts. Migrant populations are criminalized for the simple fact of appropriating public space, and simple idle activities are persecuted. The following phrase accompanying a photo taken from a police car showing five 'migrants' wandering the street is most telling: "you can see, from inside a patrol car, a group of neighbours of different ethnic groups passing the time on the street. It is a classic image in certain areas of Salt; people loitering in portals with no apparent occupation." (La Vanguardia 2011).

PACIFICATION AND EMBELLISHMENT OF PUBLIC SPACE

The media focus on the town created a sense of insecurity. However, a series of measures were implemented to solve this and, at the same time, attend to the complaints of the native inhabitants. These measures can broadly be described as punitive and supervisory policies and civic measures to improve the 'convivencia'. This result is based on what is understood as a causal relationship between petty crime problems and the feeling of insecurity perceived as a product of these; and a similar relationship between the degradation of social cohesion and convivencia conflicts and what is described as uncivil or vandalism behaviours (based on the broken windows theory).

Punitive and Supervisory Policies

Between 2005–2015, due to the alarm promoted by the media and the political pressure exerted by many 'native inhabitants', more punitive measures were adopted to deal with the 'insecurity'. From the first tense moment in 2010, a hegemonic consensus was established regarding the need for an urgent intervention, which led to repressive and supervisory measures carried out by the Mossos d'Esquadra. In this sense, the idea of insecurity was mobilized politically and justified a series of policies that I have called *strategies of pacification of public space*. These include punitive and supervisory measures such as the harassment of young people in the squares at night and patrolling in private buildings with the prior consent of the community of neighbours.

During the years 2008–2010, the municipality and the police responded firmly to the aforementioned change in crimes in a supervisory and punitive sense. The mayor and the councillor with the security portfolio had publicly demanded more significant police presence and that judges and prosecutors be tougher on multiple offenders. According to the then councillor in charge of Security, David Estevez:

> Mossos d'Esquadra in Girona, when we have only seven-eight people here, could not sit still when the mayor called for more Mossos d'Esquadra in Salt every day. They could not ignore that the neighbourhood and other local associations in Barri Centre would continuously be asking for more Mossos d'Esquadra.

Secondly, as denounced by many young migrants, local and regional police forces carried out stop-and-search campaigns, often using ethnic profiling, despite being illegal and ineffective (García Añón et al. 2013; Harcourt 2008):

> They had to do something, they had to let themselves be seen, and their way of letting themselves be seen was this. . . . Both Mossos d'Esquadra and the Local Police, as well as the National Police, the Civil Guard, and so on, work a lot with extensive statistics and here we realized that we had to put a name on these statistics, face and eyes. Moreover, we saw that there were four, five, six, seven, eight, nine people, all with one, it's no longer a stereotype because, unfortunately, they all coincided: a young Moroccan migrant. Of course, if you run a list of ten people who are all Moroccan, and the first thing a pair of police officers do is stop a Moroccan man and ask for his documentation, what would you do?

From 2010–2012, 23 closed-circuit television (CCTV) cameras were installed, which is a fairly large number for Spain, especially considering the town's size. Furthermore, in 2011, a pioneering program called *Passadissos nets, segurs passadissos* was introduced, inspired by a similar programme in New York called the Clean Halls Programme (Diari de Girona 2012 and Cosculluela 2012). The programme allowed the canine unit of the police to patrol in the neighbourhoods that had agreed to the initiative; which in 2015 counted 56, representing a total of 1,143 homes, the majority in Barri Centre and Catalunya Square.

According to a complaint issued by the Research Group on Minorities (GRAMC 2010) and partly confirmed by a report in the Catalan Ombudsman published in 2010 (Síndic de Greuges), new rules on the evaluation reports issued to the regularisation process of migrants had been introduced by the town council, which were clearly discriminatory. They had introduced new supervisory measures when assessing 'social rooting' (whereby a foreigner claims the right to obtain a residence permit) of the applicants and the family reunification process. The administration would then check the applicant's personal record at the local police station. If the person had committed an offence in the municipality—be it a misdemeanour or even a simple administrative issue—the authorities would issue an unfavourable report. Thus, the applicants would have their residence permit or renewal denied. They also demanded more months of residency registration than generally applied, and they would not issue any explanation when applications were denied. Moreover, a motion asking for the reports of the town council to be binding was approved (Julbe 2010).

Civility Policies

In the last decade, there has been increasing use of civility policies. These strategies include measures based on the discourse of 'civility' such as a reform of the civility ordinances (Galdon-Clavell 2016), civility officers, the removal of satellite dishes on the facades of buildings and junk on the balconies, surveillance, control and the displacement and criminalization of informal workers, the closure of public fountains, and so on. These policies are based on the idea that there has been an "invasion of (public) space" by undesirable subjects, the 'migrants'; hence I have called them strategies of embellishment.

In 2003, a local civility ordinance was adopted in Salt. Salt was a pioneer in the approval of a civility ordinance. The object of intervention was already the shared urban space, while attention was focused on the 'uncivil attitudes', which should be hindered through fines:

> The occupation of sidewalks and squares by some groups constitutes another of the attitudes that annoy the residents of Salt the most. "There are youth gangs that have taken over some squares and have made no one feel comfortable in

> them. Some invade the sidewalks and obstruct the passage of pedestrians," says the chief of police. (Taberner 2003)

However, it seems that the ordinance was not rigorously applied until 2007 when a first modification of the text was made. Among the new features introduced were: a) extending the prohibition (established in 2004) to install parabolic antennas (Iglesias 2008 and Julbe 2008) on the facades of buildings and to leaving junk on balconies under penalty of financial penalties; b) hiring civic agents who would ensure compliance of these ordinances, initially from an informational and educational point of view (not sanctioning).

Finally, they closed the public water sources during the summer of 2008, a measure that became permanent in 2010. At the same time, two campaigns were launched in line with what some called, 'urban patriotism' (López Sánchez 1993): "Un Salt endavant" and "T'estimo Salt". The purpose of these was to promote the sense of belonging and pride and promote citizen participation and consensus regarding the repressive measures implemented.

These strategies were implemented to facilitate the 'free movement' and access to public space for "all the inhabitants" and foster a sense of belonging among residents, in addition to promoting coexistence. However, following other investigations in the field (Mitchell 1997; Lundsteen and Fernández González 2021), I argue that these policies had social effects which had little to do with the stated objectives. Instead, we should consider them revanchist policies (Smith 1996), aimed at reducing or avoiding social conflict which could, and usually would, take place in public space through the displacement and expulsion of actors deemed to be a "menace", "invader", "transgressor", or simply "troubling", with the ultimate goal of regaining access for the 'natives' and middle-classes.

Social Effects

> The dominant perception is that crime in the city is the fault of the migrant other, thus obscuring the larger picture of increasing crime facing the entire urban society. This view does not merely reflect or distort the reality, but is itself a form of social ordering, with real political consequences. Because the migrant population is constructed as a high crime group and to a certain degree a social anomaly (being out of place), it has been subject to arbitrary official campaigns of 'cleaning and reordering' (Zhang 2001, 157)

One autumn night, I crossed the old canal Monar, where I met two men who were climbing the ravine with big bottles of water. About 100 meters away, two girls sat on a bench, and when I passed, I heard one explain to the other: "Maybe at home, they don't have water, or they can't pay for it." An important question, although more importantly: why do they make such an effort just to take water from the canal, instead of taking it from a drinking fountain, for example?

In order to understand, we must go back to mid-2011, when the local council decided to close almost all the municipal drinking fountains, except for four "strategically located" ones and another one outside the town (see La Vanguardia, Redacción 2011 and Cosculluella 2013). The previous government implemented a similar measure in 2008 due to the drought. As the then-mayor Iolanda Pineda says: "We closed the public drinking fountains in the summer of 2008 due to drought. . . . After this period, they were reopened, and these problems took place, and we decided to close them again."

The justifying reasons now included: (a) *public health*, according to the council, there was a possibility that tiger mosquitoes would breed in the surrounding puddles, and some neighbours did not like that people washed their face or feet in the fountains; (b) the *inconvenience* that they supposedly caused some neighbours and the "long lines" that sometimes occurred in front of them; (c) the *tremendous cost* that the "excessive" expense of water from the fountains supposed according to the local council. In the words of the former mayor, Iolanda Pineda:

> After the drought, yes, we started to receive complaints that there were people who queued at night looking for water. They did not know if they did not have access to water at home, or they just didn't want to spend water from their house and take it from there. Okay . . . and then there was a use or misuse of these fountains, dogs drinking from them and behind a child is waiting to drink water. . . . And another complaint was that children washed their feet and heads.

The first argument is related to hygienic and public health issues. However, in that case it would have been inconsistent not to close all the fountains from the beginning. And the fact that they were still closed four years later showed that perhaps the arguments that weighed the most were the other two: the 'annoyances' of what is considered an excessive use (both in terms of the appropriation of public space and water as a resource) by some neighbours, and the excessive cost that this reports to the council, as we see from the following quote: "The complaints of some neighbours about the concentrations that were formed in some areas have also had a lot to do with the decision of the council: 'As of seven or eight in the afternoon, up to fifteen people have gathered', explains Valentí. On occasions, these concentrations have ended in a fight" (La Vanguardia, Redacción 2011).

It is crucial that both arguments refer to the 'excess' of some users (not conceptualized as 'neighbours') who exploit municipal resources to which they have a 'doubtful' right. The closure of the fountains was taken with both political (supposedly to prevent an intensification of conflicts) and economic intention (save municipal resources and privatize water consumption). But, as I will discuss later, this reading also leads to the perverse conclusion that migrants are to blame for the 'cut' in accessing a material resource which by habit has always been accessible because of their 'uncivilized' use. An argument that ends up dovetailing with the postures of the extreme right (especially the Plataforma per Catalunya) who ask for differential treatment and accuse the migrants of stealing or depleting resources that should be for natives.

It is irrefutable that water is a fundamental resource, a natural and social condition as Karl Polanyi (2001, 99) called it. Today this essential resource is usually accessed through the market. As an alternative to buying (in the supermarket or through the domestic consumption network), one can also access it through the public drinking fountains (free public service), an option many may be forced to consider during times of scarcity. Since, far from being a practice that only people with few resources employ to satisfy their basic needs, it can also be an economizing practice for people who are in a stable situation: if a person has little money and is scarce in resources, resorting to the drinking fountain or the canal constitute a way to save money. It is undoubtedly in times like these when the nature of water as an essential and social resource is clearly shown: without water, one suffers dehydration, cannot cook or clean oneself. In this way, one might, to some extent, be excluded from normative sociability. Thus, water is essential for social reproduction. The consequences of closing the sources are that people with the greatest needs must resort to alternative, and often, unhealthier practices to access resources. This, in turn, has the effect of reinforcing hygienist and racist discourses and increasing their social marginalization, as Martínez Veiga (2001) in El Ejido.

The social effects of the police and judicial measures on petty crime, as Fassin (2013) recalls, can be extremely humiliating and violent. Under the pretext of solving the insecurity, the policies have devastating effects on young people who resort to these practices: they are marginalized and pushed towards social exclusion, and many end up in jail, while some are expelled or, in extreme cases, end up dying from police persecution, as happened in the cases of Mohammed Reda, the youth of Clichy-sous-Bois, or by the knee, as George Floyd.

Other social effects were particular geographical markings: (a) territorially, the problem is related to Barri Centre, which is the main area of action, and (b) bodily for 'young migrants', especially Moroccans.

a) Although these measures were supposedly created to promote a sense of belonging among its inhabitants and improve coexistence (due to a greater sense of security and therefore mutual trust), they have ended up avoiding or redirecting any underlying conflicts and stimulating an atmosphere of tension and distrust towards some indicated groups. All this has favoured the continuous identification between Barri Centre, migration, ghetto and conflicts of convivencia.

b) Likewise, many 'native' inhabitants confirmed an initial racist hypothesis about who was problematic. As Alim recalls: "Sometimes reality speaks for itself, and the people who have spoken out have used this argument to say 'if we went to the town hall to complain, those who reacted are those who felt alluded to, which means they are the ones who commit this."

Moreover, despite apparent universal intentions and effects, the civility policies mainly affected the public space and the 'foreign residents' of the Barri Centre. This we can conclude from reviewing and analysing two of the most famous and controversial measures: the case of satellite dishes and the closure of the public drinking fountains.

Hence, the prohibition of parabolic antennas, a typical mark of immigration, is, according to the former mayor, an action whose purpose lies in questions of security, aesthetics, and economy:

> The reasons for these actions were, first, because there was already an ordinance approved; it's a question of safety and aesthetics. It's true, but the other is also a matter of economy [laughing] in the sense that is it indispensable for each neighbour to put up their own satellite dish on the house if putting two of them in the community is enough? Does everyone need to have their own at home? Of course, this was first a matter of security because many were glued directly to the façade. Secondly, it is an aesthetic issue, it is true, it is not pleasant to see an entire facade full of antennas, and moreover, all oriented (towards) the same place, and to see it is just stupid, could they not put one on top of it all pointing in that direction and that's it?

However, this measure also seems to reside in other reasons, since the council had promised to act in the face of complaints from some 'autochthonous' neighbours during the municipal election campaign, as pointed out by one of the EINA workers, Alim:

> The issue with the satellite dishes was something that visualized the presence of specific people, and therefore it was rejected by a part of the population. So when they won, this was an essential issue for the government because it is a fact that, this has already come out in the newspapers, back then in 2007 there was a lot, even the socialists did a kind of photoshop thing in which they visualized. . . . A community with antennas and a community without antennas and it was an actual photo of a community with antennas. They erased them with

photoshop, and they said that Salt would be like this with them in power. So, it was a real issue for them, and they insisted on this quite a lot.

The fact is that the town council decided to act on the neighbourhood complaints instead of using more pedagogical tools, such as a public campaign, to solve the conflict between the neighbours. In this way, the policy had the effect of criminalizing the poor without solving the underlying problems of the conflict, which may have included access to employment, housing, or even drinking water. In effect, the logical conclusion from this handling is that the underlying problem is simply one of uncivil behaviour or other forms of being, i.e. a cultural problem.

In this sense, the program "Passadissos nets, passadissos segurs" (lit. Clean halls, secure halls)[2] is paradigmatic. While it has, in my view, a double objective: 1) to create a sense of security through police presence, and 2) to symbolically order the urban space and with it the social relations. It was presented as a plan to curb uncivil attitudes and behaviour. However, other objectives such as peace and becoming familiar with the situations of the communities, and "to act as a deterrent to all those who want to complicate life in a specific community", as the then-mayor stated, were also apparent. According to the town council, they wanted to respond to the real problems of the neighbourhood communities, defined as: "neighbours who illegally tap into utility lines to obtain electricity, people who urinate in the halls or problems of illegal occupation" (Diari de Girona 2012). Moreover, the program would deal with other problems such as drug possession and what was seen as a 'problematic' appropriation of public space by migrants.

As the following excerpt from the ethnography shows, this intervention is like other public police interventions, such as raids or frisking, in the sense that they *order* the social space. They criminalize the subjects handled and police the boundaries of belonging-in-space (see Duneier 1999; Fernández Bessa and Di Masso 2018; Ilan 2011, for similar findings). Although in general, these measures might even have had positive effects for some of the neighbours or people who frequent the areas where such policies are in effect, the fact is that yet again, another large proportion of people living or simply hanging around have had an opposite experience: that of not feeling welcome.

When [Joana and I] arrived, we saw many young people, especially very young 'black' boys and girls. Gathered in groups, they were both very young and teenagers. They were basically grouped talking and listening to music or playing games. As soon as we arrived, some said "the police are coming", indicating that we were police and we considered [what we should do since we felt we were meddling], having turned around, the real police arrived. In total, three or four cars from the Local Police and Mossos d'Esquadra arrived while we were

> in the square in front observing everything. First, we saw some older Spanish or Catalan couples, then a small group of Moroccan men in the square right in front of us. The couples showed concerned faces and close attention with their eyes on the group, while the men didn't pay much attention. The police came, and one got out of the car with the baton in his hands, then put it on his belt while he approached the main group, others were circulating through the square, and one car entered the square closer to the group of the oldest ones. The very young ones had already left running almost as if playing "the police are coming; the police are coming" laughing. . . . The police approached the group and began to talk with them and review the documents of some of them. . . . It was twelve (0:00) something. After a while and nothing happened, the police left little by little. (23/07/2012, Diary 5: 8–10)

As we saw in Chapter 3, the police response often responds to calls from neighbours who complain about the noise caused by young people, but, as the observation shows, the interpretation by the spectators must have been different. Although some of these measures may have had positive effects for many of the residents of the Barri Centre and the people who frequent it, they have also had perverse effects on others, which has motivated a mobilization against them. Thus, we see that punitive and supervisory measures are imposed to pacify, embellish, or promote public space for 'the disappeared' under the excuse of civility, which ends up affecting specific groups of people despite its apparent neutrality. In this sense, the response of the former mayor to the accusations of racism in the case of the reports of social integration is very significant: "The mayor, Iolanda Pineda, rejected these accusations in plenary session and ruled that the only thing that is intended is precisely 'to eliminate the uncivil attitudes of a few that can lead to the criminalization of an entire group based on its origin'." (Julbe 2010)

What is striking here is how contradictory the argument is: discriminatory policies are implemented to avoid racism. This type of argument is essential because it is paradigmatic of a trend in policies that social-democratic political parties started applying in Europe at the beginning of the 21st century as a political response to the rise of far-right parties and the flight of their voters towards those parties. The argument goes that one must confront the uncivil, regardless of nationality or ethnicity, while at the same time, any existing inequalities are disdained.

In the first place, 'migrants' (people without Spanish nationality and non-EU citizens) are subject to assessments on their civic adaptation, while 'natives' and EU citizens are not. No matter how uncivil a native may be, he cannot be expelled. In contrast, a 'migrant' may have problems with renewing their residence permit and, ultimately, may be expelled. Secondly, no matter how much they integrate or even achieve nationality, migrants remain migrants in the eyes of many natives, who are in a better sociocultural position to pronounce on the authenticity of your nationality. Third, that which is considered "civil" or "uncivil" is also a product of historical-geographical processes particular to each place and interrelated with changing political-economic systems. Consequently, in the resulting sociocultural fields, not everybody is equal, and by employing this kind of discourse or symbolic ordering of space, these unequal positions are reaffirmed and, at the same time, endowed with a sense of normalcy that is not be questioned.

These policies may help in the short term, but they do not address the underlying problem that, as seen in the previous chapters, often has to do with particular neglect of the State, precariousness, and poverty. I argue that they are symbolic policies, the final consequence is that they may criminalize and further marginalize precarious individuals who struggle to survive in a hostile environment. They brush aside any structural analysis of everyday problems and conflicts. Furthermore, instead of addressing the underlying problems, they implement cosmetic and surgical changes. In addition, the conflicts that arise from inequalities are redirected, disguising them as mere behavioural problems. Consequently, the effect of this psychologization and culturalization of the social conflicts through the implemented political practices is extremely perverse in that they legitimize the inherent structural racism and social inequalities.

SOCIAL EFFICACY AND POLICIES OF QUIETING

One night, when I was coming back from the municipal swimming pool, I saw a large group of people gathered in the street at the intersection of Torres i Bagès and Ramón Sambola St. Normally, one would not see that many people gathered in such a small space, so I assumed that something had happened. As I got closer, I saw several vans of Mossos d'Esquadra, and when I reached the intersection, I realized that something had happened in the Igloo cafeteria. Around the premises, forming a human cordon, at least 100 people witnessed the police exhibition. A few people came out of the cafe accompanied by the police, who escorted them to the police van. Meanwhile, I went to a nearby bar and ordered a small glass of beer. With the beer in hand, I went out to watch the show. People asked me if I was a 'secret police' or a journalist. I told them I was neither, but they did not believe me because, as one explained, "we have never seen you around here." Alerted by my presence, some of the customers were commenting on the events of the bar opposite. Thus, I was able to hear comments about the supposed frequency of events of this kind: when a newcomer asked about the accumulation of people, another answered him, "what's so strange? For a change, there is a mess". Others distanced themselves from the conflicts by singing a now-famous strophe: "I am Spanish, Spanish, Spanish!" The next day I figured out what had happened: a large police operation (the municipal police, the Mossos d'Esquadra and the National Police intervened) had raided several bars in Barri Centre (Santiago 2011). As a result, 92 people were identified, of whom 22 were taken due to a "lack of documentation". After being at the police station, where documentation checks were carried out, only seven detainees remained for "non-compliance with the immigration law." Six of whom were subsequently released after the police had opened an expulsion file. The last, an Algerian man considered 'multi-recidivist', was arrested: the police had requested authorization from the court to transfer him to the Centre for the Internment of Foreigners (CIE) in Barcelona (Zona Franca) and subsequently expel him from the country.

Through this vignette, we see reflected several of the issues discussed so far. They constitute examples of how some measures and the theatrics they involve, imbue the way people perceive and live together in these spaces, as well as the definition of the groups that conform to the social fabric of the neighbourhoods: the policies separate those who have a right to be in the space from those who do not. The measures are, in their essence, symbolic policies, the principal aim of which is to show that politicians have listened to their constituents and that action is taken to revert the perceived state of the neighbourhood; they act by reordering the social reality and space symbolically, and yet they have material consequences for those targeted (even though unintendedly).

The policies fall within the category of what has been called "punitive populism" (Aranda Ocaña et al. 2005): visible measures are taken to respond to popular demands. It is about responding to the growing concern shown by the 'native working classes', primarily residents of the Barri Centre, even though many 'migrants' (workers too) are also victims of crime. In the end, the social efficacy of these reactionary measures and their popularity resides in their ability to redirect or displace the conflicts by giving them concrete form whilst offering a solution. This has much in common with the concept of 'symbolic efficacy' used by Lévi-Strauss (1963, 186–205), since at the same time they state the problem, they make abstract problems or feelings visible and tangible, and activate a solution. Hence, we observe how the canine patrol, a quintessential part of the Clean and Clear Halls program, produces the perception that the space is ordered and calm, clearing the area of all that is considered undesirable, including the Others. Hence when under ethnographic scrutiny, we see how more than a few people had the experience that all the "foreigners" left the space when the dog patrol came through, thus implying that they were shady, although that was not the case:

> While I was waiting at Passeig Elisenda de Montcada, the new canine patrol came by. I saw two police officers pass by, and later I heard a Spanish woman exclaim, "now suddenly nobody's here!". She must've been implying that it had something to do with the presence of the patrol, but the fact is that nothing had been cleared; in fact, there had hardly been anyone, just some Spanish children who had been there playing. (29/08/2012, Diary 5: 142)

This kind of intervention is what I call *policies of quieting*. Intended at calming and preventing social conflicts and frictions that could arise between what was generally perceived as the autochthonous population and immigrants, they divert the discomfort by implicitly blaming outsiders for the ills inflicted on the 'national body'. While they convey a sense of calm because they relieve the increasing social insecurity and uncertainty in terms of labour conditions, the social side-effects of the ongoing economic restructuring in the labour market.

SOCIAL POLICIES TO TACKLE CULTURAL DIVERSITY

From the beginning of the 21st century onwards, new measures to address cultural diversity were implemented in Salt. As a result of the growing arrival of migrants from countries outside the EU, mainly Africa, the need to implement new measures arose. In January 2000, the *I Jornades per la Integració i la Convivència* organised by the consistory were created (Roura 2000). Two years later, in September 2002, the local community learning centre, *Escola d'Adults*, in collaboration with the autonomous government, *Generalitat de Catalunya* (GC from now on), and the University of Girona, launched the Local Welcoming and Training Plan because

> [M]ore than 25 per cent of the 27,000 inhabitants are of foreign origin . . . an increase in population, which has generated new demands and needs, has on top of it all come up against the already existing significant shortcomings with regards to the expansion and quality of public services, and the absence of programmes destined to improve *convivencia*, a fact which has resulted in discontent and conflicts amongst the population (Town Hall Minutes LAOS-Salt on 31 January 2005).

A couple of years later, local authorities implemented the first series of policies based principally on the experiences of community organizations. In this sense, a substantive change took place in 2004 due to the allocation of funding from the GC through the *Llei de Barris*. This allocation led to important changes in social policies at the local level and created a board called *LAOS-Salt* ('A Space for Integration and Convivencia'). This included a stakeholder board with representatives from the different political parties present in the town council, and whose principal functions were to observe and report, and finally propose different actions, policies, services and activities related to the 'migration phenomenon'. Although other third sector agents were working in the terrain (mainly NGOs), at this point the execution of the proposals would rest mainly in the hands of local community organisations whose main focus was on the social aspects of integration in the local neighbourhoods, employing no kind of distinction between native and foreigner whatsoever. A local association called *EINA* would be in charge of the neighbourhood interventions regarding mediation, community management, and 'welcoming policies'.

Among the most significant measures implemented, we find the elaboration of a *Pla de Convivència Ciutadana* [Ordinance for Living Together], and contracting of civic agents through the Salt70 project, in addition to the appointment of a coordinator for the LAOS-Salt program, whose work would be that of "coordinating all the teams of people who work on issues of immigration and convivencia." (LAOS-Salt 2005, 6); a position that Andreu Bover, the now technician from the Area of Coexistence and Integration, would take up.

The objective of these measures was to improve social cohesion and coexistence in the municipality (implicitly affected by the new immigration). Take as an example the proposal of the *Patis Oberts* [Open Patios]: "Create a play and meeting space for the children and young people of Salt, which would encourage coexistence and avoid the conflicts and incidents that children's playing caused among the neighbours." (LAOS-Salt 2006, 41) Or the Community Swimming Pool's Mediation Service:

> Achieve a swimming pool that stands out as a space for convivencia and integration where everyone has a place, reducing the conflicting and insecure image that the people of Salt have of the swimming pool.
>
> Carry out a daily work of cultural mediation and awareness of habits of convivencia, reducing conflict situations and preventing the rescue team from having to intervene and be able to carry out their work without interference. (LAOS-Salt 2006, 42)

From then on, the Town Council assumed the Escola d'Adults' projects and decided to hire a civic agent who would act as a mediator and support the neighbouring communities. In a pilot test, this role would be filled by Alim, who would later join with other workers from the Local Plan to form the EINA association. The Town Council finally hired an association that proposed a series of actions and work to do community work and foster care, in addition to the *Cercles de Conversa* [lit. Conversations circles] that the Escola d'Adults had previously carried out. EINA undoubtedly dominated the interventions on mediation, community management and reception policies until 2010. It consisted of nine members and was able to propose alternative lines of action and philosophy as a result of the relative freedom they enjoyed:

> The agreement was signed with Torramadé, and back then there were no problems, because at the economic level there was an economic abundance, and no one questioned anything. . . . The approach we adopted through EINA was an approach, not that we would work on migration issues but that we worked with community issues in the town. *Alim*

Thus, the focus is more on community aid and management, although initially, they focus their attention on those places with the greatest probability of conflict, as reflected in the memory of their activities:

> The initial territory of intervention is Grup Verge Maria, due to the current deterioration of buildings and homes, which are also included in the process of urban remodelling of Salt 70. In addition, the profile of the current inhabitants is that of new residents of non-EU origin who are living in those homes that the native population has been leaving. These two characteristics are elements that can hinder the convivencia and management of neighbouring communities (LAOS-Salt 2006).

From then on, LAOS-Salt seems to have lost importance, while EINA maintains its focus and intense activity until the change of government in 2007 (where ERC remains in government and the mayor's office passes to the PSC). In Alim's opinion, this change introduces transformations: "The issue is that PSC had a vision, I would not say different but, Iolanda [Pineda], for instance, was the person in charge of migration issues or so in the Girona region of her party, and she wanted to promote some things."

Due to disagreements in action strategies and visions about the meaning of social work, conflicts began to arise between EINA and the local government. In the end, the agreement between both was ended. The tasks they had overseen would still be carried out, but the council chose to contract other entities, including Vincle (community and mediation work) and the SER.GI Foundation (educational and reception work). These associations were more professional and apolitical—for example, the SER.GI Foundation has a board of trustees in which members of various political parties and the business world participate. Furthermore, they were not exclusively local in scope but instead worked in more extensive areas (Vincle throughout Catalonia and the Fundació SER.GI in the Girona region).

Funding would still come from the Generalitat de Catalunya, the Ministry of Foreign Affairs or the European Fund for Integration, although private foundations would finance more and more projects. In mid-2010, the entities that work in the municipality and the different projects multiplied, but substantial changes would come from the conflicts of 2010 and 2011; this included changes in terms of how to deal with both the migratory event and the problems that supposedly arise from this.

First, based on previous experience in other municipalities regarding the management of *convivencia* conflicts (Lundsteen 2010), a *Taula de Convivència* (literally a board aiming at working for *convivencia*) was created. Alongside this, we also saw the appearance of the Intercultural Community Intervention Project, a vast social project which has been implemented in several other hotspots in both Catalonia and Spain, covering 17 neighbourhoods and municipalities registering 'high cultural diversity'. The project in Catalonia is the result of an agreement between the *"la Caixa" Foundation*[3] and the *Casal dels Infants* (a historic NGO operating at the regional level and with roots in the Barcelona neighbourhood of Raval), with the collaboration of Salt's town council:

> The municipality of Salt (Gironès) has been chosen from 227 projects by Obra Social 'la Caixa' to carry out a project whose primary objective is to promote social cohesion in a population with 43% of the population of immigrant origin. The project, three years old, is endowed with 465,000 euros. This money will go to the entity 'El casal dels infants' in Barcelona, which will be responsible for developing the actions in Salt to create a new model of intervention that can be applied to other places where there is also much immigration. Children and young people will be the target audience for the program, which revolves around education, health and community relations. (ACN 2010b)

Its main objective was 'to generate a community-based intervention model regarding the management of cultural diversity', and thus 'promote peaceful *convivencia* and the development of the community through the participation of all its citizens'. Among the activities carried out in Salt, we find *See you downstairs*—an activity carried out in the village squares to promote 'intercultural encounters'. There is also community work for childhood and adolescent *convivencia* in some squares called *Let's Play?*, an urban garden, and, finally, a so-called time-bank (Casal d'Infants 2013). Third, through a 2010 grant, the Pla de Ciutadania a Salt [Citizenship Plan for Salt] was developed. A novel and exciting proposal for "an inclusive citizenship" that, however, was never institutionalized, due to the change of government that occurred just after it was written.

Likewise, the Taula de Convivencia never had continuity, and later, in 2012 and under the new government, it would merge with LAOS-Salt into the *Consell de Ciutat—l'órgan de participació ciutadana* [Town Council—Body for the Citizen's Participation]. The character of this body was still consultative, and the decisions only have the rank of recommendations for the municipal government bodies. Its main objective is to carry out the functions of, a) To advise the Town Council on the definition of the main lines of the municipal policy and management to generate citizen consensus in subjects of convivencia. b) To learn and debate the projects operating in the field of the convivencia in Salt. c) To act as a guarantor of the participation of the different citizen agents in the analysis and proposals on issues related to convivencia. e) Promote actions to develop social cohesion and improve the quality of life of the citizens. g) To debate other subjects entrusted by the mayor, the Board of Local Government, or the Town Council's Plenary session. f) To channel individual and collective citizen initiatives to promote convivencia, social peace, etc. g) Disseminate and inform the public about the proposals emerging from the Town Council through its Presidency (Town Council 2012).

Two important considerations should be made regarding the recent changes that have occurred: first, we see that the word convivencia replaces the word migration, and, secondly, the composition of the table, the component, has changed. Although the concerns of 'migrants' used to be considered, a position certainly criticizable for its quasi-multicultural approach to community representatives, now they seem to be ignored. Now the body is presided over by the mayor or a delegated councillor, and the committee is made up of: a) a representative of each municipal group with representation in the plenary, b) two representatives of the neighbourhood associations registered in the municipality, c) three representatives among the entities and associations legally constituted and registered in the municipality of a cultural, sports, and social nature, d) a representative of the board of religious entities, e) a representative of a non-local public institution with a presence in the municipality, f) a representative from the media, journalist, and collegiate sphere, g) two representatives from the schools, h) two representatives from the business sector, i) four citizens chosen according to age criteria (18–25, 26–40 , 41–60, and over 61 years old), j) an expert in citizenship and community action policies, k) two representatives from the third sector, l) the citizen ombudsman); in addition to this, a technician will act as secretary without vote.

One could argue that everybody is treated equally this way, leaving aside 'the cultural' in the sense that I am criticizing it here. The problem, as I will argue later, is that this egalitarian presentation of civil society is illusory.

At the same time, socio-economic inequalities (the most recurrent criticism made of this idea of governance) and ethnocultural ones, structural and institutional racism (Bonilla-Silva 1997), are entirely ignored.

(RE)DISCOVERING THE CULTURAL OTHER

The main problem to be solved with the implemented measures is the failed sociocultural integration of 'new residents', which supposedly brings with it problems of convivencia. They aim to ensure a 'good social cohesion' by guiding the social integration of a group of people seen as cultural strangers within the dominant (naturalized) sociocultural order. Thus, policies are implemented to promote coexistence through mediation and sociocultural dynamization. A brief genealogy of the dominant discourses on migration in Spain and the strategic plans at the State and regional level can help us uncover the inherent assumptions.

In the mid-1980s, with the obtainment of EU membership and in response to what is perceived as a new social phenomenon (non-EU immigration), a set of new social policies was implemented and promoted in Spain (Zapata-Barrero 2003). However, these differed from region to region (Gil Araujo 2010) in practice due to decentralization and regional socio-political disparities (Hepburn and Zapata-Barrero 2014). These socio-regulatory practices were aimed at the 'new migration' and, driven by the directives of the EU, emphasized three aspects of management: 1) the control of migration flows, 2) the prevention of the causes of immigration, and 3) the integration of legally residing immigrants and their families. This was reflected in the first Aliens Act, the *Ley de Estrangería*, passed in 1985. Since then, Spain adopted the European discourse and practice of stricter border control and began to problematize the presence of non-EU foreigners who had been identified as a 'problematic population' requiring control by specific public policies (Agrela and Dietz 2005, 25).

Although the first policies aimed at the integration of migrants were indeed reflected in both the Catalan I Interdepartmental Plan for Immigration 1993–2000 (1993) and the Spanish Plan for the Social Integration of Immigrants (PISI) (1994), it was not until the beginning of the twenty-first century when migration became increasingly politicized, ushering in what Cachón calls 'the third stage of integration' (2008, 32). Particularly in the media, immigration was increasingly presented as a problem; the newly arrived 'other' cultural beings had to be integrated, thus emphasizing the (inter-)cultural aspects of an otherwise highly complex social phenomenon (Gil Araujo 2010). In this sense, paradigmatic social conflicts during the late 1990s and the beginning of the twenty-first century prompted significant changes in the discourse on migration and how to handle it. The way the media treated the conflicts, and the way civil society, including parts of the academia, NGOs, and political parties, interpreted these 'social observatories' gave way to a culturalization of the social problems, most clearly expressed in the critique exposed by the Federation of the Anthropological Associations of Spain in response to the inauguration of the Forum of the Cultures (2004) (see also Narotzky 2005). More importantly, this problematic representation would lead to essential changes in how the State would handle migrants and migration from then on.

Since the turn of the century, integration and cultural policies—reflected in the development of plans and programs at the State, regional and municipal levels, such as the Second Interdepartmental Plan for Immigration 2001–2004 and the Global Programme for the Regulation and Coordination of Foreigners and Immigration (GRECO)—became the primary solution to what was seen as the main problem: ever-growing cultural diversity. Even today, little has changed despite the critique (Gil Araujo 2010; de Lucas 2016; Solanes-Corella 2015)[4]. The more recent strategic plans drawn up by the Spanish State (Spanish Ministry of Science and Education 2007, 2011) and the pacts of the Autonomous Government of Catalonia (Generalitat de Catalunya 2008, 2009, 2014) have followed in the footsteps of these initial policy frameworks and paths in the sense that they have not challenged the underlying ideas on cultural diversity. Take, for instance, the concept of 'ghettoization' mentioned in these documents (clearly influenced by the culture of poverty thesis, as initially proposed by Lewis 1969): although inequality is mentioned as a factor to bear in mind, the primary assumption in these documents is that it is the concentration of cultural minorities that leads to urban poverty and segregation. Therefore, to overcome 'potential situations of hostility'—indeed an example of 'not racism' (Lentin 2018) at work—'intercultural *convivencia* amongst the citizens in these neighbourhoods' must be promoted (Spanish Ministry of Work and Immigration 2011, 116).

In Catalonia, this translated into the programme known as *Llei de Barris*, a socio-urban renewal and integration programme started in 2004 aimed at targeting deprived neighbourhoods and small towns, and financial support schemes for people in 'danger of social exclusion', specifically to pay rent, as 'there are immigrants in danger of social exclusion on the housing market' (Generalitat de Catalunya 2008, 58). The main aim was to improve the social life of the suburbs, to promote (intercultural) *convivencia* and social cohesion in public space (Generalitat de Catalunya 2008, 66), to develop a politics of urban cohesion, measures in favour of community projects, neighbourhood renewal, and the participation of citizens.

One way or another, these key documents generally involve measures targeting 'diversity' to solve the problems ostensibly deriving from the same phenomenon (Gil Araujo 2010; Agrela Romero 2006). They outline a governance model to be followed at the local administrative level in which the 'residential concentration' of immigrants must be avoided because otherwise, it might lead to 'ghettoization', which in turn would lead to hostilities between the Spanish residents and foreigners. The underlying assumption of all this is that the recent incorporation of non-European migrants into Spanish society has produced new urban scenarios, often stigmatized as 'powder kegs', highly diverse places, which will eventually and unavoidably, lead to tensions and conflicts between neighbours often labelled *convivencia conflicts* (Aramburu 2001, 23–40). This is a phrase increasingly employed to describe conflicts in these neighbourhood communities, in practice serving as a substitute for 'ethnic conflicts', 'racial conflicts', or 'cultural conflicts'. Salt would here serve as an exemplary laboratory for these new policies.

In fact, Jordi Moreras supports this hypothesis by arguing that, in the context of Catalonia, it was the conflicts in the Ca n'Anglada de Terrassa neighbourhood (1999), the conflict in the Erm neighbourhood of Manlleu (1999) and the conflict of the mosque in Premià de Mar, were decisive for future political actions:

> These three cases may have represented an important turning point in how the local intervention policies on immigration are thought, designed and formulated. The new paradigm that seems to be proposed passes through the field of "diversity management", which starts from a double preventive and regulatory assumption of the circumstances involved in intercultural coexistence. (Moreras 2007, 66)

In the case of Salt, we have seen that from 2004–2005 and from the Salt70 project, financed by the *Llei de Barris*, a different perspective was institutionalized, and non-welfare structures were created—as the head of the area, Andreu Bover, confirmed in an interview—to face the problems derived from the (new) migratory phenomenon. Migration and cultural diversity were paid more attention to, particularly with a growing concern for intercultural convivencia. This results in measures, programs and policies aimed to prevent and mediate conflicts and facilitate "intercultural coexistence", as with the Intercultural Community Intervention Project. They proposed dialogue and mediation to avoid social conflicts, here interpreted as pure "conflicts of (inter)cultural coexistence" ("la Caixa" Foundation 2013).

A great majority of the actions taken to remediate this, aimed at ensuring that 'native' and 'migrant' populations would get along, were derived from the assumptions of the contact hypothesis conceived by Allport (1954).

Inherent to these measures was an organicist view of society. Since by virtue of identification and familiarity, the product of the contact between 'us' and 'them', the negative and stereotyped perception of the Other would be attenuated, and thus prejudice, rejection and conflict would be reduced. In the last decade, this type of program aimed at fostering contact or encounter has multiplied (Koutrolikou 2012).

In general terms, I argue that a culturalization of interventions (social policies) can be observed to address social problems that are understood as products of social conflicts identified as (inter)cultural convivencia. A hegemonic interpretation and framework of action which has its own particular dispositive, in the way Michel Foucault conceived it: "A resolutely heterogeneous assemblage made up by discourses, institutions, architectural qualifications, regulatory decisions, laws, administrative measures, scientific statements, philosophical, moral, and philanthropic propositions (Foucault, Dits et écrits, vol. iii, pp. 229 y ss)" quoted in (Agamben 2011, 250).

Other authors also detected a fact (Agrela 2006; Agrela and Dietz 2005; Gil Araujo 2010). In turn, it is part of a hegemonic project of knowledge, which, as I argue elsewhere (Lundsteen, Forthcoming; see also Wolf 1982), was born with the social sciences in the 19th century, and which separated the domains of the social (where culture relates to migration) from the economic and political. This project also finds its expression in bureaucratic spheres that do not relate to each other, an idea which I believe is crucial when analysing the neoliberal mode of organization of the social. A conceptualization that encompasses a wide range of discursive and political practices, which, as we have seen, are various and not at all homogeneous, under a shared axis of 'cultural differentialism'.

We are facing a paradoxical situation, where most political practices regarding the phenomenon of extra-community immigration are based on similar assumptions, namely: a primacy of cultural factors. In the words of Delgado (2006, 2), "These two positions—the "intolerant" and the "tolerant"—are not too different, and both agree that what matters is to consider cultural diversity not as what it ultimately is—a fact and enough—but as a source of serious problems that require an adequate and energetic response."

As Etiénne Balibar says (Balibar and Wallerstein 1991), this new discourse has two political consequences. First, a destabilization of the defences of traditional anti-racism, insofar as its argumentation is used against it. It contradicts the arguments of biological racism: it confirms that there are no human races, nor can the aptitudes, defects, or behaviour be explained through blood or genes, but as the result of belonging to historical cultures. These arguments had been provided by anthropologists and were used against racist arguments and policies. As Balibar argues, we see that 'culture' can also naturalize 'human behaviour' and social affinities: "and it can in particular function as a way of locking individuals and groups a priori into a genealogy, into a determination that is immutable and intangible in origin." (Balibar and Wallerstein 1991, 22)

Second, the new discourse can explain or even legitimize racism. The mixing of cultures, or the idea of the melting pot, is seen as the death of 'cultural diversity'. Therefore, if indeed cultural difference is natural, when we are faced with a possible cultural mixture or the possible incorporation of undesirable cultural elements, there will necessarily be defensive reactions, 'interethnic' conflicts and in general, an environment of insecurity and susceptibility. These reactions represented as natural, almost causal, and dangerous are situations that must be avoided. A political consequence which promotes a need to prevent racism from 'sprouting', since, in the practices and representations of migration from outside the EU, a relationship is taken for granted between the presence and characteristics of migrant groups and feelings of concern, fear or alarm that their presence provokes, as well as the spread of national-populist and neo-racist formations and rhetoric (Santamaría 2002, 164).

SOCIAL EFFECTS

The social consequences of this dispositive can be diverse. However, as usually happens in these cases, the object of the intervention (the social reality assumed at the beginning, or the epistemological point of view) materializes and the subjects and their relationships are delimited to their cultural expression.

One might argue that the practices derived from the culturalist paradigm foster interrelations based on cultural affiliation (although not exclusively) since the inhabitants internalize these devices through teaching, the awareness of social workers and mediators, and the media. For example, the contact hypothesis at the base of many of the proposals intercultural interventions, is socially useful and politically necessary, since contact can effectively reduce anxiety between one and the other, in addition to offering the opportunity to establish cross-cultural bridges of identification and, above all, to allow the Other to be seen as someone with a biography and personal characteristics beyond their 'cultural' belonging.

However, in practice, at least two problems arise that hinder the transformative political potential of these actions. First, the fact that the benefits of contact are determined mainly by a wide range of socioeconomic and political factors is not recognized. Thus, trying to end a problem of structural racism based on the premise that "liking each other more we can find a solution" seems misleading, if not directly ideological. Second, we find possible consequences of reification. In general, contact with the Other not only tends to establish and develop social ties but also confirms the Other as a cultural other. This is the logic of reified cultural differences. The reduction of anxiety towards the Other is as closely linked to the perception of similarities as the certainty that the verification of the essentialized cultural difference of the Other allows us to preserve certain identity privileges (the local 'us', bearer of the exclusive 'native culture' which is different from 'them' and 'their' culture). This circumstance represents the perverse part of the much-acclaimed multiculturalism, which turns the celebration of the cultural difference of the Other into a subterfuge of apparent tolerance adjusted to the desire of the dominant 'native' groups to feel controlled by a latent threat: the possibility that the Other may one day be like 'us'. This contradictory mechanism is based on the benevolent racism of the 'native'.

In this way, through political practices, social education or cultural mediation (remember, for example, the mentioned Catalan classes or community mediation sessions), one learns to identify oneself and others according to their belonging to a certain distinct nationality or ethnic group, with its specific culture (an ethnocultural distinguished collective). Thus the (cultural) devices take on materiality, and the groups become cultural collectives, social facts to which each of us is naturally affiliated.

The internalisation processes occurring through what Michel Foucault (2007) called governmentality, form the nexus uniting the 'cultural differentiation' at an abstract level with the everyday social practices. In this sense, Margaret Wetherell and Jonathan Potter (1992) make an interestingly similar observation from their study in New Zealand. They describe how certain discourses by whites in New Zealand construct the categories of culture, race, and nation in concrete ways. These devices would hinder readings of another type (for example, the neighbour) since they are conceived as the natural way of understanding social reality. Consequently, the representation of the problem is the following: the problem, in general, is migration and the difficult subject is the migrant. This kind of logic reinforces a differential inclusion of 'foreign subjects', under constant threat of expulsion and, above all, kept in a subordinate position (De Genova 2002), and through this potentially more docile and likely to accept the harmful socio-economic labour conditions.

Thus, we see a generalized tendency amongst the public administrations to perceive that these populations generate new demands that derive from their cultural difference (and not, for example, from their working-class condition or from the precarious situations in which many sometimes live). This way of managing what is perceived as a new 'social question' has changed in recent years, as responsibility is increasingly relegated, although not exclusively, to the third sector due to political-economic pressures at various scales. This, and the public services, direct their interventions towards certain population groups instead of offering a universal service; a tendency to manage inequalities based on cultural differences, which we will further discuss in the final chapter.

These policies aimed at cultural diversity may be harmless and even superficially helpful (in the short term), but if we want to improve the problems of impoverished and marginalized neighbourhoods (in the long term), the more structural problems (racism and socio-economic inequality) must be confronted. In this sense, we should remember that racism is not a psychological (attitudinal) issue but rather a social phenomenon and, at the same time, a concrete and tangible praxis. Race, ethnicity, and culture are much like gender and nation, systems of classification and social differentiation which in many ways are meaningful for the human being, but which is also functional for maintaining privilege. Indeed a group of people designated as native and local may maintain symbolic and material privileges over other people constructed as migrants, newcomers, foreigners, and so on. In this sense, it is also important to remember that these systems of differentiation are often arbitrary; they are based on some attributes (the colour of the skin, the clothing) as distinctive markers as they could be any other. However, the truth is that the different systems of differentiation have historically been functional for the enrichment, well-being, and maintenance of positions of domination of some people over others.

Furthermore, even though these policies may superficially help—the reason for their success (i.e., the consensus that exists around them)—I question their harmlessness because they seem to serve as a screen for the option of addressing the underlying problems (to frame problems that have to do with fundamentally economic inequalities, in a culturalist spectrum). Hence, we might say they do something to avoid doing something else. The money that funds these programs could have been used to fight structural problems.

This new social management through cultural diversity dovetails with the repressive policies, apparently universal yet profoundly discriminatory, which I call *policies of quieting*. They are policies implemented to control increasingly destitute and desperate populations, who do not fall into the formal categories of citizenship or labour, and who are perceived and represented as disturbing and possibly dangerous (hence, their connection to the 'social question'), in addition to redirecting their discomfort, confronting them with the police (Diari de Girona 2011) and society in general. At the same time, they convey a sense of calm because they alleviate increased insecurity and uncertainty (both socially and in terms of the workforce), which are the social effects of the ongoing economic-political restructuring. That is why these are effective and socially comfortable policies because they blame strangers for the evil inflicted on the national body.

Thus, everything seems to indicate that the implemented policies self-confirm the vision that we are facing a problem of convivencia and, subsequently, that the guilty are the migrants, who cause problems due to their different way of being (being out of their 'natural place'). The final consequence is that the socio-economic factors inherent to existing social problems are obviated, and thus they end up being ethnoculturalized, while they reproduce social inequalities, both ethnocultural and socio-economic. In this way, they end up ethnoculturalizing the social conflicts that initially emanate from a socio-economic and ethnocultural marginalization, and above all, they end up providing arguments for the right and extreme right parties that operate on the ground and that generally make use of culturalist and racist discourses.

In this chapter, I have dealt with the social policies implemented in Salt; in the following chapter, I will deal with the urban policies implemented to also deal with the increasing social and cultural diversity or, as I will show, to promote a specific kind of mobility.

CHAPTER 4 NOTES

1. A reduced version of this chapter has been published previously (see Lundsteen 2020b).
2. The equivalent is the controversial Clean Halls program, ruled unconstitutional by a Federal Judge in New York: http://blackandbrownnews.com/nypd-clean-halls-ruled-unconstitutional/
3. "la Caixa" Foundation was established by one of Spain's major banks (now known as Caixa Bank) that carries out or funds 'social work' as the social, philanthropic aspect of its activities. It is ironic that they call it 'the soul' of the bank.
4. Although see also Pasetti (2014).

Chapter Five

Between Territorial Stigma and Rural Gentrification

An Urban Village for the Middle-Class?

As we saw in the introduction, Salt experienced, much like many other cities in 21st century Spain, the effects of capitalist urbanization through rapid urban transformations and human mobility. In this chapter, I will show how a dominant representation concerning the problems in Salt emerged—a representation that has been influenced by other social conflicts in Spain and around the world (see introduction) and portrays the town as plagued by 'too many' migrants, which according to the argument, complicates the convivencia in the town. Most of the urban policies implemented during the last two decades share this underlying problem identification. Politicians, journalists, and eventually some inhabitants were worried about the agglomeration of migrants in town, especially in areas such as the Centre district. This might seem noble; after all, who would not be worried about segregation between inhabitants based on their ethnicity or race? However, here, the problem is neither perceived nor presented as a consequence of the underlying social inequalities and, more concretely, the result of a racist and capitalist real estate market and its spatialization (as we saw in the introduction and chapter 3). Instead, the problem is presented as one emanating from an apparently conflictual presence of a cultural Other (i.e., a high percentage of migrants cause social fracture and [cultural] conflicts between neighbours in these spaces).

Consequently, alongside the policing of uncivil behaviour analysed in the previous chapter, politicians and urbanists propose and implement measures to stop or even revert this phantasmagorical phenomenon (indeed, one might argue that they are concurring strategies in a complex political ensemble). Therefore, anti-ghetto policies of urban renewal and restructuring (including demolishing parts of the urban fabric and expelling residents) or social mixing policies are enacted. On the one hand, the aim is to avoid the arrival of migrants by raising the prices and limiting low-income housing and, on the other, to attract young natives by promoting the existing positive aspects of the town via cultural events, infrastructure, and middle-income housing. So, specific mobility and human composition are desired and heeded when planning.

As has often been the case, social reform and improvement for the people in areas of deprivation and social marginalization overlap and are superimposed by political and economic interests, such as gentrification (Macleod and Johnstone 2012). Of course, there might be several varied and even antagonistic political-economic ensembles. Nevertheless, in any case, the inherent socio-spatial process of organization, the production of space, although subjugated to the capitalist economy in general, requires extra-economic factors. In fact, any projected spatial transformation requires narratives of either stigmatization or revalorization. In other words, they need what Franquesa (2005) calls 'legitimizing narratives' to attain legitimacy and the needed consent to project and accomplish the projects. These discourses aim to justify the interventions and the logic of the capital scientifically and morally. A whole set of actions that might operate on a symbolic level but include economic, political, and police actions, as we have seen—a process labelled territorial stigmatization (Wacquant, Slater, and Pereira 2014). Through a critical analysis of media, government, and resident discourse, we see how the stigmatizing attitudes in Salt both serve to devalue certain areas, justify projects of urban renewal, and allocate public funding to promote a new economic sector and, at the same time, produce the famous rent gap (Smith 1987). We see how certain inhabitants are deemed problematic only because of their ethnicity, culture, origin, or looks, while other cultural expressions are explicitly promoted and desired. In the end, it becomes clear that these local expressions collude with a more generalized global economic transformation tendency from the industry towards the fourth sector, based on the production and consumption of information, knowledge, and culture.

TOO MANY MIGRANTS: TERRITORIAL STIGMATIZATION IN ACTION

At the beginning of the 21st century, migration became one of the main issues in Spanish society. In Salt, there was a particular focus in the media and among politicians on the concentration of migrants in the town. When looking through the newspaper articles and magazines of the 1990s, we can see how the first time this problem was mentioned was when dealing with the pupils of other nationalities at the La Farga school (in 1997, it was 23.39%). A series of newspaper articles appeared in the 1990s and, at the beginning of the 21st century, denouncing incipient segregation in the local school system

(Soler 1997; Taberner 2001; Sandoval 2002). This is an ongoing concern and not without reason. However, this initial worry evolved into a worry concerning the percentage of foreign-born residents in the town at large.

In 2004, 200 residents protested 'against the public insecurity which they attribute to the migrant collective' (López 2004). Let us take a look at the interpretations made in this article. We see that the mobilization linked with insecurity as a problem of adaptation and integration, which again ends up as a problem of convivencia that is supposedly threatened as the headline, 'Salt has serious troubles managing without tensions the phenomenon of the newly arrived', indicates. The article is covered by a photo of a woman wearing hijab walking a buggy with a footnote stating, 'The streets of Salt show a mosaic of nationalities.'

The rhetoric is based on two fundamental observations: First, that more than 70% of the pupils in the schools are children of immigrants, and second, that there has been an increase in the number of non-national residents in the town. This way, importance was given to the percentage when non-nationals only make up 22.7% of the population at large, which does not defer compared to other towns with similar socio-economic and geographical characteristics. Most other towns with a 'high percentage of migrants' have between 15% and 20% of non-nationals as part of their residents. Compared with other towns in the Girona region, the figure is distinctly lower: Castelló d'Empúries, 36.38%, Lloret de Mar, 26.11%, and Sant Pere Pescador, 26.02% (IDESCAT). It is also revealing that the journalist was wrong about the percentages concerning the Catalan average. He said that the number of non-nationals in Salt tripled the Catalan average when back then the average was 9.44%, and the triple would have been more than 28.32%. Furthermore, it has not been proven that this should negatively influence social cohesion.

Nonetheless, the journalist warned that 'apparently normal people' are increasingly employing racist language that only 'skin heads' had been using until then. He assumed that the first premise, an increase in the number of migrant residents, leads to unrest and rejection by the native inhabitants in a causal way. However, researchers such as Carles Serra (2006) have observed that skinhead creeds were present and relatively widespread in Salt already during the late 1990s, despite little migrant presence. The then Mayor Jaume Torramadé (Democratic Union of Catalonia—[UDC] *Unió Democràtica de Catalunya*) expressed his worries that the convivencia in the town was indeed at stake (Sandoval 2004).

Thus, a specific causal relation was engendered: A high migration rate or percentage of migrant residents leads to convivencia or intercultural conflicts, which in turn leads to social fracture; thus, it is expected that natives adopt racist attitudes. This tendency to represent the town's problems in a certain way still dominates today. It is linked to social developments at other scales of society and, more importantly, the public administration, where the 'new migration phenomenon' is increasingly emphasized, and with it, what some—especially, but not exclusively, the conservative and right-wing—present as its social consequences: crime and insecurity, and in general, tensions, and disputes.

Some years later, the mayor expressed his worries regarding the town's evolution again (Sandoval 2007a). He pointed out that 36% of the residents are non-Spaniards, following which the journalist emphasized that the migration flows arriving in town tended to concentrate in the Centre district, where the percentage according to 'municipal sources' reached 70%. Although this might have been true for some buildings or areas, the data did not corroborate in general terms, much less in 2011. Nevertheless, these numbers are repeatedly used when referring to Salt and migration, until three years later when the percentage was around 40% in the town and 80% in the Centre (Playà Maset 2010b).

An additional idea appears in the article. The increasing number of people moving to the town can lead to a 'social fracture' (Sandoval 2007a). The mayor, surprisingly the only person interviewed for the article, confirmed that immigration levels are too high. Though not explicitly stated, it is clear that he meant people from outside of Europe, ignoring both migrants from other European countries and other regions of Spain. It became clear that, according to him, the problem was not that people settle but, instead, the culture of those who settle. Some people are seen as a problem to the convivencia.

In another article written by the same journalist (Sandoval 2007b), two weeks later, natality is of concern. Originally an article on decreasing numbers of child vaccinations, it is clear that the journalist was worried about something else. The title read, 'More than 63% of the newborn babies in Salt are children of migrant families', and the subtitle, 'The population of sub-15 represents a 49% in total in Salt; the majority are from African countries'. He wanted to reflect on the migration numbers and underscore that there are more migrant kids than Spanish. Five days later, he returned. Following the Catalan prime minister's visit, the journalist concluded that he had been acquainted with one of the 'most worrying realities of Salt: immigration.' (Sandoval 2007c).

The following year, similar articles were published. For instance, an article published in La Vanguardia titled, 'Salt, the gateway for immigrant', dedicated two pages to migration in the town. Another article read, 'Two out of every three births in Salt corresponds to children of migrants.' In this, the former Mayor Jaume Torramadé stated:

> It's a negative figure because 'Salt lives with the problem, but it needs global help from outside to rebalance the municipality.' Torramadé highlights the fact that the 'real' problem is not that of that actual government, nor the prior one,

> he recalls that he has been asking for help from the Generalitat to balance the 'singular problems' of Salt: 'Economic funding for the Centre district is much needed. However, there's been a lack of willingness.' (Batlle 2008)

Four months later, the then-mayor, Iolanda Pineda (PSC), publicly stated that the town was undergoing a state of social emergency due to the arrival of migrants. She asked for the government's help, claiming that the social cohesion was endangered and that the 40% percent of migrants complicated the convivencia (J.B.M. 2008). Although she qualified her argument in an interview published a month later, she reinforced the idea that the arrival of 'many migrants' in a short time might create conflicts of convivencia (Oller 2008a). After all, if there is a lack of funding and budget to face the challenges of migration, then it is not a migration problem but, rather, a symptom of institutional and regional inequalities and the economic crisis.

The Catalan Prime Minister took note (El Punt, Editorial 2008), and some months later, the Spanish Minister of Work and Migration visited the town (Barrera 2008). A series of articles in *La Vanguardia*, the front page of the local section and the following two pages, reported his visit and put Salt in the limelight once more. Again, the central theme of these articles was migration and, above all, the problems it supposedly creates (Oller 2008b). From this moment onwards, the media attention de-escalated.

As an example, a report made by Antena 3 (a Spanish private television channel) some days after the demonstration in February 2011 portrays a rather nasty image. The critical (read anti-migrant) voices were in the spotlight, as one of them stated, '"they" [foreigners] do not know how to live together with other people because they break staircases, doors, everything' (Antena 3 2011). In general terms, the report purveyed an image of deprivation and insecurity, where nobody dares walk the streets due to fear. Rhetorically, this is linked with the idea that migrants do not adapt to the cultural values of the local society. Furthermore, there is a sense of the Spanish population feeling encroached on and forced to leave the imminent formation of a ghetto. Thus, the idea of Salt as an indicator of a Catalan banlieue/ghetto phenomenon gained force.

The percentage thus turned into a social indicator of a political struggle over meaning and symbols, and statistical figures were used as weapons, similar to what Jean and John Comaroff (2006) observed regarding the crime statistics in South Africa. In the end, a specific interpretation and representation of the problems in Salt became hegemonic; a large number of migrants was seen to lead to bad or no integration, which in turn leads to social and public disorder. This idea, inspired by the white flight hypothesis (Martínez Veiga 1999), means that a high percentage is a negative indicator for the convivencia, social cohesion, and the stability of society in general. According to this argument, many migrants (a high percentage) motivate the flight of natives and people with high social and cultural capital. Although one can observe a recognition that there are problems in town, there is also a clear tendency among the social analysts and the media to reduce these to a problem of convivencia. They all share the idea that the conflicts are fruit of a cultural encounter between residents labelled native and others that are foreign, basically extra-EU migrants.

To summarize, from the beginning, the percentage of migrants were seen as a problem, even when the numbers were low. However, as the figure rose, so did the worry and social alarm among a part of the population, most notably politicians and the media. Although most conflicts in the Centre district and the town at large were due to the increasingly precarious conditions in which the inhabitants were living, a deprived neighbourhood and insufficient public funding. The framework of the clash of cultures offered a much simpler and even self-fulfilling explanation. For more than a decade, news stories had overexposed specific problems at the expense of profound analysis and, with it, a better understanding of the field. In this way, the tense moments described in chapter 1 led to intense media coverage, which felt like a siege for many residents.

The consequences of this problematization are multiple. First of it creates a social problem, in the words of Bourdieu, Wacquant, and Farage (1994, 2): 'It is in the realm of symbolic production that the grip of the state is felt most powerfully. State bureaucracies and their representatives are great producers of "social problems" that social science does little more than ratify whenever it takes them over as "sociological" problems.' To this, a particular space in which interventions must take place is conceived along with associated practices of control and discipline. To use the term coined by Michel Foucault, this dispositive orders the social reality in specific ways and creates, through the process of conceiving and intervening, an object of intervention. In this case, the problems are in the ghetto (Duneier 2016) among marginalized social groups. Following Justus Uitermark (2014), this is mainly so in the policies of integration, which we have dealt with in the previous chapter. Here, I will first focus on the urban policies and review the different cultural and historical narratives.

ANTI-GHETTO POLICIES AND STRATEGIES OF NEOLIBERAL URBANISM

Against the stigmatizing images and portrayals, and to combat the supposed socio-urban erosion of the community, the local governments took several actions—measures that can aptly be divided into two: (a) programs of social and urban intervention and (b) policies of social mix.

Urban Renewal against Deprivation

At the beginning of the 21st century, the dominant idea among the politicians in Salt was that something had to be done in Barri Centre. Although the main worry was the decay of specific spaces and buildings, a group of mainly Spanish residents and some local politicians were confident that a significant transformation to revert the socio-human decay was needed. They wanted to avoid what they saw as the incipient formation of a ghetto. See for instance the following ideas of the then-mayor, Jaume Torramadé:

> 'We have to take action via both policing and education, and deal with the issue in a calm, discrete and gradual way', says Torramadé, who criticizes what he believes is an institutional abandonment of the local administration on migration issues. According to him, Salt lacks the funding needed to resort to urban measures of the geographical dispersion of the immigrants and thus to avoid the formation of ghettos. Why do so many newcomers settle in Salt? 'They arrive and settle where they can, usually in areas with low rent, which ends up lowering it even more' the mayor explains. In fact, the real estate prices are much higher in the neighbouring Girona. 'While there are almost no immigrants in the other towns of the region, we are overloaded; the municipalities create industrial estates which benefit from the labour force in Salt, but they do nothing to take in the workers so that they will settle in their town. In fact, they try to avoid it' Torramadé denounces. (López 2004)

Salt70 (2004–2008)

The first urban intervention planned for the town emerged from within the framework and funding of the *Llei 2/2004, de millora de barris, àrees urbanes i viles* (Generalitat de Catalunya 2006), also known as the Llei de barris (literally, the neighbourhood law). It was the first law in the Spanish State to work with the improvement and intervention of neighbourhoods. It was implemented during what became known as the Tripartit, the first coalition government in Catalonia after 23 years of right-wing government at the hands of CiU, formed by PSC, ERC, and ICV and in charge from 2003 to 2010. The main aim was to establish an integral rehabilitation programme in those urban areas that required special attention, alongside a planned €600 million funding until 2011 to improve the conditions of the inhabitants living in those areas:

> This law, already tested in three rounds with 46 projects up and running and a budget of 600 million euro, shared equally between the local government and the autonomous government, is an invitation to optimism to solidary activism, the generation of urban dynamics of social and urban change which we have already confirmed are possible and which can be measured in terms of income, investments, quality and reform. (Generalitat de Catalunya 2006, 6)

The law was based on the idea that certain areas of Catalan cities and towns were experiencing social, economic, and urban order problems. The main argument followed the ideas of the urban interventions in the United Kingdom called Urban Renaissance, in which, for the first time, social aspects were included in the policies aimed at deprived neighbourhoods (Arbaci and Tapada-Berteli 2012). According to this, it is necessary to direct the interventions towards the population as a whole and not only through sectorial interventions:

> The added value of the law is its capacity to concentrate resources and strategies in an action plan that aim to help envision the change of mentality, attitudes, collective psychology, and approach facing with the opportunities that society has to offer, the positive orientation of the attitude up to the point of becoming a change in trend in the life perspective of a neighbourhood. (Generalitat de Catalunya 2006, 6)

A fund was created to finance these projects of comprehensive intervention to promote the 'municipal profoundly', although other social and economic agents were to be involved as well: 'the Catalan Government will offer resources and provision municipal programmes that the city councils will co-finance and execute under the supervision of the Generalitat and in participation of all the social and economic agents.' (Generalitat de Catalunya 2006, 5). Hence, following the ideas of mixed funding and 'horizontal government' that the political idea of governance promotes, every stakeholder and interested party were included in the decision-making and planning of actions.

Later that year, Salt was among 12 locations selected out of 66 projects presented. The main objective was to improve public space and equip it with facilities and programmes to boost local business, employability and attend to vulnerable groups. In Salt 70, the objectives crystallized in the following actions: (a) re-urbanization of the streets; (b) improvement of the streetlight; (c) installation of 12 lifts; (d) rehabilitation and equipment of common elements in the buildings; (e) refurbishment of the old factory Coma-Cros for public use and the fitting out of Mas Mota for Community Centre; (f) a campaign to promote the connection to the drinking water network; (g) programmes for the social, urban, and economic improvement (including the LAOS-Salt as mentioned earlier, a citizen committee, and the Pla

Civisme, an action plan that included the contract of Civil Agents); and (h) land purchase for public facilities and green areas.

The area of intervention of the first project of comprehensive intervention "PII – Salt 70" covered 45 hectares, corresponding to 23 percent of the urban fabric and 70 percent of the population, and paid particular attention to the areas of Teixidores, Veïnat, Plaça Catalunya, and the Centre (GMG Plans i projectes 2010). The first phase would last four years, from the beginning of 2005 to 2008, later extended to 2010.

The particular areas were selected on account of a series of factors (figure 5.1): a high residential density, low cadastral value, general deprivation of the buildings, lack of tap water, lack of lifts in tall buildings, lack of green areas, a considerable increase in population over the last decade, and a high percentage of extra-EU citizens, a lack of public spaces, and a lack of public facilities.

The evaluation of the project, published in 2010, revealed that the project had not been entirely successful (GMG Plans i projectes 2010). Some of the actions were not carried out and were not prioritized sufficiently. For

Figure 5.1. Ámbito de actuación del PII – Salt 70 del "Pla de Barris. *Source*: GMG Plans i Projectes. 2010. Informe d'avaluació final del projecte d'intervenció integral «Salt 70» 2010. March 2010. Retrieved from: http://territori.gencat.cat/web/.content/home/01_departament/actuacions_i_obres/barris/projectes_2004/documents/salt70._informe_avaluacio_final.pdf

instance, no community centre was created, Mas Mota did not function in practice, and what was destined to be the Community Centre in the street, Àngel Guimerà, was the Local Housing Office. It was not until 2007 that Salt got its first community centre, the Ateneu Coma-Cros. On top of that, some of the actions were controversial, especially those that aimed to refurbish the common elements but should instead be considered policies of embellishment of the public space, as shown in the preceding chapter.

A Large-Scale Project for an Urban and Social Transformation of Salt (2010–2022)

In May 2010, a large-scale project for an urban and social transformation of Salt was presented. The project was based on the recommendation and proposed lines of action of the Local Urban Plan (GMG Plans i Projectes 2009) and the evaluation report (GMG Plans i Projectes 2010). It was signed by the architects Ricard Pié and Josep Maria Vilanova and presented alongside all the political parties present in the town council and the local government. The main objective was to radically change the urban fabric of the Centre district in around 12 years, and it projected a global budget of €200 million (Ramon Mòdol 2010).

As of the Neighbourhood Law, several actions were implemented to improve the urban and architectural conditions of the neighbourhood. According to the then municipal architect, the conditions were not that bad:

> In our project, there were only a few actions in the buildings. Actually, the buildings were in quite a good state. In the Centre district or any other of the ones included in the plan, the buildings were not deprived; they are in good shape, they were built when the construction was getting much better. There might have been some problems in terms of maintenance and conservation, but there were no important structural problems. *Ramón Artal*

Despite this, and the fact that the migration did not play an important part in the proposal (remember how among the aims, the focus was mainly on the state of the buildings, green areas, and so on), the media did indeed emphasized the migration, sometimes mentioning the formation of a ghetto explicitly:

> Salt projects the demolishment of 600 flats at the heart of the town during the next 12 years, an ambitious urban operation that will affect the most deprived part of the municipality where a ghetto of migration and marginality has been formed. Moreover, 1,200 flats will be refurbished. To do this, an economic injection has been granted from the public administration of 200 million euros.

> The area where the renewal will occur is the same area where racial tensions took place in February. (Fuentes 2010)

This implicit meaning of the socio-urban project was later criticized. Apparently, the chief aim of the renewal was to create a process of gentrification, which would predominantly harm the most vulnerable group. Thus, it was indeed an anti-ghetto policy:

> The Neighbourhood Law is an anti-ghetto law; that is, we have to help certain areas or neighbourhoods in Catalonia that need it not to become ghettos. What does ghetto mean? Areas where only migrants go to live because the rent is cheaper, or the real estate market prices are lower. So, what does the Neighbourhood Law pursue? That the prices increase in those areas. That is, the Neighbourhood Law is no aimed at reducing the prices in general, but rather that the prices in areas where there are more migrants increase. That's why I say it is somewhat perverse *Ramón Artal*

The actions are divided into two areas (figure 5.2): the Area of Comprehensive Restoration (ARI) and the Area of Urban Renewal (ARU). The ARI consisted of 94 hectares and included a large part of the town, only the newer part Massana was excluded. In this area of action, a rehabilitation was visualized of up to 1,200 flats by granting subsidies. The ARU instead, consisting of about 13 hectares, was constituted by the buildings in the far-east and

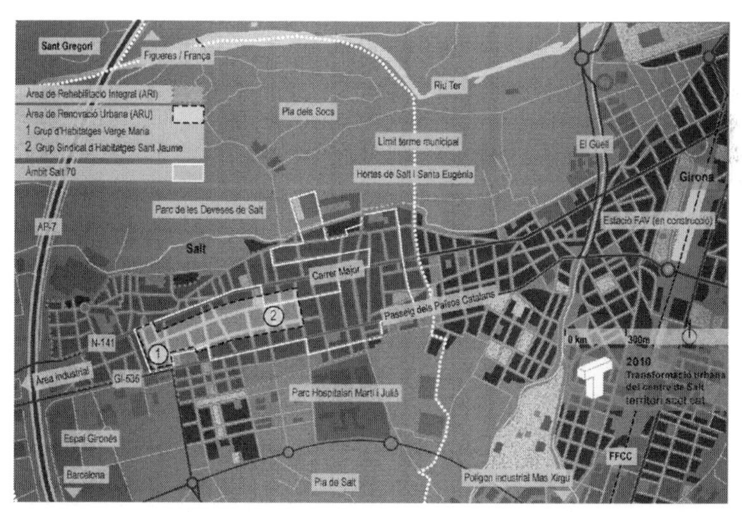

Figure 5.2. Urban Renewal of the Centre in Salt. Areas of Intervention ARI y ARU. ***Source*****: Territori. Observatori de projectes i debats territorials de Catalunya. Retrieved from: http://territori.scot.cat/cat/img2/2010/10/transformacio_urbana_del_centre_de_salt.jpg**

far-west of the streets Àngel Guimerà and Torras i Bages and circumscribed by the streets of Ramon y Cajal and Esteve Vila. In this area, a profound politics of demolishment was proposed to reduce the high density of buildings in the area. Among other measures, it included purchasing and demolishing around 600 flats to create more green areas in the town centre.

However, there was an uncertainty about which properties would be affected from the beginning. First, a selection process had to be carried out following the criteria of the age of the buildings, the number of empty floors, and the state of conservation of the buildings. Secondly, and in line with the objectives of the Pla Territorial Sectorial d'Habitatge (PTSH), the intention was to limit the speculation in the process as much as possible.

Initially, there was broad support among the parties of the town council, and the urban project was approved in the plenary session. However, despite this positive stance, the residents were not excited, and little by little, opposition was mobilized. This, together with the crisis, put a halt to the plans.

Although there were mixed opinions among the inhabitants in the affected areas, the lack of information soon became apparent as a cause for concern. The residents were especially concerned with the lack of definition surrounding the selection process for the homes destined for demolition:

> Yesterday the neighbours didn't know the intentions of the council. Some, such as Joseph, a Moroccan owner of a flat 'see the initiative in a positive light: 'This area is not pleasant, there are too many people." While others are unclear about it, like Josep Maria: 'It's a good idea to distribute people, but only the foreigners' (Fuentes 2010).

Therefore, a group of residents requested an explanatory meeting. At the beginning of June 2010, the first step was taken to start the project. An agreement was signed between the Ministry of Housing, the Department of Medi Ambient i Habitatge (DMAH) and the Town Council of Salt to carry out the investments planned in the first four years of the project (2010–2013), in which it was expected to demolish or rehabilitate around 300 homes. According to the mayor, the project would not involve the expropriation of homes. However, around 500 residents later that month attended another meeting held with the specialists who designed the project. Once again, the uneasiness generated by the lack of information regarding the affected buildings was clear. Members of the Moviment Anti-ARU, expressed their discomfort. The movement was born as a protest movement, especially in response to the proposed urban plan (ARU) and in defence of the interest of the affected inhabitants. The project allowed for new construction on some of the demolished sites as they saw it. Others warned about the lack of information due to language issues. Moreover, the incessant story of the conflicts of convivencia reappeared: 'The atmosphere was tense, on several various occasions when treating the problems of convivencia in the centre of Salt, and also the project and the uncertainty that it's producing in thousands of families' (Mas 2010).

From this moment, the unconditional support of the opposition began to break down. In early July, CiU distanced itself from the project, arguing that it was too far from the initial municipal agreement (Diari de Girona 2010). Furthermore, in mid-August, the CiU candidate and former mayor, Jaume Torramadé, affirmed that he would organize a referendum on the ARU plan if he was elected. The rest of the groups nuanced their support for the project in mid-September. PPC and IPS-ICV still considered the project a good idea on paper but disagreed that the majority of the investment must be assumed by the local administration, either through the town council or private initiative. At the municipal plenary session on 20 September, it became apparent that PSC and ERC, the local government team, were left alone because CiU and IPS-ICV voted against and the PPC abstained (T.C.C. 2010). In the end, the ARU plan was paralysed, mainly due to the public budget halt (austerity policies) and the change of government in 2011.

Policies of Social Mix

In late 2011, the new local government executed an alternative socio-urban improvement strategy. The main aim was to 'attract young people in this area to integrate and fix the population' (J.N. 2010). In other words, they implemented social and urban policies to promote a 'social mix' in the town through a social rental project aimed at young students, who were offered low-cost housing in exchange for social work in the community (such as community mediation, community debts management, or neighbourhood civil officer), and a public award for seven rental flats, some with an option to buy.

The explicit objective of these policies was to attract young people, often of a specific profile: with a high cultural or social capital, middle class and, although not explicitly stated, 'Spaniards'. This rhetoric seemed to have been successful and was a more general demand among the associations of the Centre and other neighbourhoods in the town. The inherent logic of these policies, based as they were on the assumptions of the 'social mix' theories (Koutrolikou 2012; Lees 2008), was that these populations with their social, cultural, and economic capital would improve the social fabric of the neighbourhood, thus reversing any process of socio-urban degradation. In the words of the then councillor of Community and Housing:

> If you have got young people, the milieu will also change, so we believe this is where we must work. I know how in other places, in other big cities, well

> that at some point, in an area artist had so to speak taken over, and with it, a transformation had taken place, and now that the neighbourhood it's amazing. I don't know if it was in Holland. . . . So we've thought that, well maybe not a lot of artists will come, but why don't we appeal to, obviously you have to tie in with everything a bit you know, you can't just appeal by saying 'hey, in Salt we are very cool'. . . . So, in this case, why shouldn't Salt be a university town? But to make it a university town you must articulate several aspects, and one of them, for example, is housing. So, this is where we are working, and it's our understanding that we must work all these things together to transform the town.

Despite what seemed to be good intentions, other kinds of underlying interests and maybe even the most important ones were quickly revealed. In the end, the urban planning strategies and policies were gentrification strategies (Smith 2002; Glass 1989; Wacquant 2008b). In recent years, the local administration has put effort into an idea from 2004, which was implemented throughout the following years: promoting a transformation of the town towards a 'university town' around the central productive axis of the Cultural Factory Coma-Cros (partially funded by the European Integration Fund). The objectives were several, but two interrelated stand out: to improve the image of the town and stimulate the arrival of affluent young people, Spanish or from the EU but, especially students, to reverse the trend of the last decade of extra-EU immigration, and to change the main productive sector of the town, from the industry to that of knowledge or information. At least, this has been the fundamental aim of promoting the old Coma-Cros factory as a university and educational hub and through the various socio-urban policies implemented.

The Cultural Factory Coma-Cros; Towards a New Cultural Salt?

In 1995, the Institut Català del Sòl, a public company whose primary area of action is the urbanization of the territory for economic activities and residential purposes, acquired the old Coma-Cros factory and, in 1998, transferred the ownership to the municipal administration with the objective that it would serve as public equipment. In 1999, a public tender was published for the preparation of a programming study, and based on this Master Plan—elaborated by a mixed team of architects and cultural programmers—the rehabilitation works began in 2002, intending to make it a cultural centre of reference for the town of Salt and the other counties in the Girona region (Bover i Pagespetit 2003).

The main objective of this rehabilitation was to create a space for cultural production and promotion, and it aimed to stimulate a productive change towards the fourth or fifth sector (production and distribution of knowledge, information, and culture). The project mentioned the implementation of an Ateneu d'Entitats, a sort of horizontal management made up by the groups and associations in the municipality, and a bar-restaurant. Although both had recently been implemented, the use of these facilities at the time of the fieldwork was still subject to the request and prior granting by the local administration (i.e., it did not function as a meeting place, but rather as a closed space with exclusive use).

Gradually, cultural institutions were installed, such as the headquarters of the Open University of Catalonia (UOC), the regional headquarters of Spanish Online University (UNED) and the EU ERAM, an interdisciplinary centre attached to the Universitario de Girona, and

> connected to the communication and arts, which promote a transdisciplinary and creative education oriented towards the professional world. The centre, a pioneer in Girona in the educational areas of audiovisual, multimedia and design, is perfectly integrated into the surrounding social and industrial fabric and is leading in the educational areas.[1]

Additionally, a supra-municipal body, the Consorci Alba-Ter, was placed in the town. Designed to promote the territorial development of the fluvial space, unite the territory using the river as the axis of union, enhance the cultural heritage linked to the traditional uses of water and natural heritage, and develop the economic (tourist) potential of the territory.[2] Similarly, the Viver d'Empreses Creativo-Culturals, co-funded by the European Regional Development Fund (930.583,46€) and created with the main aim of

> Lending support to entrepreneurs and new businesses through a series of services and spaces aimed at helping in the start-up, growth and consolidation of business projects in the creative and cultural areas. . . . Finally, in a moment where the economic situation generates uncertainty, it becomes ever more important to support initiatives that aim at creating value and generating confidence in the future.[3]

In 2012, another cultural centre was set up: El Canal, a Centre for Performing Arts in Salt and Girona. Co-funded by the European Regional Development Fund, in collaboration with the cooperation programme Spain-France-Andorra (POCTEFA), the Department of Culture and Media of the Generalitat de Catalunya, the provincial government of Girona, the Town Council of Salt, and the Social Work Fund of 'la Caixa'. According to the director Salvador Sunyer, the main aim was to become a reference point in the performing arts of South Europe (ACN, ARA 2012).

These strategies conflated in an overall political-economic tendency of change in the labour-market regime from an industrial economy towards one based on information and culture. When considering the strategies promoted during the last decade to solve the town's problems, one can see a clear desire for selling and producing culture and, with it, attracting young people with high cultural capital. Indeed, this might explain why a covert multiculturalism was maintained, that is, as mere symbolism—because an image of a multicultural town sells well among the younger generations, especially the middle classes, as is seen in several locations such as Hackney (London) or Raval (Barcelona).

It is thus assumed that the arrival of these new populations will lead to a socio-urban transformation of the town. In this way, the commitment to high-class culture and the socio-urban policies in general certainly show an interest in promoting a process of gentrification, which in its essence encourages a change of population: attracting young people (students) with high purchasing power and high cultural capital. These middle classes are essential because they must carry out the desired socio-urban transformation.

Several interests of different actors converge, with various and sometimes antagonistic agendas. First, those, mainly Spanish inhabitants of the Centre, are interested in reversing the so-called ghettoization process. Second, some inhabitants of the Old district and Veïnat want to refurbish the deprived urban space of their older neighbourhoods and avoid the process of stigmatization and ghettoization. Third, there is a possible gain in reversing the devaluation process because the vast majority of the houses and flats in the Centre are privately owned and, as a result of the crisis, many of them are owned and managed by investors and banks. Thus, it is not surprising that there are speculative interests in the area due to the possible revenue from revaluation.

The seeds of this are already apparent in the Old neighbourhood, where an increasing number of young middle-class people from Girona and Barcelona have settled. Although often not considered foreign, these populations move into old houses that they help reform. They live out a neo-rural fantasy without losing their urban roots, and, more importantly, they preserve and reinvigorate a hereditary and historic-cultural capital invested in these buildings and the neighbourhood at large, achieved through the work and consumption that they invest in them (Morell 2014). They constitute the avant-garde of the desired gentrification and contribute an added value to the neighbourhood and houses through the symbolic value that they incarnate. Hence, they change the human composition of the neighbourhood (or simply repossess it) and create a surplus value to be earned when the houses are sold, as has happened so often in other studied cases of gentrification in the larger cities.

Another desire with the proposed urban policies is to attract more students and make Salt a university town. However, this 'studentification' also attracts middle-class young people (more so as the public universities are privatized and have increased tuition fees), and they undoubtedly have high cultural capital and, therefore, could easily be considered part of a gentrification process, as argued by Smith and Holt (2007).

Interestingly, these cases show indications that gentrification strategies are extended to smaller cities that until now had only been interested in implementing large industrial areas. Undoubtedly, Salt remains a small city or town near the Ter river and the entire natural park of Les Deveses, just a few minutes from Girona, with a town structure and parts with a high heritage-historical and cultural value. Additionally, it has many future possibilities for development, with two crucial urbanization projects open, the factories of Frigorífics del Ter SA and the one of Gassol, whose primary purpose would be again to accommodate new low-rise houses very close to, or in Barri Vell (with its traditional heritage), the Les Deveses, or the new Coma-Cros. In this sense, the area of Gassol is exemplary, in the words of the previous municipal architect:

> Gassol is actually bigger than the whole Old district. It is an abandoned factory, closed less than ten years ago. About five years ago, its owners made proposals to the town council, mostly speculative in the real estate bubble era. Proposals of 800 homes or 1,000 homes have continuously been submitted to the town council, and the town council has always reacted by saying yes, but smaller buildings. And when they were still negotiating and discussing all this, the economic crisis blew it all into the air *Ramon Artal*

In an article, the same person imagines how Rec Monar (the irrigation channel running right next to the Old district and the factory) could become an axis through which this new socio-spatial configuration would be articulated (Artal 2014). He also spoke about promoting workshops, artisan shops, and artist studios in the Naus Guixeres (like the Camden or Hackney in London), with restaurants and cafes, ‘a kind of town of artists and craftsmen’ (Artal 2014, 17).

If everything would follow recent trends of other European countries where there is an increasing return to rural values and environments among the middle classes (Scott et al. 2011, 596–605), Salt would certainly offer an exciting mixture of urban and rural, centrality and periphery, which might seem attractive to this type of consumer. Hence, these projects might suddenly not seem utopian.

At this point, one can only observe the direction of the policies and what their explicit objectives and inherent assumptions were. The future will show the practical changes and their real social effects. However, what is evident is that, although capitalism implies and requires a specific socio-spatial organization, the same is the case for particular social relations. So, the geography of capitalism needs both the mobility (migratory movements) of some and the fixation of others. In other words, for these strategies to give the desired results, particular mobility and immobility of the subjects involved in the process are required (Franquesa 2011). So, the socio-urban project is necessarily based on a specific set of social relations, while at the same time, it promotes others (those that favour the reproduction and social production of the space).

If we apply this to what we have seen so far, the people who come to the town play an essential role in these processes, one way or another. For example, in the case of the district, young middle-class people, who have mainly come from other regions and provinces of Catalonia, allocate the capital invested in renovating their homes. Therefore, we can say that they contribute their cultural and economic capital. However, this mobility and labour appear invisible, mainly because they are generally Spanish (sometimes from outside Salt, sometimes from other neighbourhoods) or EU nationals. Therefore, they are often white (as in a socially constructed category of privilege and power) and have symbolic capital and greater purchasing power.

One such example is Verónica, a 45-year-old Portuguese who after some time in Barcelona in 2009 decided to move in with her partner, Jaume (originally from Valencia), to his mortgaged apartment in Salt, in the neighbourhood La Massana:

> Yes, I really liked this place, even though I don't know, well, Jaume doesn't like it, that is, he doesn't like it. He says yes that if he could, of course, once bought, you are caught up, you have the mortgage on you cannot leave as easily. Well, but he says that it was not like that when he decided to buy it. There was not as much migration. That is, the migration seventeen years ago didn't exist; there wasn't any. And it was much better, but he says that if he had been a fortune-teller, he wouldn't have bought it [laughing] . . . Even though we are quite well here. That is, it's not the same to live in this neighbourhood compared to the other, in the centre.

It is significant to revisit the dominating idea between officials and social theorists that high mobility is bad for social cohesion and leads to marginalization. Because they only refer to the mobility of non-Spanish immigrants and not to that of the invisible migrants, be they EU citizens or Spaniards. Thus, for instance, the mayor Jaume Torramadé stated that 'Salt is an ecosystem, and we need to show the advantages of the 21st century Catalan and Western town, and you simply can't do that when [new] people arrive every day' (Torramadé 2011). But who are these new people that he refers to?

LEGITIMIZING NARRATIVES

Extra-economic factors are essential to promote and legitimize this urban economic project. For this purpose, the State apparatuses are fundamental as the only actor with the capacity to carry out the necessary tasks of consent and coercion. This they do, for example, through urban planning as well as strategies and policies of pacification and embellishment of public space, as seen in the previous chapter. Moreover, 'legitimizing narratives' (Franquesa 2005) are also employed to achieve the necessary legitimation and consensus. These are discourses and narratives that scientifically or morally justify the interventions and logic of capital.

In this case, we see how visions of the town are promoted from the administrative instances. The main objectives of these are, on the one hand, to create consensus around the political measures taken and thus unite the population as a whole around the political-economic project and, on the other, to promote a good image, one that can be sold among new potential buyers and therefore future inhabitants.

In this sense, one should understand the different advertising campaigns ('I Love NY' style) implemented in Salt. First, it was 'Un Salt endavant' (promoted by the PSC-ERC government), and then 'T'estimo Salt' (promoted by the CiU government). In my opinion, these campaigns aimed to promote a sense of belonging and pride in being from Salt, a kind of 'city patriotism' as López Sánchez (1993) called it, whose primary purpose was to achieve consensus regarding the measures taken.

We see something similar in a book published in 2011 under the CiU government: *Salt és el meu poble*. Although, at first sight, it might look like a children's book, it is written for the general public. I, for instance, was given one after participating in a poetry reading for Catalan students at the Ateneu Coma-Cros. In the introduction, the Mayor, Jaume Torramadé, and the Aldermand of Culture, Robert Fàbregas, say:

> Some things—maybe many—you already knew, but others will be new to you and surprise you. Salt has had and still has a fascinating history, environment and people that we need to know because this knowledge is what makes us love it, and enable us to say, proudly and without fear: 'Salt is my town.' (Ajuntament de Salt 2011)

If we take a closer look at the book, we see how the first chapter illustrates the town's history.[4] The second chapter comprises eight pages dedicated to what they call 'the heart of the town': Barri Vell and its samples of cultural-architectural heritage (no such space is dedicated to any other neighbourhood of the town). In the third chapter, there is a section with samples of the natural wealth of fauna and flora, and the fourth chapter is devoted to old productive activities: agriculture, basketry, and industrial activity. In the fifth, some typical houses of the town are presented, and in the sixth, there is a section on 'Festivities and Culture' where the theatre and different sculptures in Salt appear. The seventh is a section called 'We are all important' that deals with the issue of the town's culturally diverse human population (until then, it had not appeared). There is a world map in which different people are located depending on their origin, and next to it, we have a table with all the countries represented in Salt. They speak of a great variety of cultural samples coexisting in Salt, but the only samples that later appear are the different languages and some references to typical Senegalese food. Although this is not one of the majority nationalities of Salt, it is undoubtedly the one that receives the most attention. Perhaps this overrepresentation is due to the active role a lot of Senegalese associations play in cultural activities such as the local colla castellera (human tower) Els Marrecs. However, I suspect it might also have to do with the historical relations of international cooperation. At the end of the book, there is a 'map of activities' in which only Spanish activities appear, although many of the activities might be considered global as well.

Likewise, we find certain campaigns and cultural activities trying to promote specific cultures with the explicit purpose of revaluing the town and encouraging the arrival of other populations, especially those belonging to the wealthiest classes. I would mention the International Basketry Fair (Fira internacional del castell). It is a fair related to the world of basketry, held every year since 1997. Until six years ago, it was held at the Centre neighbourhood, but as a result of a confrontation between the organizers and the Town Council (then PSC-ERC), it was moved to the Old neighbourhood. The neighbourhood association AVV de Barri Vell began promoting it with pennants and baskets on balconies and façades. Since then, the fair has acquired a new look, and, especially with the arrival of the new government, it has become yet another example of this eagerness to promote the town both on a commercial (tourist) and symbolic-cultural level:

> The Basket Fair in Salt closed yesterday with a successful number of participants, as usual, among many of its peculiarities that it is a great showcase of the Old neighbourhood of Salt, a place unknown to many who visit it for the first time. "'t is an opportunity to discover Barri Vell in the framework of a fair that is unique because it only focuses on the basket, leaving aside other proposals,' said the mayor, Jaume Torramadé. Probably, for this reason, to enjoy and discover the Barrio Viejo, an Instagram your Town route has been made to show the *patios* of the neighbourhood. (Trillas 2014)

> Until, well, it became an attraction. I mean, for the neighbours involved. And they want the fair to come and for the people of Salt from certain places they come and walk and well it's a place, well it's very nice. Moreover, to promote Salt at the foreign level, at the level of the Girona region, and of Barcelona in different places, right? I mean, it has a bit of an image, this bad image of Salt doesn't, it's always just about immigration and conflict, and I don't think that's it; there's another reality. *Jordi*

In 2014, the Office of Promotion and Commerce of the Town was established, and in early 2015, a promotional campaign was launched titled 'Salt is a lot more' through a guide and a website: viusalt.com and later a promotional video. The image conveyed was that of (a) an active town with a natural environment (Les Deveses) and rich infrastructures (sports clubs, horse riding, canoeing) that invite people to do sports; (b) a popular town, rooted in Catalan culture (through samples of local folk associations such as the colla castellera); (c) an ecologically sustainable town, close to nature (Les Deveses, the allotments and the Ter river) and the land (allotments and local produces); and (d) a university and cultural town (due to the various university and cultural facilities)—altogether, both a modern and traditional town, young and with history. It is an image, in their words, projected to attract tourism, but it is clear that it is also done to show another image for potential future students that of a new university town from which they speak—a kind of face wash and make-up for a future source of capital, the gentrifier or the tourist.

It is clear that all these strategies to promote and project another type of image of Salt find their justification and general support in the grievance that may have existed among the population due to the negative images projected onto the town. Thus, in the wake of the many stigmatizing campaigns launched by the media and the political responses that seem to confirm racist hypotheses, a large part of the population, both Spaniards and migrants, seems to internalize the degrading representations. Consequently, gradually a consensus is reached around the idea that there *is* a socio-spatial degradation to which action must be directed:

> And it is a neighbourhood that you must work hard to make attractive, a neighbourhood where I would invite you to come for a walk, and where you feel safe living. However, this requires work that currently is not being done. Right now, the balconies, I think the balconies should . . .The image of your neighbourhood tells you a lot about who you are or who you are not, or about the people who live in your neighbourhood. If you have a clean neighbourhood, a polished neighbourhood. . . you come with a different attitude. If you who come from outside and upon encountering the neighbourhood you see a dirty neighbourhood, a neighbourhood where every balcony has a closet or a staircase, and you see what you see, you leave with an impression, which at best is not real,

> but with what you have seen, with the image, you got an impression of the neighbourhood. I think it's something that needs to be worked on, a day-to-day pedagogy that needs to be done (Toñi)

Thus, the stigma and its devaluation find its revaluative response, behind which there is widespread support, in the exclusion of what has been perceived as degrading: the cultural Other. In this way, native cultural exhibitions and the Old district are constantly promoted (around 90% of the images on the 'Images from the town' tab are from the Old district), thus leaving out much of the town in the portrait.[5] A similar observation was made concerning the campaign 'we want a decent neighbourhood' in the Barcelona neighbourhood of Raval (Fernández González 2016).

Paradoxically, however, both the triggered and 'consensual' processes of gentrification can end up expelling the native working classes. Of course, the negative and degrading views of the town and the Centre are not shared by all Salt residents. In fact, most people find them distorted and even consider them third-party inventions. Other people live elsewhere in the town and simply have not experienced any such problems, whereas others have had largely positive experiences. Some consider that the negative images are strategies employed by social actors who try to profit in one way or another from the misery of some inhabitants or exert violence on them to appropriate social space for speculative purposes.

In any case, part of the local society mobilizes and resorts to various strategies to reverse what they generally perceive as an unfair situation. They react by promoting the cultural expressions of natives, 'those who have always been there' and are now considered a minority. They are promoted as if they embodied the authentic ways or essence of the town, a group in extinction faced by globalization and the continuous promotions of multiculturalism (the promotion of other cultures) carried out by NGOs and State administrations.

Hence, some people attempt to visualize or promote the local culture, *the authentic*, such as the *traditional commerce* (i.e., that of the native popular classes). The purpose is to recover or revitalize the traditional neighbourhood threatened by cultural diversity that turns the neighbourhood into a lifeless ghetto. Therefore, it is an anti-stigmatization strategy to maintain the natives. These initiatives are primarily promoted by local (cultural) associations, such as the Local Merchants Association of La Massana and the Centre, the Neighbourhood Association of the Centre, and the Neighbourhood Association of La Massana.

Another case is the local television channel, Televisió Vila de Salt. They say they broadcast the *Informatius Saltencs* with the vocation of giving voice to the 'simple and hardworking people who live in their neighbourhood.'

However, the overemphasis on the Spanish cultural expressions and absence of migrants is surprising.

Although there are apparent exceptions, compared with the other initiatives that want to promote the old (disappearing) commerce, the president of the Neighbourhood Association of the Centre proposes to strengthen the

> Trade, make it more attractive, or even more specialized. Make a specialized neighbourhood with this multiculturalism and promote it in this sense but well, well it would be attractive to outsiders. . . . Taking advantage of the ground floor to make a gallery, samples and make it, a very different look and make it attractive for people to come, just like they go to the Old district, they should come to the Centre which is noteworthy for its diversity

However, if we analyse the narratives, discourses, and initiatives as a whole, what is striking is the fact that there is an overwhelming absence of migrants. Instead, what we see is a position, sometimes implicit and sometimes explicit, against the stigmatizing images of Salt that have been spread mainly due to the social conflicts and in which much of the responsibility has fallen on the immigrants. This way, they are strategies for visualizing a set of cultural traits and practices as the native in front of the existing plurality of cultures.

In fact, certain cultural traits are rejected for being degrading, such as the case of the mosque in Torremirona and the opposition to the small places of worship in town.[6] In the end, these campaigns (both for the recovery and promotion of certain businesses and for opposition to places of worship) are part of a struggle for the urban space of the Centre, about what kind of inhabitants can live there and what cultural traits can and should be visible.

They are reactionary and revanchist responses to the changes in the neighbourhood and the town, such as the opening of 'ethnic shops' (e.g., halal butchers, phone booths, cafés, etc.) and places of worship. Faced with a perception of ethnocultural loss and threat and based on what Hage (2000) calls the 'fantasy of white supremacy', some natives feel a need to promote 'their culture' in front of the wide variety of 'foreign cultures' and the process of stigmatization taking place. They often shielded themselves behind the idea that the others receive much attention through aid or in the media, albeit negatively, an observation quite in line with what Rogaly and Qureshi (2013) explain in the case of Peterborough. The social effect of these romantic visions of the past and the strategies of recovery and (mono)cultural promotion of the neighbourhood is that the existing social divisions among the populations end up being reproduced along ethnocultural lines of us and them.

Thus, the project is presented not only as classist but also as revanchist-nativist and, therefore, extremely racist. In the end, the goal is to limit the number of poor migrant residents in the town and favour the arrival of native youth.

When the public authorities say, 'young people', they refer to native or young people from any other population group with a high cultural and economic capital. In fact, Salt does not lack young people. The local housing plan of the town already detected that there is a significant number of young people in the town: 'The population pyramid incorporates a significant number of people in the age of emancipation, higher than other towns in the area.' (GMG Plans i Projectes 2009, 3). Hence, the problem is instead that they are not native.

In this chapter, I have dealt with the different urban policies implemented in Salt in the last decade. I have shown how anti-ghetto policies of urban renewal and restructuring (including demolishing parts of the urban fabric and expelling residents) or policies of social mixing are enacted to avoid the arrival of migrants by raising the prices and limiting low-income housing, and, on the other, to attract young natives by promoting the existing positive aspects of the town via cultural events, infrastructure, and middle-income housing (i.e., specific mobility and human composition is desired and planned for).

Through a critical analysis of media, government, and resident discourse, we see how the stigmatizing attitudes in Salt both serve to devalue certain areas, justify projects of urban renewal, and allocate public funding to promote a new economic sector and, at the same time, produce the famous rent- gap (Smith 1987). We see how certain inhabitants are deemed problematic only because of their ethnicity, culture, origin, or looks, whereas other cultural expressions are explicitly promoted and desired. In the end, it becomes clear that these local expressions collude with a more generalized global economic transformation tendency from the industry towards the fourth sector based on the production and consumption of information, knowledge, and culture.

The following chapter is meant as a concluding chapter and an attempt to draw the issues together to a close, although several questions are left open as well.

CHAPTER 5 NOTES

1. ERAM 2021.
2. Consorci del Ter 2021,
3. Factoria Cultural Coma Cros 2021.
4. Divided into the following periods: (a) prehistoric, (b) Roman, (c) medieval, (d) modern, (e) industrial, and (f) current.
5. Contrary to the amazing portrait that the photographer Martí Artalejo has made of the town and its inhabitants.
6. See in this regard the view of the old Spanish nationals in the web of the Anti-ARU Platform, and particularly the video 'Enquesta sobre la nova normativa de locals de culte'.

Chapter Six

Openings and Closures

In 2007–2008 Spain entered a state of economic crisis after 10 years of significant economic growth. The Spanish economy had evolved mainly based on tourism and property development and was thus strongly affected by the UK and US housing bubbles and the global financial crisis (López and Rodríguez 2011). The economic crisis turned into recession, which, alongside the implementation of austerity measures in the public sector and labour-market restructuring, had disastrous consequences for a society that had been trying to build up a Welfare State, with massive unemployment rates, especially among young people, and daily foreclosures and lay-offs.

These political and economic transformations comprised the scenery of this book, which aimed to study its social and political consequences through an ethnographic study of convivencia in a small town. It comprehended a long-term immersion and living in the town to study the relations between the inhabitants of Salt, focusing mainly on the Barri Centre, where several crucial conflicts had taken place between groups defined as immigrants and natives.

Quite interestingly, through this, we see how convivencia is a much more conflictual and complex phenomenon than is often presented. In fact, in mediating migration as a social phenomenon and social reproduction, I argue that convivencia is an essential concept to think with and through and, therefore, for understanding contemporary Spanish and Catalan politics and society.

Although a rich ethnography always leaves more questions than answers, the present one shows us how the crisis is experienced on various scales and in different domains, creating a situation of profound anxiety and insecurity, similar to what some authors have denominated as 'ontological insecurity' (Giddens 1990; Bauman 1992; Young 1999). It is a situation mainly produced by the flexibility of the labour market and the worsening of labour-market conditions and unemployment (Marle and Maruna 2010, 8), and that profoundly affects the lives of the working classes and precarious populations, resulting in constant instability and uncertainty in their livelihoods and concerning their prospects, alongside a perpetual competition for primary resources in a situation of scarcity.

Similarly, we see how many inhabitants have been evicted from their homes or are struggling to pay high mortgages. Meanwhile, in the neighbourhood communities, debts are high, and consequently, essential community services cannot be maintained. Despite this, we see how everyday social conflicts in these social spaces of dispossessed neighbourhoods pit working-class residents against each other, in conflicts, often expressed by the ethnocultural group markers and moral frameworks linked to discourses of civility and an imagined neighbourhood identity that is the product of historical struggles for improvement.

Questions of community and well-being are indeed at the centre of the debate when new residents are depicted as invaders and breakers of moral codes, who create feelings of insecurity and alienation among the older native residents. Similarly, we can observe exclusivist claims of belonging, again defined by ethnocultural markers, which reproduce unequal power structures and access to resources.

Faced with this social situation, the local governments, be they left-wing or right-wing, have in their majority adopted punitive, penal, and criminalizing policies alongside minor social reforms, usually applied through the third sector and discriminatory in their reach. These strategies (principally guided by the ideological principles of the Third Way famously proposed by Anthony Giddens) are implemented with the aim of 'ordering the social' in response to the insecurity felt among some of the residents (Wacquant 2008c) and preventing social fracture through the strengthening of 'social cohesion'. Unfortunately, by doing this, they adopt the racist premises that associate insecurity with petty crime, often committed by young migrants. Likewise, although in a much subtler way, they disqualify any juvenile discontent or protest, branding it simply as problematic and loutish behaviour, despite an objective problem of juvenile unemployment that offers few prospects, especially for the ethnocultural Others.

Hence, although the expression of social conflicts can indeed be varied and various, the hegemonic narratives in contemporary European societies present the social conflicts merely as cultural conflicts. This discursive arrangement constitutes an ideological displacement of the conflicts; the actual differences in culture have nothing to do with the practices frowned upon or used to explain social conflicts in the neighbourhoods where interaction between people of different origins is frequent. However, the dominant interpretations overemphasize cultural difference, treating it sui generis, separated from other equally important factors such as ethnocultural, race, or gender inequalities and obfuscating the material underpinnings of the conflicts; a move that ends up naturalizing these self-same inequalities (Wieviorka 1998). Throughout the book, I have shown that many of these are merely daily conflicts that emerge due to close relationships between neighbours or fruit of the precarious situation in which many of them have ended up due to the crisis, while others are indicators of ethnocultural and socio-economic inequalities.

I argue that the main reason the ethnocultural explanations are dominant is that they are articulated within a political-symbolic field that favours these kinds of classification and differentiation because they are both functional for the enrichment of a few, the secure the unequal welfare provision of the privileged (e.g., the native), and the simple maintenance of these unequal power positions. In this sense, adopting culturalist policies is a step in the wrong direction because it assumes the inherent culturalist logic of the abovementioned political-symbolic field.

Let me be clear: I am not arguing against the concept of culture as such. On the contrary, I am advocating somewhat more responsible use of it. I aspire to pivot the categories as they are used in the fieldwork, where other categories can be equally important and even clarify the meanings of translocal categories such as culture. Instead of discarding cultural explanations altogether—thus running the risk of overemphasizing economic explanations—I have proposed to scrutinize the role that culture or cultural explanations play in their connection to economic, political, and moral factors at different scales.

Although the data described and analysed here are locally grounded, they are nonetheless articulated on multiple scales within specific historical and geographical dynamics. We must, therefore, always aim to show how the ethnography might reveal interesting trends that go beyond the local, as Wacquant (2009c, 119) states it

> "go native" but "go native armed," that is, equipped with your theoretical and methodological tools, with the full store of problematics inherited from your discipline, with your capacity for reflexivity and analysis, and guided by a constant effort, once you have passed the ordeal of initiation, to objectivize this experience and construct the object—instead of allowing yourself to be naively embraced and constructed by it. Go ahead, go native, but come back a sociologist!

Accordingly, from the analysis of the ethnography, we can deduce several tendencies that have contradictory purposes. In any case, despite the anthropological attempt to construct a coherent narrative, the ethnographic enterprise, as usual, leaves more doors open than closed. In what follows, I will merely address some of the fundamental debates and openings that emerge from this, as I see it.

THE FIELD IS A PRODUCED AND SOCIALLY CONSTRUCTED SPACE

I argue against conceiving the site of fieldwork as merely a spatial container. Given that the site is local-globally (re)produced and constructed in socio-cultural and political-economic senses (Gupta and Ferguson 1992), I believe it is quintessential that we as anthropologists consider the geographical and historical factors of the field we study.

In this vein, and as an example, I find it productive to comprehend marginalized spaces such as Barri Centre and Salt as spatial fixes in the Harveyian sense. When the capitalist economy enters an accumulation crisis, it turns to 'accumulation by dispossession' to reproduce itself through a process of 'spatial fixes' (Harvey 1985). In this sense, I argue that in Salt, we see a contemporary spatial fix that entails the extraction of a surplus (through debt enforcement and subsequent evictions) in a peripheralized space and the subsequent creation of surplus through gentrification. To this end, non-economic factors are required, epitomized in the case of Salt by territorial stigmatization (Wacquant, Slater, and Pereira 2014). In fact, to justify socio-urban projects such as gentrification, massive urban reforms, or evictions, spaces of exception and social alarm are often created, a process in which the media play a quintessential part.

In the wake of the crisis, banks and real estate developers have been, and still are, interested in profiting from and making liquid the variable capital they invested in the space. If we extend this out to a larger scale, we see how German banks had capital invested in Southern Europe in general, especially in the real estate sector. With the financial crisis, they suddenly found themselves with fixed capital from which they could not profit, and the problems were thus transferred to their South European branches, which went bankrupt and needed to be supported by public funds, which again meant public debt. To justify this move, the age-old imagery of the lazy Southerners, renewed through the acronym PIGS (referring thus to the countries of Portugal, Italy, Ireland, Greece, and Spain), came in handy. Furthermore, suddenly, the problem fruit of the accumulation crisis was rendered as one of public overspending in the South European states. This way, the debt was displaced and territorialized in the South, a tendency that was repeated within the Spanish State towards the working classes, whom sackings or cut-offs had already hit, and especially taking advantage of the defencelessness of the migrants.

Thus, a division was created between long-term residents (old migrants from the south of Spain, often in possession of their own houses, or with cheaper mortgages or extensive social networks making it easier to defray the costs) and the newly arrived (migrants from the Global South, often with expensive mortgages and less extensive social networks, or poor in economic terms, making it difficult to defray the costs).

Nonetheless, the dominant interpretations emphasize other local-global processes, such as migration, and specially bound the problems in cultural differences. So, behind the theatre of cultural conflicts, we find another political-economic battleground: Inherent socio-spatial antagonisms of the town. For instance, we have seen that one of the critical political-economic projects in the town is to attract human and social investment to the town (i.e., to revalorize the town through gentrification. A socio-urban project of creating a cultural or university town that has been promoted to boost a fourth and fifth sector through a trinity of interventions: (1) promotion of the town, aimed at attracting new young native inhabitants and avoiding the flight of the native inhabitants who do not feel at home; (2) urban politics of gentrification and social mixing aimed at attracting more young native people; and (3) pacification policies aimed at making the natives feel secure and remain in the town instead of moving away.

This project, however, goes against the interests and social reproduction of the majority of residents in Salt. In that sense, Salt is a paradigmatic example of growing political antagonisms between different economic projects and models, a political-economic transition towards a post-industrial and post-Fordist society. In reaction to the social consequences of this restructuring, political measures have been implemented in Salt to cope with the urban poor, working-class, and migrant populations, both to keep them in place, prepare their displacement, and in an ideological sense justify their misery.

TOWARDS A POST-FORDIST MANAGEMENT OF THE POOR?

Following the magisterial theorizations of Michael Mann (1984) and Phillips Abrams (1988), in the words of Gupta and Sharma (2006, 291), the State does not appear here as a monolithic entity but rather as a multi-scalar and conflictual assemblage (Gupta and Sharma 2006, 291), with internal antagonism and conflicts. Different interests of the partaking actors of society converge in and through it, and consensus is supposed to be guaranteed by the State. Inherent to theories of 'governance', the work carried out by the technocrats and officials that make up the different departments and bodies of the State (urban planning, public-private companies for urban development and construction, the police, teachers, etc.) is that of a supposed 'mediation' of these different interests.

However, as Marx famously argued in his critique of Hegel's theory of mediation (Marx 1970), there is no such thing as an equal encounter between equal forces; not all have the same power of representation nor influence. In reality, the different groups and classes can influence through deploying their symbolic capital. Think, for example, of the academics who exercise a specific power of influence in terms of the production and construction of the social problems on which we must act, their composition, and the measures.

Therefore, I consider it crucial to reflect on the functioning of the contemporary State. To this end, I will use Bourdieu's conceptualization of the bureaucratic field (Bourdieu et al. 1994), tracing the most recent historical transformations in general terms of the Western State, finally locating it in the case of Spain. Through doing this, I detect two interesting trends in the case of Salt that are linked to transformations observed in other European and Western States in recent decades: More significant dependence on private funding and new management of poverty through group-specific claims, such as culture, gender, ethnicity, and age.

PUBLIC FUNDING IN NEOLIBERAL TIMES

The first one refers to the fact that the State, be that in the guise of the local or regional administration, is increasingly pushed to seek financing via the third sector or external funds to carry out actions in the regime of social policy, a need primarily generated by decreasing public spending, quintessential of the neoliberal policy regime. One of its primary effects is an intensified political and economic integration between private and public and the dominance of economic reasoning over the sociopolitical. This change was already observed in the late 1980s by scholars such as Harvey (1989). He argued that changes were taking place in the bureaucratic field of local and regional administrations, moving from a 'managerialist' to an 'entrepreneurialist' administration, a change, he argued, that was the product of the crisis of the 1970s. It had brought the prevailing State model into crisis, resulting in a widening gap between the economic and sociopolitical spheres. Thus, since the late 1990s, the tendency has been for the State to reconfigure from a Keynesian National Welfare State (KNWS) towards a neoliberal model (Rodríguez Cabrero 1991; Wacquant 2009b). Alongside this, there has been a slow transition from a so-called socialized economy towards a (corporate) market with substantial social costs (Agrela 2006, 118).

Consequently, local and regional administrations increasingly receive fewer financial resources from the higher State administrations. In light of this situation, city councils often feel obliged to promote different financial management of their town, attracting resources now available in the private sector. Because reductions have been made in public interventions, the continuation of these activities depends on external funding through projects, which tend to privatize access to public services. In the words of Agrela, 'the state loses centrality and the social policies are increasingly blurred with the intricacies of the market, commodifying itself, and where the governments are becoming mere managers of the processes' (2006, 118). As a result, we see a slip of State responsibility towards social reproduction. At the same time, due to the increasing desperation, marginalization, and insecurity that this new socio-economic situation also creates, we observe a tendency to monitor and penalize the most disadvantaged groups as a new way to manage and control them.

Second, in terms of governance, the incorporation of Spain into the EU in 1986 is of utmost importance. The political project of integration in EU was based on a concept called *subsidiarity*, an inherited concept of the social doctrine of the Catholic Church, which originated from Leo XIII's encyclical papal *Rerum novarum* (Holmes 2000). The use of this concept in the entire financial organization of the EU has led to financing through project funding, thus supposedly transferring sovereignty to adequate local parties on the ground. This new form of regional governance (Lovering 1999; MacLeod 2001) changed the type of interventions implemented and had consequences for detecting deficiencies and how to tackle them. At the same time, it provided small municipalities with more room for political manoeuvre because they would have access to larger funding budgets. However, we also see a growing phenomenon of external financing, operationalized through the creation of Development Funds or similar programs with external funding, which generally operate outside the traditional sectoral structures' (Cardarelli and Rosenfeld 1998, 83). Hence, aid programs targeted at marginalized groups or populations at 'risk of social exclusion' are carried out by NGOs especially. These programs, which might favour some over others, ultimately divide the population and possibly even create grievances between groups, while they tend to individualize the attention or base it mainly on group demands and, at the same time, perceive the groups and their demands in culturalist terms.

Faced with a limited municipal budget that did not allow for large public investments as in other municipalities, Salt created a material need to attract financial resources, investments. In the words of the former mayor, Iolanda Pineda:

> We started looking for everything we could because it became clear that we needed the support of other administrations as the town council alone could

> not put 200 million euros upfront [laughing]. The municipal budget of Salt was about 28 million back then, and now it's 23 annually. Therefore, to finance part of the operation, you either get support from other administrations who will then make a significant contribution, or you generate profit from urban rezoning.

Thus, to increase the capacity to act, three lines of action were used (a) a request 'framed projects' financed by public and transnational administrations, such as the EU; (b) promote the town to attract public-private investment, which together with the social policies studied would motivate a social change; and (c) the urban requalification that allowed new constructions, and with them, jobs.

These actions are encompassed in two meta-narratives. The first is that of a state of emergency that needs urgent financing. It serves as a regional creative brand to which avant-garde policies, as seen in chapter 4, are applied—a social laboratory. The other is the cultural and university town, i.e., the process of local development from an industrial town towards one based on services, technology, and information, as we saw in chapter 5.

It was June 2008 when, for the first time, the former mayor, Iolanda Pineda (PSC) began to create a public image of a 'social emergency':

> [Iolanda Pineda] yesterday exposed the municipality's emergency due to the avalanche of immigrants who have arrived in recent years to the President of the Generalitat, José Montilla. Pineda asked for help from the government because 'the social cohesion of Salt is at risk' and the fact that it has 40% of the new population is difficult to live with (J.B.M. 2008)

This discourse reinforces the already existing readings, although in a more implicit way; the lack of resources in the local administration to face the challenges posed by migration does not seem to have anything to do with institutional-regional inequalities or with the recently launched crisis. Be that as it may, it demonstrates the importance of creating an alarming image to obtain resources in a new public financing model based on grants and projects. Later, Salt's tense moments provided the opportunity to request more resources from the Catalan government. The close relationship that the former mayor had with the Tripartite and the then president of the Generalitat de Catalunya, José Montilla, was an important factor in raising funds (Sandoval 2007c) but, without a doubt, the crucial element was the media coverage given to the conflicts in the town. In this way, a local government with few economic resources obtained an extension of the financing for the social projects carried out in the Salt Area 70. Focusing on urban planning and immigration, resources were obtained to improve the urban fabric of a large part of Salt and, especially, of the public space.

I am not saying that there was no need to intervene, nor that the whole set-up was exclusively due to political interests. Many actors with diverse interests intervened in this process, and the town council's interest must also have been diverse: At first, it did want to attract attention and thus obtain more resources due to its unique situation. However, later it took advantage of a moment created by other instances to ask for financing again and thus avoid responsibility.

Everything points to the fact that to obtain financing, in many cases, it is as essential to know how to communicate specific needs as to problematize according to a particular logic. Furthermore, it is convenient to present a catastrophic and singular image in times of public austerity. Thus, in the case of Salt, the emphasis was placed on immigration and degradation, although these factors did not seem to constitute a problem at that time (at least, they would not be until later). One could argue that they saw it coming and were visionary; others would say that the intervention might have caused the problem. In this sense, resorting to migration statistics would draw attention because numbers are indeed powerful (Comaroff and Comaroff 2006). This placed Salt in a superior position than other towns, which supposedly required action. An exceptional moment was created using sociological and bureaucratic indicators (such as the percentage of immigrants). The argument was based on the idea that the percentage is something significant (which has been denied) and that migration was the leading cause of social problems (of convivencia). I propose that this way of problematizing reality has social effects: The idea that there *is* a problem is naturalized, and to attract economic resources, attention is continually drawn to it.

The other way to get financing has been through European development funds. To this end, the idea of a cultural and university town has been essential. The rehabilitation of Coma-Cros and the urban improvements for the future installation of cultural facilities have been financed by trans-local institutions, following the idea of creating a kind of cultural-university node that even transgresses the borders of Spain and France. This idea, however valuable and interesting it may seem, as it is inserted within the geography of capitalism, means that the desire to commercialize space for the return on capital tends to dominate this transformation. As I have shown in the previous chapter, gentrification processes are promoted that displace dispossessed populations and favour the arrival of more affluent populations. At the same time, the latter's cultural expressions are promoted, in the act excluding other popular or folk cultural expressions.

NEW WAYS OF MANAGING POVERTY

> [T]he assertive rolling out of the penal state has engendered new categories and discourses, novel administrative bodies and government policies, fresh social types and associated forms of knowledge across the criminal and social welfare domains. In sum, the penalization of poverty has proved to be a prolific vector for the construction of social reality and for the reengineering of the state geared toward the *ordering of social insecurity* in the age of deregulated capitalism (Wacquant 2009b, 295)

As we have seen in the previous sections, alongside punitive and repressive policies (right hand), two important trends are detected in terms of social policies (left hand); on the one hand, a series of social policies tend to be confused with those of integration and are directed in a less universal and much more selective way through the third sector, and on the other hand, civility becomes a hegemonic framework that justifies divisions and the harshness of punitive policies.

In other words, we see a tendency to manage social inequalities less and less in terms of labour and economic rights (social question = poverty) through universal social services. Although several attempts have been made in Spain, there is still no workfare; currently, the subsidy after the benefit of accumulated unemployment is minimal, and not everyone has access to it. The result is that a separation is created between regular and irregular at a legal-political level, a separation of citizenship, which entails greater or lesser security and social stability. At the level of social stratification, there are differentiations, both at the inter-subjective level and in public administrations (structural racism), based on moral ideas of belonging to a community and of access to rights and economic resources, which are based above all on structural changes in the labour market and social austerity policies. The result is that a whole set of 'surplus people' are emerging, who are not recognized as legitimate subjects by the State or formally enter the labour market (although often informally they do). Until recently, this population group was treated more or less equally (although in the Spanish case, the third sector and, above all, the Christian charity, has played an important role and the level of self-government of each autonomous community). However, these relatively universal policies have declined in recent years, and the third sector has gradually filled out the vacuum of responsibility.

Following Peck and Tickell (2002, 387–92), this new trend was born out of a neoliberal critique of public services. This extension ('roll-out') of the neoliberal project is different from the previous phases, what Peck and Tickell (2002) call 'roll-back' and 'proto-neoliberalism', in that instead of attacking the Welfare State, it reformulates its operation, introducing new forms of 'institutional hardware. This eventually leads to a concentration of resources in social policies aimed at the groups characterized as vulnerable or at risk of social exclusion (Cardarelli and Rosenfeld 1998). Although migrants are often among the most affected in terms of unemployment and generally live in precarious situations, what is surprising is the lack of effort to direct policies to these socio-economic inequalities. Instead, we see a rise in policies targeting cultural aspects, paired with a penal treatment of the informal activities related to the specific socio-economic and legal situation in which these populations find themselves.

Gavin Smith (2011) instead prefers to speak of different hegemonic projects, and he distinguishes between an 'expansive' and 'selective' hegemony. The first one referred to the post-World War II phase and was based on the KNWS and public services for all. The second, the current, is characterized by the logic of financial capitalism. Although the population surplus existed in the previous hegemony, the project of hegemony was expansive, universal, and inclusive (on a universalist basis). The project of selective hegemony is characterized by defining projects aimed at selected populations (such as 'indigenous women') instead of addressing the population in general and universal terms (citizens of the nation-state). Therefore, two categories are formed, the 'relative surplus population' and the 'absolute surplus population'. Therefore, the selectivity of the contemporary hegemony project leaves out the absolute surplus population (Smith 2011, 22). Then this population is 'integrated' through correctional and penal institutions. With this, we should not understand reinsert. Instead, the post-industrial society tends to understand that there is no longer any need for these populations; therefore, integration should here be understood as integration through exclusion, based on the impossibility of their reinsertion or 'normal integration'. This shows that the State has not stopped managing the social consequences of the capitalist system but, rather, that its strategy has been transformed.

Hence, we might say that it is precisely because they do *something* that they do not act differently. A reform-oriented politics aimed at reproducing the system and the money that funds these programmes could have been used to fight structural problems. Therefore, the State has not failed to manage the social consequences of the capitalist system; a specific political project, which some have labelled neoliberalism, has purposely used and perpetuated its crisis as a pretext to transform its strategy. As Wacquant puts it:

> [T]he generalized hardening of police, judicial, and correctional policies that can be observed in most of the countries of the First World over the past two decades partakes of a triple transformation of the state, which it helps simultaneously to accelerate and obfuscate, wedding the amputation of its economic arm,

> the retraction of its social bosom, and the massive expansion of its criminal fist (2009b, 4).

In our case, particularly visible in the present context of economic crisis and great structural changes, migrants from North Africa seem to be the scapegoat for all societal ills. A reading promoted by the right that equates migration with crime and coincides with the 'absolute surplus population' described by Smith. In this case, and as Smith also argues, the extreme right promotes discrimination in favour of what they call the native, based on the assumption of hegemony. This way, they offer a coherent reading of the changes produced in society and blame the negative effects mainly on the working classes and directly on the new migration and its visible Otherness. In fact, the recent growth of right-wing parties such as Plataforma per Catalunya should be understood in this sense. The explanatory system that they propose is based on a simple but effective reading of the social reality of a proportion of the working class: Inhabitants of the peripheries of the metropolis, the industrial working-class areas and neighbourhoods (such as Salt or Vic), where former migrants from the south of Spain and impoverished workers live. It confers a group identity that promises them a preference to access scarce public resources in terms of selective hegemony. Pierre Bourdieu described it well:

> With the eruption into the political field of a party like the National Front whose whole strategy is based on xenophobia and racism, political debate as a whole has more or less directly turned on the problem of immigration: in the political struggle between opposing authorities, political parties and trade unions in particular, each of which lays claim to the legitimate principle of vision and division, the question of redistribution has become absolutely central, along with the question of determining who has the right to claim all the advantages attached to membership in the national community. For that matter, it is this claim to monopolize access to the economic and social advantages associated with citizenship that lets dominated 'nationals' take sides with dominant 'nationals' against the 'immigrants.' (Bourdieu 1999, 187–88).

A NEOLIBERAL STATE?

This state-in-formation is what Wacquant (2012) calls the Centaur State. At the top, it is liberal because it acts to leverage the resources and expand the life options of the holders of economic and cultural capital. At the bottom, it is paternalistic, castigatory and restrictive when 'managing the populations destabilized by the deepening of inequality and the diffusion of work insecurity and ethnic anxiety' (Wacquant 2012, 74). However, despite my profound acknowledgement and admiration for the work of Wacquant, I do not believe that the State is a monolithic leviathan, as several authors have rightfully criticized (Collier 2012; Hilgers 2012).

As explained earlier, the crisis of the 1970s brought a crisis of the prevailing State model, the consequence of which was a deepening of the gap between the economic sphere and the social sphere. Thus, since the late 1990s, there has been a trend towards the reconfiguration of the KNWS model towards a neoliberal type model, and slowly we see a transition from a so-called socialized economy to a market (corporate) with high social costs.

This sociopolitical development corresponds to institutional changes regarding the management of the State apparatus, changes that have weakened it and made it possible to function more in line with the economic and mercantile premises of capitalism. In this way, reductions are made in public interventions, increasingly dependent on external financing through projects (frequently involving private-public collaborations), whereas access to public services tends to be privatized. In the words of Agrela: 'The State loses its centrality and social policies are increasingly blurred by the ins and outs of the market, becoming commercialized, and governments becoming mere process managers' (2006, 118).

Similarly, there is a growing slippage in the State's responsibility concerning the social reproduction of citizens. A trend that started in the 1970s and has gradually intensified following the political-economic doctrines of neoliberalism (Harvey 2005). Execution is increasingly delegated, although not necessarily management, to third-sector NGOs, which, instead of offering universal and public services, allocate them to small groups following parameters according to the risk of exclusion (of necessity, it is understood). At the same time, given the growing despair, marginality, and precariousness that this new socio-economic situation creates, there is an increasing tendency to control and penalize the most deprived classes as a new way of managing and controlling the social body.

An ideological transformation of the State that promotes changes in its reason for being and the ways it acts, which cannot be understood in political terms only. If this were the case, we would make the mistake of accepting the ideological trap of neoliberalism, which wants to separate the sociocultural, economic, and political spheres (Wolf 1982), especially when it comes to the responsibility that the State has regarding the reproduction of subjects. The functioning of the State, that is, of the bureaucratic-administrative system that makes it up, has been transformed with the different changes in the economic-political system. This is understood in relation to, on the one hand, the role that the economic domain plays for the social and political and financing of administrations:

> This project involves the retooling and redeployment of the state to buttress market-like mechanisms and discipline the new postindustrial proletariat while restraining the internal disruptions generated by the fragmentation of labor, the retrenchment of social protection schemes, and the correlative shake-up of the established ethnic hierarchy (ethnoracial in the United States, ethnonational in Western Europe, and a mix of the two in Latin America) (Wacquant 2009a, 172)

And it is also understood in relation, on the other hand, to the institutional changes that have occurred in recent decades, among other things, as a result of joining the EU and the effects of the EU integration. In 1978, Stuart Hall and colleagues (1979; Hall et al. 1978) at the Centre for Contemporary Cultural Studies at the University of Birmingham published a series of increasingly relevant analyses of how the economic crisis of the 1970s was being handled politically and economically during the administration of Margaret Thatcher in the United Kingdom. They detected back then the implementation, at the hands of Thatcher, Ronald Reagan, and Augusto Pinochet, of the 'neoliberal doctrines' (Harvey 2005).

Indeed, in these moments of 'systemic crisis', it seems that we are seeing an intensification and amplification of these political measures (Hall 2011). State apparatuses are increasingly influenced by neoliberal dictates, the market, and financial institutions such as the IMF, World Bank, TROIKA, etc. We are facing a minimalist State in terms of its role as economic redistributor and social manager and powerful and repressive in terms of political dissent or alternative economic practices. It is a corporate State, a neoliberal state model and utopia, that Wacquant has called the Centaur State:

> *[T]hat displays opposite visages at the two ends of the class structure*: it is uplifting and 'liberating' at the top, where it acts to leverage the resources and expand the life options of the holders of economic and cultural capital; but it is castigatory and restrictive at the bottom, when it comes to managing the populations destabilised by the deepening of inequality and the diffusion of work insecurity and ethnic anxiety. Actually existing neoliberalism extolls 'laissez faire et laissez passer' for the dominant, but it turns out to be paternalist and intrusive for the subaltern, and especially for the urban precariat whose life parameters it restricts through the combined mesh of supervisory workfare and judicial oversight. (Wacquant 2012, 74)

Obsessed with finding funding and legitimating its singular use of force and violence and its raison d'être, this State is highly contradictory and unstable. It promotes certain changes, maybe to attract resources, that later have some devastating effects that must then be alleviated or funnelled.

Consequently, certain clarifications are required regarding the historical development of the Welfare State in the Spanish case.1 It is based primarily on the pillars and achievements carried out at the end of the Franco period. With the social policies implemented in the Transition Era, the aim was to universalize the existing measures rather than carry out a radical change, thus leaving the task of renewal in the hands of the autonomous administrations. This has given rise to specificities of each region, above all regarding social services (Agrela 2006, 100). Equally important is to highlight the role that the Catholic Church would continue to play in the post-Franco state, as Agrela (2006, 100) writes: 'The political and ideological control role assigned to the Catholic Church during the Franco period—through national Catholicism—, as well as the weight of its care intervention via its charitable action program, left their mark on the beginnings of the model of the Spanish Welfare State.'

According to her, despite the consolidation of a publicly guaranteed social services system, it was deficient, and for this reason, the church managed to maintain its function as a provider of services, especially assistance and concerning those needs not covered by the public system of social services. This solidarity assistance space continues today, albeit no longer exclusive to the church's social work (although a large part of the NGOs operating in the field is indeed based on charitable works and ideas).

However, I do not believe that this particularity challenges the applicability of the theories. In fact, the foundations, sediments perhaps from the Franco era, although not simply the product of neoliberal doctrines, end up converging with the dominant objectives within the (neo)liberal ideology, as they have been applied in the EU—perhaps precisely because they stem from a Catholic social philosophy.

SALT: A SOCIAL LABORATORY?

> Salt is a social laboratory for what is going to happen with migration. (Pineda 2010)

> I like to say that Salt is a laboratory of social practices due to its peculiar situation. Salt, a unique municipality, a challenge for everyone. (Pineda 2012)

Given the descriptions made so far, the reader must ask, as I did, why is so much attention shed to the case of Salt? A first and plausible explanation is that Salt was considered a paradigmatic case in sociological and political terms, a situation that in one way or another could be extended to the whole of Catalonia or Spain. Perhaps there was an interest in spreading an alarmist image and taking advantage of the particular-exceptional moment that aroused all the media attention. Be that as it may, time has shown that the case of Salt has served particular purposes, and hence the idea of a social laboratory has been useful to analyse and understand how the various political-economic and symbolic processes interrelate.

It goes without saying that the idea of a social laboratory is a construct: It presupposes an exceptional moment while requiring a spatial limitation to subsequently implement special measures, which would be evaluated for later use in other similar contexts or at a general level. According to the meaning of the word *exceptionality*, much studied by Giorgio Agamben (2005) and recently rediscovered in times of pandemic, exceptional moments imply a suspension of normality (largely legal-political) for an indefinite amount of time, at least until the problem has been solved.

Although in Spain the concept of a social laboratory has a long history, it was first applied to the case of Salt by the former mayor Iolanda Pineda (Pineda 2010, 2012) in 2008:

> "'It is yet another consequence of the migratory fact. We have the feeling that we are a laboratory in Catalonia and we think that what happens in Salt will happen later in Catalonia", says Pineda, who admits that the municipality cannot be left alone "in this struggle" and therefore needs "all the help possible"' (Batlle 2008)

In this sense, locations such as Ca n'Anglada, El Ejido, Premià de Mar, and Salt constituted social observatories in terms of new culturalized sociabilities and social conflicts. They were also social laboratories in the sense that new forms of political conflict management were deployed, which used the cultural variable both in the way of understanding the problem and of solving it.

The fact is that since the first conflict in Ca n'Anglada in 1999 and subsequent attempts to solve the problems that were considered inherent to them, policies have been approved and implemented and experiences evaluated and exchanged between Catalan municipalities with a high percentage of immigration or high cultural diversity. In this sense, the same Catalan municipalities always appear: Salt, L'Hospitalet de Llobregat, El Vendrell, Figueres, Premià de Mar, Badalona, Terrassa, Manlleu, and Vic, to name just a few.

Some will say that what we see in Salt are the social consequences of the crisis, whereas others would reply that it is instead the possible consequences of 'multiculturalism' and Salt a sort of Catalan banlieue. However, as the former mayor recalls, what makes Salt a social laboratory is perhaps the interrelation among a high percentage of migration and feeble economy and high marginality—a juxtaposition that somehow allows bringing together various social problems that have been built on various scales and that constitute the logical-symbolic foundation.

Without a doubt, what made Salt famous, and marked a before and after, were the clashes in February 2010. Now, the ideological-symbolic formation of the conflict came from afar, both in a spatial and temporal sense. The interpretations proposed by officials and journalists, the only ones that I have been able to analyse from this point of view, had been elaborated during the years prior to the most critical moments. Attention had been drawn to the town in such a way that an exceptional social situation was being built (Wacquant 2007), which would require extraordinary measures or solutions, a genuine 'social laboratory'.

Many social actors intervene who do not coincide with each other, neither in their way of working, nor in their way of seeing the world or in their interests; yet a shared symbolic spectrum is formed between them all that has effects while it is constantly repeated and reified through opinion articles, news, policies, and.

Since the first incident in Salt, the media placed great emphasis on describing the social situation of the town as fragile, on the verge of chaos, constantly referring to the high number of immigrants and the difficult convivencia resulting from this. Largely also a consequence of the fact that the third sector organizations and the local administration, pending as they are more and more external funds and their continuous renewal, would benefit from promoting this state of fragility to justify their reason for being and the influx of resources.

During fieldwork, I observed a dissonance between the sensationalist journalistic image and social alarmism and the daily social reality, so it is certainly not unreasonable to talk about a stigmatizing campaign of Salt. A hypothesis shared by several of the interviewees residing in Salt, including a local police officer I interviewed:

> 'The truth is that the media has distorted it all quite a lot. The media focus has created precisely an insecurity but subjective of all, all, have created the same media a sense of insecurity to which must be added that there was an immigrant community that created much suspicion in the say in the native neighbour.'

This incongruity between the representation and the lived reality is neither a banal nor an arbitrary question because it often serves specific political purposes. Several reasons are underlying these campaigns denigrating Salt. One possible explanation is that they serve to apply a kind of moral geography—localized legitimizing narratives—with which the creation of a place of exceptional social intervention is justified. Campaigns also serve political purposes at the regional and local levels. At the regional level, the case of Salt comes to light in the media, along with other towns and neighbourhoods such as Lloret de Mar, Raval or Terrassa, in the course of a journalistic campaign by *La Vanguardia*, which encourages its journalists to search for news about matters of 'maximum political and moral importance', to portray a kind of moral geography of the crisis in Catalonia, closely related to migration. At the local level, there is interest in portraying the failure of the local government (in the hands of the PSC-ERC) in the management of social conflicts to demonstrate its weakness and obtain political revenue in the municipal elections held in May 2011. In short, we see that conservative interests converge at the regional and local levels, so it should not be surprising that there have been convergent manoeuvres between them.

In economic terms, there may also have been underlying interests. The social conflict around convivencia seems to have served as an argument to justify the large number of evictions in this area, the Barri Centre, even in comparison with other significant places in Catalan geography. At the same time, behind the bureaucratic appearance is the economic desire to transfer bank debt to the precarious private hands and, more concretely, Salt's lumpen-proletariat, in its majority immigrants from the Global South. This is achieved through structural violence based on what I call the 'geography of economic restructuring' (financial); through foreclosures and evictions, the State participates in what some authors describe as an exercise in 'state crime-corporation' (Bernat 2014), which consists of the lower layers of society assuming by force the losses created in the real estate sector. To this, we must add the future earnings for investors who acquire homes at derisory prices (if one compares them with the price at which they were purchased just 10 years ago). This zeal for accumulation by dispossession is undoubtedly an act of institutional and symbolic violence that is truly dangerous for social cohesion and convivencia. It ends up marginalizing a population group and inhibiting its settlement and social integration in the life of the town.

The preceding problematization reminds me of the persistent social problems and the resulting political landscape and projects that arose in the industrializing countries during the 19th and 20th centuries (see Lundsteen forthcoming for further elaboration).

In this sense, I argue that we see the reappearance of the discourses of the dangerous classes and with them a strong hint of (ethnocultural) differentialism. As with the 19th-century social question, several themes are at the foundation of the social conflicts in question: Urban space and housing, a criminalization and severe punishment of petty crime, and a massive mobility. Furthermore, like then, while the conflicts emerge as symptoms of the frequent crises of capitalist accumulation, the State and its satellite organizations (such as NGOs) play a quintessential role in managing the social outcome. They enable the reproduction of the conditions and social relations bound in culture, this way favouring unequal social relations and hindering radical social mobilization through a combination of repressive policing and cultural politics.

However, social sciences have played an equally important role, alongside the media (Champagne 1999; Gönen and Yonucu 2011), portraying and naming the social problems (Bourdieu et al. 1994), and continue to do so. In this sense, our entrenchment in society is more than obvious; trying to avoid or ignore this fact implies embarking on a neocolonial enterprise to which I hope contemporary anthropology especially is vehemently opposed. We are at an impasse that has been recurring since the origin of the social question and the political-academic (bourgeois) response to it.

In times of political crisis, and maybe due to a loss of legitimacy, the State clings on to the reminiscence of the KNWS, employing a series of punitive interventions hitting mainly the most vulnerable populations (constituted mainly by the Other in the national imageries of Catalanness and Spanishness) to create a sensation of security for the others (the native populations). Meanwhile, the accelerating political-economic restructuring weakens the social ties and the fabric sustaining the self-same system.

In this sense, zero-tolerance policies aimed at petty crime tend to hit the most marginalized and precarious populations, often the migrant Other. Moreover, while doing this, these are portrayed as disrespectful and morally corrupt people, a characterization that perversely naturalizes their social marginalization and supplies the conservative parties with discursive weaponry.

So, contemporary capitalist states depend on disciplinary and regulatory practices and social control, despite—or perhaps *because of*, as Desmond King suggests (1999)—their (neo)liberal foundation. Despite noticeable geographical and historical differences (and at the risk of sounding reductionist), when going back to the origins of capitalism, it seems clear that the (ab)use of power (colonialism, enclosure movements, forced migration, and so on), as an integral part of the control over populations through 'science', policing, and regulation of behaviour, and so on, with the aim of 'integration' into an exploitative political-economic system, has somehow always been present (Li 2014). How these are enforced, however, have changed. The free market does seem like an illusion (Harcourt 2011) when the great majority of the stable capitalist economies are progressively more and more dependent on punitive policies, increasing incarceration rates, and the criminalization, punishment, and stigmatization of petty crime (the kind of crime that poor people and working-class people resort to in times of [capitalist] crisis).

The elements of control gained with implementing punitive and restrictive actions are essential. Though they serve to discipline a group of people to ensure their entry into the formal labour market, it is also true that a lot of them have no place in it. In this sense, an important question arises: Have some sectors of the population of today's late capitalist society become superfluous, left to die, rather than serve as the old reserve army of labour, as Li (2014) suggests? Or are they, instead, occupying the lowest and most precarious positions in a segmented and informalized labour market, as recent developments in the app or gig-economy seem to suggest?

Although informal economic practices such as those expressed by the 'virtuous musician' in the metro are often appraised and well-received, the Roma street musician, the sub-Saharan street vendors selling sunglasses and handbags, or the scrap dealers are often frowned upon. Instead of praising their creativeness, independence, and entrepreneurship (words so often called for in these neoliberal times), their productiveness and contributions to the formal markets are made invisible and even criminalized. Thus, another positive effect that these practices might have is social reproduction. Of course, we should worry about petty crime because its effects on social relations and social cohesion in the neighbourhoods can be severe. However, instead of criminalizing these practices, I think we should rather go to the root of the problem; in these times where unemployment rates among young people exceed 50 percent, we should instead spend money on regularizing already existing informal (non-destructive) economic practices (such as the mayor of Bogotá did with the scrap dealers),[2] thus assuring better social conditions for these already working people.

SPACES OF HOPE AND THE PITFALLS OF THE LEFT

Finally, I want to contend the hegemonic problematization concerning Salt. Utterly contrary to what is often put forward, and despite worsening social conditions, I believe that Salt is a somewhat positive example of well-functioning diverse coexistence.

The struggle for social production of the space is inherently conflictual, and although these spaces are marginalized and dispossessed, one could argue that they show attractive signs of hope that might contribute to a reformulation of politics. In this sense, I propose to see these social conflicts as 'events' in the Badiouean sense. The popular mobilization and organization in response to and opposed to the socio-economic restructuring of the capitalist system take place in particular locations and focal points, places (the peripheries of the peripheries) that can possibly convert themselves into the centres of future alternative and hegemonic mobilizations. This way, the peripheralized spaces are 'spaces of hope' (Harvey 2000) and sites of potentiality that 'open[s] up the sociopolitical space for a multiplicity of new, though not always necessarily rosy, possibilities' (Hage 2010, 236). In this sense, I find two phenomena in the town exciting: The occupation of an empty building, named Bloc-Salt, by the foreclosure movement PAH, and the Ateneu Popular Coma-Cros.

In the wake of the new situations of defencelessness and structural violence, a foreclosure movement (Movement for the People Affected by the Mortgages, known as PAH) arose in Salt, a movement that started by organizing several meetings to inform people of their activities and (resorting to civil disobedience) mobilizing against new evictions. Interestingly the central axis of mobilization, the ground identity, seemed not to be based on ethnocultural markers, and a new identity of 'affected peoples' emerged. In time, this local section of PAH was able to mobilize itself. With the help and support of a great portion of the civil society of Salt' they managed to occupy an empty building (Europa Press 2013)—the property of a State society for the management of assets originating from the restructuring of the banking sector (Gestión de Activos Procedentes de la Reestructuración Bancaria, SAREB), also known as the 'bad bank'. This action was part of a new strategy that the PAH was beginning to employ, the purpose of which was to rehouse families of PAH who had been evicted and to negotiate future social housing.

Several (seemingly justified) critiques can undoubtedly be made about the movement's inner workings. Apparently, paternalistic and patronage dynamics ruled the social space (on several occasions, the members described the groups as a great family). However, when it came to allocating the flats—16 families had registered to live there—necessity always seems to have prevailed, instead of origin, for instance. All in all, the movement created a horizontal mobilization that shattered the native-migrant dichotomy and achieved significant participation of the affected and precarious peoples—an achievement that many previous mobilizations had failed to achieve.

In a similar vein, in 2013, several years of hard community work and organization to gain a civic centre seemed to produce results. Until then, the town had had two failed experiences of creating such a centre, Mas Mota and Can Panxut, and something similar seemed to be happening with Coma-Cros, where a socio-urbanistic project aimed at promoting the town as a cultural and university town (clearly favouring private and capital interest above the needs of the inhabitants of Salt) was originating. In light of this situation, a group of inhabitants mobilized under the name of Espai Salt. The main aim of this mobilization was to recover the popular or working-class spirit of the space and set in motion a collective project of the numerous entities and inhabitants of Salt: The building of a self-organized community centre, Ateneu Popular Coma-Cros, in this way providing a shared space for all of the inhabitants of Salt. They mobilized demonstrations and public actions to claim the space, and after some time, the local government started what they called 'a participatory process'. In the beginning, the process aroused much excitement, but the government only offered feeble promises, and still, after 18 months of negotiation, no real power had been transferred to the assembly by 2014. Nonetheless, in 2017, and after much struggle, an agreement was finally reached with the Town Council, and the place has been work in process since then.

So, even though the working-class populations are pitted against each other in the political realm following concepts of civic and national belonging, not everybody follows this line of argument; a small group of people—both native and non-native—see things differently. They do not emphasize cultural difference as the groundbreaker but rather endorse a shared (neighbourhood or working-class) identity. In this sense, I believe that the fate of the industrial sectors of Gassol and the Ateneu Popular Coma-Cros are crucial points of future antagonisms: Whose 'right to the city' are we talking about, the right to capitalist accumulation of the social space of Salt, and further gentrification, or the social production of spaces for the contemporary inhabitants of Salt?

Many horizontal mobilizations of left-wing associations and formations obviate other inequalities, mainly along the lines of race or ethnicity (Bonilla-Silva 1997, 2010) and gender (Roberts 2014); inequalities that structure the social world in equally important ways. Thus, any alternative or popular movement in the town will have to take the growing antagonisms between the use and exchange value of the urban space alongside power inequalities per ethnocultural, racial, and gender lines (Goonewardena and Kipfer 2005) seriously. By failing to consider these structures and mobilize them coherently, the movements are bound to reproduce them and thereby leaves the terrain open for right-wing readings but, above all, hinders a radical change of the hegemonic structures,3 or they will end up doing the labour of a new societal model for the town that in the end will displace a significant part of the working-class and poor inhabitants, who will not be able to afford to live there.

SKETCHES TOWARDS A RADICAL POLITICS OF DIFFERENCE

Although some might righteously claim that diversity is a sociocultural construction, I propose considering diversity to be a natural fact for the sake of argument. The way we understand this diversity, classifying it, conferring on it one meaning or another, is a human construction. Meanwhile, instead of fighting against contra-natural acts, too human indeed, which promote separation and the purification of species, races, or culture, minority expressions are often politically fostered (through cultural politics UNESCO-style).

Instead, I believe that if we are to support the flourishing of diversity, it is necessary to create equal opportunities, not only in a liberal-economic way: '[W]e must recognise that the promise of the city consists *not* in simply celebrating the plurality of *actually existing differences* given to us under the signs of "cultural diversity": multiculturalism, diaspora and creolization' (Goonewardena and Kipfer 2005, 676). The only way to achieve a real plethora of differences is by fighting and annihilating the inherent injustices of the social world in which we live today, where socio-economic inequalities reign: Inequalities that have to be addressed both in their origin (socio-economic exploitation) and in their political, academic, and bureaucratic institutionalization, expression, and foundation.

In this sense, I believe that we, in both academic/scientific and political terms, have been avoiding the need to take a stance concerning this new social question derived from migration from the Global South as a social phenomenon. Uncritically employing conceptions of multiculturalism, interculturalism, and tolerance promotes latent ideas of nativeness, exclusionary belonging, and whiteness, which give more voice to some and silence others, thus reproducing the underlying unequal power relations. Instead, we must become aware and, thus, more critical of our position within the relations of social domination (based primarily on ethnocultural or racial, gender, and class identities) and the equivalent concerning the knowledge that we produce and how we produce it (Santos 2014).

In this social context, another simplistic narrative has been working for too long among those on the left: The problem is *neoliberalism* or *finance capitalism*. In this sense, a great majority of the European left-wing parties are struggling with a fantasy: The return of the social and the praise of the (long-lost) virtues of the Welfare State. I believe, on the contrary, that the findings of this book suggest—although a more refined analysis and further study are undoubtedly necessary—the confirming of an underlying systemic contradiction: that a social State and equal society is increasingly difficult if not impossible to incorporate within a (neoliberal) capitalist economy.

CHAPTER 6 NOTES

1. Furthermore, this new formation of the State should be analysed and compared in relation to other Western State formations, among others considering its racial and colonial foundations and principles (Goldberg 2002; Anderson 2013)—a task that I have been forced to postpone due to time and space limitations.
2. See http://www.wiegoinbrief.org/bogota-colombia/
3. In this sense, Islamophobia also seems to be significant, both in the context of the field work and in Europe in general, and although I would have liked to be able to consider in depth this phenomenon and its material and ideological basis, due to the limits of time and space I have not been able to do so, see Lundsteen 2020a.

Appendix

Dramatis Personae

The characters described here are all people I had lasting relationships with during fieldwork or interviewed and quoted during the book. They appear under a pseudonym except for the known public persons.

Abdul: 30 years old.[1] Resident in Santa Eugenia St (Catalunya Square, Barri Centre). Born in the Kolda region of Senegal, he had lived in Salt since 1995. He shared a flat with his parents, three siblings, his cousin, and his wife and children. He worked in various sectors, construction, package factories, picking fruit, and had a clothing store for a season.

Aisha: 31 years old. Resident in Àngel Guimerà St (Barri Centre), where I lived for three months in 2012. Born in the Sedhiou region of Senegal. She worked as a cleaner in a hotel in Girona, although she did not have a residence permit.

Albert: 40 years old. Resident in Barri Vell and born in Salt. During fieldwork, he was unemployed but renovating the house where he lived with his French partner and children.

Alim: 38 years old. Resident in Major St (Barri Vell). Born in Oujda, Morocco. He had been living in Salt for 10 years, where he moved from Banyoles. Most of his family continued to live in Banyoles. He was part of EINA and worked for several years as a social worker, and was also studying a degree in philosophy.

Ariadna: 36 years old. Resident in Barri Vell, where we shared a flat for two months in 2012. Civil servant.

Assane: 37 years old. Resident in Santa Eugenia, Girona. Born in the Kolda region of Senegal. He is the younger brother of Demba's mother. He has a 12-year-old boy and was married to a Catalan woman. He had been unemployed for two years, although he sporadically worked as a waiter.

Babacar: 36 years old. Resident in Barri Centre, born in Senegal. He worked with all kinds of technological arrangements, small reparations, and resale of second-hand objects. He had also run a grocery store.

Barry: 55 years old. Resident in Àngel Guimerà St (Barri Centre). Originally from Senegal. After several years working as a bricklayer in the company of the former mayor's father, he was unemployed for a few years.

Bouba: 43 years old. Resident in Àngel Guimerà St (Barri Centre). He had been living in Salt since 2008. He arrived in Spain in 1994 but was later deported and came back by boat a few years later. Before arriving to Salt he spent some periods in Figueres, El Ejido, Gandia, Lleida, and Jaén. He was my flatmate before moving to Major St (Barri Centre). He had a Romanian partner while we were living together, although they separated after a few months. He was married to a Catalan woman. He worked at a slaughterhouse in Salt with another man's contract. He did not have a residence permit.

Carles: 34 years old. Resident in Major St (Veïnat). Born in Barcelona. Student.

Demba: 26 years. Main informant. Resident in several flats of Barri Centre. Born in the Koulda region, Senegal, he had lived in Salt since 2000. His mother lived in the same neighbourhood in Torras i Bagès St, with her husband (stepfather), who has been in the city for more than 30 years and had Spanish nationality, the cousin, and his half-brother. His sister lived in Barcelona. Demba mainly worked in the informal economy and had only worked for short periods in the Haribo factory and the Central Market in Girona.

Edgard: 34 years old. Resident in Barri Vell. He worked at La Mirona as a sound technician and on a community music project.

Francesc: 32 years old. Resident in Barri Vell. Originally from Mataró. Unemployed.

Houri: 40 years. Resident in Barri Vell. Born in Guinea-Conakry. Manager of the bar Fouta.

Ibrahim: 43 years old. Resident in Torras i Bages St, next to the local market (Barri Centre). Born in Larache, Morocco. After five years in the Netherlands, he moved to Salt in 2007. His wife was from Morocco, too. He was working as a hairdresser at Catalunya Square.

Joana: 35 years old. Resident in Sant Romà (Veïnat). Joana worked at the University of Girona, was part of EINA and worked in various places both in Salt and Girona as a social worker. She had a degree in sociology and completed a master's degree in Youth and Society. She was originally from Sant Andreu (Barcelona) and lived in Salt since 2004 (in Girona since 2002).

John: 34 years old. Resident in the housing project Teixidors, originally from Nigeria. He studied economics, but the studies were not validated. After working in different jobs, such as security guard, he engaged in illicit businesses such as selling drugs or buying tickets through the internet. His partner is the cousin of Abdul, a 31-year-old Senegalese woman.

Julius: 38 years old. Resident in Torras i Bagès St (Barri Centre). Born in the Democratic Republic of the Congo. He ran a bar with Demba in Torras i Bagès St. He was convicted of a scam.

Mahmadou: 34 years old. Resident at Doctor Ferran St (Barri Centre). Originally from Casamance, Senegal. He lived with his two cousins. I met him in Catalan classes. He did not have a residence permit, although he was in the process of regularization. He lived in Salt for more than three years. He was an amateur photographer and recorder of videos, especially for weddings and other celebrations.

Mansour: 32 years old. Resident in Belgium, born in Dakar, Senegal. Aisha's husband. He was a musician by family tradition, from a musicians' caste, griou/djeli, but he had no papers and was not employed.

Marc: 26 years old. Resident in Sils, born in Salt. Unemployed, worked in construction, sometimes worked in a casino. His parents had a bar in Salt where they dealt drugs and laundered money.

Mostafa: 34 years old. Resident in Josep Irla St (Barri Centre-Veïnat), where we shared a flat for eight months. Originally from Al Arroui (Mount Arruit), Morocco. He had previously lived four years in Vic and shorter seasons in Frankfurt (Germany), the Netherlands, Belgium, and France. His partner was originally from Honduras.

Omar: 39 years old, resident in Girona. Soccer companion. He was a Catalan speaker and professor of religion at an institute.

Taino: 32 years old. Resident at Major St (Barri Vell). Fellow professor and researcher who was doing a doctorate at the University of Girona in Critical Criminology at the time of the fieldwork. Born in Barcelona.

Toqueer: 29 years old. Resident in Josep Irla St (Barri Centre-Veïnat), where we shared a flat for some months in 2012 and later Miguel de Cervantes St (Veïnat). Born in Bangladesh. He had lived in Salt for eight years. He worked as a bricklayer and had been studying engineering in Bangladesh when his brother, who also lived in Salt, convinced him to leave and go to Spain. He had a partner, originally from Honduras.

INTERVIEWEES

Andoni: 56 years old. Lived in La Massana (previously lived in the area of Catalunya Square). Member of the neighbourhood association AVV de la Massana and the platform Gent per Salt.

Ángel: 58 years old. Lived in the area of Catalunya Square. He was born in Andalusia, resident in Salt since 1975.

Alba: 33 years old. Lived in Girona. Neighbourhood community mediator, social worker of the NGO Vincle.

Andreu Bover: 48 years old. Head of the Area of Convivencia and Integration, an administrative department of the City Council.

Carmen: 46 years old. Lived in housing estate Grup Verge de María (Barri Centre). Born in Valladolid, resident in Salt since 1990. She worked as a cleaner in the multinational cleaning company ISS since 1995.

Carolina: 63 years old. Lives in Torras i Bagès St (Barri Centre). Born in Peru, resident in Salt since 1976, previously had lived two years in Bisbal d'Empordà. She worked as a cleaner of community hall rooms and stairs.

Concepción: 48 years old. Lived in the area of Catalunya Square. Born in Barcelona and later moved to Sant Feliú de Guíxols. She worked as a waitress, in a cork factory, in a grocery store, and finally, eight years as a cleaner. She was unemployed for almost two years and had little economic allowance left.

Conchita: 53 years old. Lived around Catalunya Square since 2003 (first lived a few years in Pontmajor, Girona). Born in Argentina (Buenos Aires), she had been living in Spain for 12 years. She worked as a cleaner, a property manager, ran a shop with her husband, and worked as a civic agent but was now unemployed with no financial allowance left, and even considered going to England, where one of her children lived.

David Estévez: 38 years old. Lived in La Massana. Councillor of Security in Salt from 2007 to 2011.

Federic: 65 years old. Lived in Barri Centre. Vice president of the neighbourhood association AVV de Barri Centre.

Iolanda Pineda: 36 years old. Lived in La Massana. Member of PSC, the Catalan Socialdemocratic Party. Mayor of Salt from 2007 to 2011.

Ivan: 44 years old. Lived in Veïnat. He was the coordinator of the cultural and social associations of Salt. He was originally from Girona and had lived in Salt for 10 years.

Jaume: 44 years old. Lived in Francesc Macià St (La Massana). Veronica's sentimental partner. Born in Valencia, resident in Salt since 2009, although he bought the apartment in 1995. He worked as a computer scientist at the CSIC in Barcelona.

Joan: 51 years old. Lived in the housing estate La Sagrada Família (Barri Centre). Born in Sant Gregori, resident in Salt since 1967. He was originally a construction worker. He was the president of the housing estate.

Jordi: 52 years old. Lived in Barri Vell. Born in Berguedà, he lived in Salt since 1982. He worked as a civil servant in public administration.

Josep: 73 years old. Lived in Ramón Sambola St (Barri Centre). Born in Alicante (son of an Andalusian and a Valencian), resident in Salt since 1970. He was previously a baker but was retired.

Júlia: 55 years old. Lived in Barri Vell. Born in Valencia, resident in Salt since 1983.

Marta: 34 years old. Lived in Verdaguer St (Barri Vell). Born in Salt. She worked as a Catalan teacher at the Consorci per a la Normalització Lingüística.

Nadia: 19 years old. Lived in Torras i Bagès St (Barri Centre). Born in Palafrugell, daughter of Moroccans, resident in Salt since she was five years old (1999). She studied Psychology at the University of Girona.

Pau: 38 years old. Lived in Veïnat. Small businessman of a computer company. He was born in Salt, although he had been living more than 10 years abroad (in Girona and Barcelona).

Pilar: 58 years old. Lived in the area of Catalunya Square. Born in Andalusia, she had been living in Salt since 1975.

Pere: 52 years old. Lived in Francesc Macià St (Barri Centre). Born in Salt. Member of the Moviment Anti-ARU, Consell de Presidents d'Escales and Televisió Vila de Salt. He worked in a slaughterhouse.

Ramon Artal: 65 years old. Lived in Vila Square (Barri Vell) in one of the oldest houses in the town. Born in Figueres, resident in Salt since 1986. Former municipal architect (1986–2011).

Ricard: 34 years old. Lived in Girona. Neighbourhood community mediator and social worker at the NGO Vincle.

Toñi: 50 years old. Lived in Barri Centre. Born in Sabadell, resident in Salt since 1985. President of the neighbourhood association AVV de Barri Centre.

Verónica: 45 years old. Lived in Francesc Macià St (La Massana). Born in Portugal, she lived most of her life in Venezuela. Resident in Salt since 2009, she had previously lived in Sant Cugat del Vallès since 2005. She has a postgraduate degree in bioinformatics. She worked as a cashier in a supermarket and as a pollster for the National Statistics Institute (within the Barrido Project).

NOTES

1. The age of the people is often the approximate age as estimated by me during fieldwork because I did not always get to know their age.

Bibliography

ABC. 1984. "Barcelona, Cerrada." *ABC*, March 2, 1984. Frontpage.

Abrams, Philip. 1988. "Notes on the Difficulty of Studying the State (1977)." *Journal of Historical Sociology* 1 (1): 58–89.

ACN. 2009. "Detenen un jove que acumula una trentena d'antecedents per entrar a robar en una ferreteria de Salt." *ACN*, May 05, 2009.

———. 2010. "Un projecte de l'Obra Social 'la Caixa' dóna a Salt 465.000 euros per integrar nens i joves immigrants." *CCMA*, September 15, 2010. Retrieved from https://www.ccma.cat/324/un-projecte-de-lobra-social-la-caixa-dna-a-salt-465-000-euros-per-integrar-nens-i-joves-immigrants/noticia/854909/

———. 2011. "Entitats de Salt convoquen una manifestació a favor de la convivència." *El Gerió Digital*, January 20, 2011. Retrieved from https://www.gerio.cat/noticia/52924/les-entitats-de-salt-diuen-que-la-manifestacio-pro-convivencia-ara-te-mes-sentit-que-mai.

ACN. ARA. 2011. "L'alcaldessa de Salt crida 'a la serenitat i el seny', com a resposta a la mort del menor." *Ara*, January 20, 2011. Retrieved from https://www.ara.cat/societat/salt-alcaldessa-mort-aldarulls-convivencia-immigracio_0_412159253.html.

———. 2012. "Neix la Factoria Cultural Coma Cros de Salt, nova seu d'El Canal." *Ara*, September 13, 2012.

ACN. El Punt. 2010. "Salt detecta casos d'immigrants que ocupen pisos embargats i provoquen problemes de convivència." *El Punt*, February 09, 2010.

———. 2011. "El conflicte a Salt continua amb la crema de cinc cotxes i set motos." *El Punt*, January 16, 2011. Retrieved from http://www.elpuntavui.cat/societat/article/5-societat/357586-el-conflicte-a-salt-continua-amb-la-crema-de-cinc-cotxes-i-set-motos.html.

Agamben, Giorgio. 2005. *State of Exception*. Chicago: University of Chicago Press.

———. 2011. "¿Qué es un dispositivo?" *Sociológica* 26 (73): 249–64.

Agrela, Belen. 2006. *Análisis antropológico de las políticas sociales dirigidas a la población inmigrante.* Doctoral Thesis presented at the Department of Social Work and Social Services at the University of Granada.

Agrela, Belen, and Gunther Dietz 2005. ¿Oposición entre actores gubernamentales y no gubernamentales? Emergencia de regímenes de multinivel y diversificación público-privada de la política de inmigración en España. *Migración y Desarrollo* 4: 20–41.

Ajuntament de Salt. 2011. *Salt és el meu poble.* Anglès: Pagès Editorial.

Akasoy, Anna. 2010. "Convivencia and Its Discontents: Interfaith Life in Al-Andalus." *International Journal of Middle East Studies* 42 (3): 489–99.

Alberch, Ramon, and Jaume Portella. 1978. "Aspectes demogràfics i de l'activitat econòmica a Salt, 1900–1970." *Revista de Girona* 85: 389–94.

Allen, Christopher. 2010. *Islamophobia.* Farnham, UK: Ashgate.

Allport, Gordon W. 1954. *The Nature of Prejudice*. Cambridge, MA: Addison Wesley.

Álvarez-Uría, Fernando, and Julia Varela. 1989. *Sujetos frágiles: ensayos de sociología de la desviación*. Fondo de Cultura Económica.

Anderson, Bridget. 2013. *Us and Them? The Dangerous Politics of Immigration Control.* Oxford: Oxford University Press.

Antena 3. 2011 "Los nervios a flor de piel." *Espejo público*, January 24, 2011. Retrieved from https://www.antena3.com/programas/espejo-publico/nervios-flor-piel_2011012457472a234beb287180b9a868.html.

Antonsich, Marco. 2015. "Nation and Nationalism." In *The Wiley Blackwell Companion to Political Geography*, edited by J. Agnew, V. Mamadouh, A. Secor, and J. Sharp, 297–310. London: Wiley-Blackwell.

Aramburu, Mikel. 2001. "El mito de la 'huída' autóctona. El caso de Ciutat Vella." *Scripta Nova. Revista electrónica de Geografía y Ciencias Sociales* 94 (63).

———. 2002. *Los otros y nosotros. imágenes del inmigrante en ciutat vella de Barcelona.* Madrid: Ministerio de Educación, Cultura y Deporte.

———. 2018. "Neighbourhood Memories: Bridges or Barriers? Old and New Migrants in Catalan Working-Class Areas." In *Exploring Cities and Countries of the World*, edited by Kathie Summers, 43–69. Hauppauge, NY: Nova Science Publishers.

Aranda Ocaña, Mónica, Gemma Chaves Castillo, Maika Moreno Aldea, Juan David Posada Segura, Carolina Rivas Trullols and Iñaki Rivera Beira. 2005. *El populisme punitiu. Anàlisi de les reformes i contra-reformes del Sistema Penal a Espanya (1995–2005).* Barcelona: Universitat de Barcelona.

Arbaci, Sonia, and Teresa Tapada-Berteli. 2012. "Social Inequality and Urban Regeneration in Barcelona City Centre: Reconsidering Success." *European Urban and Regional Studies* 19 (3): 287–311.

Àrea de Integració i Covivència, Ajuntament de Salt. 2012. *Proyecto Barrido.* Salt: Ajuntament de Salt.

Artal, Ramon. 2014. "El rec, canal de cultura." *Salt17190—UniverSalt* 7, 2014.

Azurmendi, Mikel. 2001. *Estampas de El Ejido*. Madrid: Taurus.

———. 2002a. "Inmigrar para vivir en democracia." *El País*, January 22, 2002.

———. 2002b. "Democracia y cultura." *El País*, February 23, 2002.

Bacchi, Carol. 2009. *Analysing Policy: What's the Problem Represented to Be?* Frenchs Forest, NSW: Pearson Australia Pty Ltd.
———. 2012. 'Why Study Problematizations? Making Politics Visible.' *Open Journal of Political Science* 2 (1): 1–8.
Back, Les. 2009. "Researching Community and Its Moral Projects." *Twenty-First Century Society* 4 (2): 201–14.
Badenes, Jesús. 2011. "Expulsen d'Espanya el conegut multireincident de Salt Morad El Hassani." *Diari de Girona*, March 10, 2011.
Badosa, Narcis. 2011. "Elaboració i pràctica d'un pla de ciutadania al municipi de Salt." Facultat de Ciències de l'Educació: Universitat de Girona.
Balibar, Etienne, and Immanuel Wallerstein. 1991. *Race, Nation, Class: Ambiguous Identities*. London: Verso.
Barrera, Montse. 2008. "El ministre de Treball i Immigració visitarà Salt dilluns per conèixer de prop la realitat del municipi." *El Punt*, September 25, 2008.
———. 2009a. "Menors amb llicència per robar." *El Punt*, August 26, 2009.
———. 2009b. "Un policia local va haver de disparar per dispersar una baralla la mig del carrer a Salt, la nit de Nadal." *El Punt*, October 29, 2009.
———. 2010a. "Pineda diu que no està satisfeta de la seguretat al municipi." *El Punt*, January 26, 2010.
———. 2010b. "Els robatoris de bicicletes es continuen produint a Salt." *El Punt*, February 03, 2010.
———. 2010c. "La problemàtica dels 'pisos ocupats' de Salt preocupa i molesta veïns, propietaris i immobiliàries." *El Punt*, February 09, 2010.
———. 2010d. "Cinc homes armats assalten un bar de Salt i apallisen la parella que el regenta." *El Punt*, February 11, 2010.
———. 2010e. "Ajuntament i entitats de Salt reclamen als jutges l'aplicació estricta de la llei en els casos de delicte reincident." *El Punt*, February 22, 2010.
———. 2011. "Aldarulls a Salt en un acte de suport al lladre malferit." *El Punt* January 15, 2011.
Barth, Frederik. 1969. *Ethnic Groups and Boundaries. The Social Organization of Culture Difference*.
Batlle, Eduard. 2008. "Dos de cada tres naixements a Salt corresponen a fills d'immigrants." *El Punt*, February 21, 2008.
Bauman, Zygmunt. 1992. *Intimations of Postmodernity*. London: Routledge.
Berg, Mette Louise, and Nando Sigona. 2013. "Ethnography, Diversity and Urban Space." *Identities* 20 (4): 347–60.
Bernat, Ignasi. 2014. "Eviction and Immigrants: Ethnography in a Damaged Community." *Revista Crítica Penal y Poder* 7: 35–63.
Boades i Raset, Joan. 1988. "La transformació de Salt per la indústria tèxtil." *Revista de Girona* 126: 75–80.
Bonilla-Silva, Eduardo. 1997. "Rethinking Racism: Toward a Structural Interpretation." *American Sociological Review* 62 (3): 465–80.
———. 2010. *Racism without Racists: Color-Blind Racism and the Persistence of Racial Inequality in the United States*. Vol. 3. Lanham, MD: Rowman & Littlefield Publishers.

Bourdieu, Pierre. 1977. *Outline of a Theory of Practice*. Cambridge: Cambridge University Press.
———. 1990. *Logic of Practice*. Reprint. Stanford, CA: Stanford University Press.
———. 1999. *The Weight of the World: Social Suffering in Contemporary Society*. Stanford, CA: Stanford University Press.
———. 2003. "Participant Objectivation." *Journal of the Royal Anthropological Institute* 9 (2): 281–94.
Bourdieu, Pierre, Loïc Wacquant, and Samar Farage. 1994. "Rethinking the State: Genesis and Structure of the Bureaucratic Field." *Sociological Theory* 12 (1): 1–18.
Bourgois, Philippe. 2006. "Anthropology in the Global State of Emergency." In *Engaged Observer. Anthropology, Advocacy, and Activism*, edited by Victoria Sanford and Asale Angel-Ajani, ix–xii. New Brunswick, NJ: Rutgers University Press.
Bover i Pagespetit, Andreu. 2003. "Factoria Cultural Coma Cros de Salt." In *Nous usos per a antics espais industrials*. Girona: Universitat de Girona.
Burawoy, Michael. 2000. *Global Ethnography. Forces, Connections, and Imaginations in a Postmodern World*. Edited by Michael Burawoy. Berkeley: University of California Press.
———. 2009. *The Extended Case Method: Four Countries, Four Decades, Four Great Transformations, and One Theoretical Tradition*. Berkeley: University of California Press.
Cachón Rodríguez, Lorenzo. 2008. "Integración, conflictos e inmigración en Europa: Nuevos desafíos desde la ciudadanía. Una introducción." In *Conflictos e Inmigración: Experiencias en Europa*, edited by Lorenzo Cachón Rodríguez. Madrid: Colección Estudios.
———. 2011. "Conflictos e inmigración en Europa: Presentación de una problemática para reforzar la convivencia." In *Inmigración y conflictos en Europa: Aprender para una mejor convivencia*, edited by Lorenzo Cachón Rodríguez. Barcelona: Editorial Hacer.
———. 2015. "Tipología de conflictos ligados a la inmigración y de respuestas institucionales: Lecciones Europeas." In *Análisis, prevención y transformación de conflictos en contextos de inmigración*, edited by Carlos Giménez Romero and Paloma Gómez Crespo, 95–114. Madrid: UAM Ediciones.
Calhoun, Craig. 2002. "Imagining Solidarity: Cosmopolitanism, Constitutional Patriotism and the Public Sphere." *Public Culture* 14 (1): 147–72.
Calhoun, Craig. 2010. "The public sphere in the field of power." *Social Science History* 34 (3): 301–335.
Cardarelli, G., and M. Rosenfeld. 1998. *Las participaciones de la pobreza. Programas y proyectos sociales*. Buenos Aires: Paidós.
Cáritas Salt. 2008. *Projecte comunitats*.
Carranco, Rebeca. 2010. "Los inmigrantes de Salt, divididos." *El País*, February 28, 2010. Retrieved from https://elpais.com/diario/2010/02/28/catalunya/1267322839_850215.html.
Carreras, Tapi. 2010. "Adhesius de protesta a comerços del Barri Vell." *Diari de Girona*, February 24, 2010.

Casal dels Infants. 2013. "Salt, trabajando por la convivencia y el desarrollo." *Casal dels Infants*, January 26, 2012. Retrieved from: https://projecteicisalt.wordpress.com/ (February 26, 2013).

CCMA, TV3. 2010a. "Es crearà una taula de convivència a Salt." *Telenotícies TV3,* March 2, 2010. Retrieved from https://www.ccma.cat/tv3/alacarta/programa/es-creara-una-taula-de-convivencia-a-salt/video/2748350/.

———. 2010b. "Salt. Assaig de convivència." *30 Minutos*. Catalan Corporation of Audiovisual Media (CCMA). April 12, 2010. Retrieved from https://www.ccma.cat/tv3/alacarta/30-minuts/salt-assaig-de-convivencia/video/2832230/.

Cervera, Jordi, Montserrat Ventura, and Diana Montsalve. 2001. "El Barri de Sant Cugat: Una Ciutat Jardí a Salt." *Revista de Girona* 207: 398–405.

Cesari, Jocelyne. 2006. *Securitization and Religious Muslims in Western Europe After 9/11: Why the Term Islamophobia Is More a Predicament than an Explanation.* Submission to the Changing Landscape of Citizenship and Security 6th PCRD of European Commission.

Champagne, Patrick. 1999. "The View from the Media." In *The Weight of the World. Social Suffering in Contemporary Society*, edited by Pierre Bourdieu, et al., 46–60. Stanford, CA: Stanford University Press.

Clara, Josep. 1977. "Salt a mitjans segle XIX. L'origen de la ma d'obra atreta per la indústria tèxtil." *Revista de Girona* 78: 39–47.

Clua i Fainé, Montserrat. 2011. "Catalan, Immigrants and Charnegos: 'Race', 'Cultura' and 'Mixture' in Catalan Nationalist Rhetoric." *Revista de Antropología Social* 1: 55–75.

Cohen, Anthony. 1985. *The Symbolic Construction of Community*. London: Routledge.

Cole, John W., and Eric R. Wolf. 1999. *The Hidden Frontier: Ecology and Ethnicity in an Alpine Valley*. Berkeley: University of California Press.

Colectivo IOÉ. 2012. *Impactos de la crisis sobre la población inmigrante. Estudio promovido por la Organización Internacional para las Migraciones*. Madrid: Colectivo IOÉ. Retrieved from: http://www.colectivoioe.org/uploads/0bae582aa3b0842a9eaf50cde16f4f97d9527bcb.pdf

Collier, Stephen J. 2012. "Neoliberalism as Big Leviathan, or a Response to Wacquant and Hilgers." *Social Anthropology* 20 (2): 186–95.

Comaroff, Jean, and John L. Comaroff. 2006. "Criminal Obsessions, after Foucault: Postcoloniality, Policing, and the Metaphysics of Disorder." In *Law and Disorder in the Postcolony*. Chicago: University of Chicago Press.

Comisión Superior de Ordenación Urbana de la Provincia de Gerona.1956. Plan General de Ordenación de Gerona y su zona de influencia. Plan Comarcal. II Memoria. Girona. https://www.girona.cat/adminwebs/docs/0/2/02-_memoria_b.pdf.

Comisiones Obreras (CCOO). 2011. Mapa de l'atur a Catalunya 2011. CCOO.

Consell de Ciutat. 2012. Normes de composició i funcionament de l'òrgan de participació ciutadana consell de ciutat.

Consorci del Ter. 2021. "Què és?" Accessed October 5, 2021. https://www.consorcidelter.cat/seu-electronica/consorci/que-es.

Conversi, Daniele. 1999. "Ideological Fragmentation, Cultural Nationalism and State Violence: Euskadi and Catalonia (1939–1968)." *Canadian Review of Studies in Nationalism* 26 (1–2): 37–52.

Cosculluela, Feran. 2008. "La población extranjera en Salt cae debido a la crisis económica." *El Periódico*, October 12, 2008. Retrieved from https://www.elperiodico.com/es/sociedad/20081210/la-poblacion-extranjera-en-salt-cae-debido-a-la-crisis-economica-69054.

———. 2010. "Las protestas por la inseguridad en Salt degeneran en un brote xenófobo." *El Periódico*, February 26, 2010. Retrieved from https://www.elperiodico.com/es/sociedad/20100225/las-protestas-por-la-inseguridad-en-salt-degeneran-en-un-brote-xenofobo-110338.

———. 2012. "La policía de Salt patrullará con un perro por los edificios." *El Periódico*, August 4, 2012.

———. 2013. "Salt cierra las fuentes públicas." *La Vanguardia*, August 15, 2013. Retrieved from https://www.lavanguardia.com/local/girona/20130815/54379455000/salt-cierra-fuentes-publicas.html.

Cruz, Helena. 2014. *Barris i crisi. Estudi de cas de Salt*. IGOP: Barcelona. Available from: https://barrisicrisi.files.wordpress.com/2014/03/salt-barris-i-crisi-igop-22.pdf.

De Genova, Nicholas P. 2002. "Migrant "Illegality" and Deportability in Everyday Life." *Annual Review of Anthropology* 31: 419–47.

Delgado, Manuel, ed. 1997. *Urbanitats. Ciutat i immigració*. Barcelona: Centre de Cultura Contemporània de Barcelona (CCCB).

———. 2006. "Nuevas retóricas para la exclusión social." In *Flujos migratorios y su (des)control. Puntos de vista pluridisciplinarios*, edited by R. Bergalli. Barcelona: Anthropos.

———. 2012. "El espacio público como ideología." *Athenea Digital* 12 (1): 241–46.

Departament d'Integració i Convivència, Ajuntament de Salt. 2011. "Proyecto Barrido"—Estudi poblacional per zones 2012.

Di Masso, Andrés and John Dixon. 2015. "More than words: Place, discourse and the struggle over public space in Barcelona." *Qualitative Research in Psychology* 12 (1): 45–60.

Diari de Girona. 1986a. "Menor detenido en Salt por robo con intimidación." *Diari de Girona*, February 13, 1986.

———. 1986b. "Tirón en Salt." *Diari de Girona*, February 13, 1986.

———.1987. "Robo con intimidación en una tienda de Salt." *Diari de Girona,* February 31, 1987.

———. 2010. "Xerrada CiU i la plataforma expliquen l'ARU als veïns de Salt." *Diari de Girona,* July 16, 2010.

———. 2011. "Detenen un home a Salt per cremar un cotxe de la policia." *Diari de Girona*, November 19, 2011. Retrieved from https://www.diaridegirona.cat/girona/2011/11/19/detenen-home-salt-cremar-cotxe-policia/530314.html.

———. 2012. "'Passadissos nets i segurs' a Salt." *Diari de Girona*, February 6, 2012.

Dikeç, Mustafa. 2007. *Badlands of the Republic: Space, Politics and Urban Policy*. Malden, MA: Blackwell Publishing.

Duneier, Mitchell. 1999. *Sidewalk*. New York: Farrar, Straus and Giroux.
———. 2016. *Ghetto: The Invention of a Place, the History of an Idea*. New York: Farrar, Strauss and Giroux.
Dymski, Gary. 2009. "Racial Exclusion and the Political Economy of the Subprime Crisis." *Historical Materialism* 17 (2): 149–79.
Edensor, Tim. 2004. "Automobility and National Identity." *Theory, Culture & Society* 21 (4–5): 101–20. https://doi.org/10.1177/0263276404046063.
———. 2006. "Reconsidering National Temporalities." *European Journal of Social Theory* 9 (4): 525–45. https://doi.org/10.1177/1368431006071996.
El Periódico. 2009. "Detenidos dos hombres por robar en varias joyerías con tarjetas falsas en Salt." *El Periódico*, September 18, 2009.
———. 2010. "Los inmigrantes que regentan tiendas y otros negocios en Salt también se quejan de la ola de robos." *El Periódico*, February 26, 2010.
El Punt. 2008. "Sobre Salt." *El Punt*, December 11, 2008.
———. 2010. "Els alcaldes gironins no es plantegen deixar d'empadronar immigrants sense papers." *El Punt*, January 13, 2010.
El Punt. Editorial. 2008. "Montilla en pren nota." *El Punt*, June 10, 2008.
El Punt. Redacció. 1986. "Per una cigarreta apunyalen i fereixen greument un jove, a Salt." *El Punt*, February 11, 1986.
ERAM (Escola Universitària). 2021. "What Is ERAM?" Accessed October 5, 2021. https://www.eram.cat/en/eu-eram/the-school.
Erickson, Brad. 2011. "Utopian Virtues: Muslim Neighbors, Ritual Sociality, and the Politics of Convivència." *American Ethnologist* 38 (1): 114–31.
Esposito, John L., and Ibrahim Kalin, eds. 2011. *Islamophobia. The Challenge of Pluralism in the 21st Century.* Oxford: Oxford University Press.
Europa Press. 2011a. "Detenido en Salt (Girona) un neonazi por quemar un contenedor." *20 Minutos*, January 20, 2011. Retrieved from https://www.20minutos.es/noticia/934110/0/.
———. 2011b. "La renta bruta por habitante de Cataluña se sitúa en 16.900 euros." *El País,* June 1, 2011.
———. 2011c. "Salt crea un fondo para ayudar a las comunidades de vecinos a cubrir deudas." *20 Minutos*, September 22, 2011.
———. 2013. "Un centenar de activistas ocupan un bloque de pisos en Salt (Girona)." *La Vanguardia*, March 22, 2013. Retrieved from https://www.lavanguardia.com/local/girona/20130322/54369513287/un-centenar-de-activistas-de-la-pah-ocupan-un-bloque-de-pisos-en-salt-girona.html.
Factoria Cultural Coma Cros. 2021. "El viver de Salt." Accessed October 5, 2021. https://comacros.cat/el-viver-de-salt/.
Fassin, Didier. 2013. *Enforcing Order: An Ethnography of Urban Policing*. Cambridge: Polity Press.
Fernández Bessa, Cristina and Andrés Di Masso. 2018. "Diez años de civismo "a golpe de ordenanza": estudio sobre la aplicación de la ordenanza de convivencia en el espacio público de Barcelona." *Barcelona Societat*, 22: 27–50.

Fernández González, Miquel. 2016. "Viejos problemas y nuevos vecinos. Consecuencias de una gran reforma urbana en el barrio Del Raval, Barcelona." *AIBR Revista de Antropologia Iberoamericana* 11 (2): 225–45.

Fernández González, Miquel, Andreu Espasa, Alejandro García, Paulina Sastre, and Xavier Zambrano. 2009. *Fabricar l'immigrant : Aprofitaments polítics de la immigració, Catalunya 1977–2007*. Edited by Miquel Fernández. Lleida: Pagès editors.

Foucault, Michel. 2007. *Security, Territory, Population.* Basingstoke, UK: Palgrave Macmillan.

Franquesa, Jaume. 2005. "Sa calatrava mon amour. Etnografía d'un barri atrapat en la geografia del capital." *Facultat de Geografia e Historia*. Barcelona: Universitat de Barcelona.

———. 2007a. "Sobre la pertinencia del barrio como unidad de observación y análisis." In *Intersecçoes Ibéricas. Margens, passagens e fronteiras*, edited by Manuela Cunha and Luís Cunha, 251–74. Lisboa: Graus Editora.

———. 2007b. "Vaciar y llenar, o la lógica espacial de la neoliberalización. Franquesa, Jaume (REIS N°118. ARTÍCULOS)." *Reis: Revista Española de Investigaciones Sociológicas*, no. 118: 123–50.

———. 2011. "'We've Lost Our Bearings': Place, Tourism, and the Limits of the 'Mobility Turn.'" *Antipode* 43 (4): 1012–33.

Fraser, Nancy. 1990. "Rethinking the Public Sphere: A Contribution to the Critique of Actually Existing Democracy." *Social Text*, no. 25/26: 56.

Fuentes, Lluïsa. 2010. "Salt renovarà la zona amb més immigració." *El Público*, May 18, 2010. Retrieved from https://www.publico.es/espana/catalunya/salt-renovara-zona-amb-mes.html

Galdon-Clavell, G. 2016. Uncivil Cities: Insecurity, Policy Transfer, Tolerance and the Case of Barcelona's "Civility Ordinance." *Urban Studies*, 53 (9): 1–17.

García Añón, José, Ben Bradford, José Antonio García Sáez, Andrés Gascón Cuenca, Antoni Llorente Ferreres, and Institut de Drets Humans. 2013. *Identificación policial por perfil étnico en España.* Valencia: Tirant lo Blanch.

Garcia, Sergio, and Déborah Ávila. 2016. "La prevención securitaria como modo de gobierno: el caso de Madrid." *Athenea Digital* 16 (1): 43–82.

Generalitat de Catalunya. 2006. Llei 2/2004, de millora de barris, àrees urbanes i viles que requereixen una atenció especial. Retrieved from http://territori.gencat.cat/web/.content/home/01_departament/documentacio/territori_urbanisme/urbanisme/publicacions/llei_reglament_millora_barris.pdf.

Generalitat de Catalunya. 2008. *Un pacte per viure junts i juntes.* Barcelona: Generalitat de Catalunya.

Generalitat de Catalunya. 2009. *Pla de ciutadania i immigració 2009–2012.* Barcelona: Generalitat de Catalunya.

Generalitat de Catalunya. 2014. *Pla de ciutadania i de les migracions: horitzó 2016.* Barcelona: Generalitat de Catalunya.

Giddens, Anthony. 1990. *The Consequences of Modernity*. Cambridge: Polity Press.

Gil Araujo, Sandra. 2010. *Las argucias de la integración. Políticas migratorias, construcción nacional y cuestión social*. Madrid: IEPALA Editorial.

Glass, Ruth. 1989. *Clichés of Urban Doom and Other Essays*. Cornwall: Basil Blackwell Inc.

Glick, Thomas F., and Oriol Pi-Sunyer. 1992. "Convivencia: An Introductory Note." In *Convivencia: Jews, Muslims, and Christians in Medieval Spain*, edited by Vivian B. Mann, Thomas F. Glick, and Jerrilynn Denise Dodds, 1–11. New York: George Braziller.

Gluckman, Max. 1940. "The Social Organization of Modern Zululand." *Bantu Studies* 14 (1): 1–30.

GMG Plans i Projectes. 2009. Pla local d'habitatge de la Vila de Salt 2009–2015. Document de síntesi.

———. 2010. Informe d'avaluació final del projecte d'intervenció integral «Salt 70» 2010. March 2010. Retrieved from http://territori.gencat.cat/web/.content/home/01_departament/actuacions_i_obres/barris/projectes_2004/documents/salt70._informe_avaluacio_final.pdf.

Goebel, Alison D. 2011. *Small City Neighbors: Race, Space, and Class in Mansfield, Ohio*. PhD presented at the University of Illinois at Urbana-Champaign.

Goldberg, David Theo. 2002. *The Racial State*. Malden, MA: Blackwell Publishers.

Gómez Crespo, Paloma, and Franciso Torres Pérez. 2020. "Convivencia y barrios multiculturales: conflicto y cohesion en contextos de crisis." *Cuadernos Manuel Giménez Abad* 7: 28–44.

Gönen, Zeynep, and Deniz Yonucu. 2011. "Legitimizing Violence and Segregation: Neoliberal Discourses on Crime and the Criminalization of Urban Poor Populations in Turkey." In *Lumpencity: Discourses of Marginality, Marginalizing Discourses*, edited by Alan Bourke, Tia Dafnos, and Markus Kip. Ottawa: Red Quil Books.

Goonewardena, Kanishka, and Stefan Kipfer. 2005. "Spaces of Difference: Reflections from Toronto on Multiculturalism, Bourgeois Urbanism and the Possibility of Radical Urban Politics." *International Journal of Urban and Regional Research* 29 (3): 670–78.

Goytisolo, Juan. 1985. *Contracorrientes*. Barcelona: Editorial Montesinos.

GRAMC. 2010. "Sobre l'informe d'arrelament", complaint presented by GRAMC (Grup de Recerca i Actuació amb Minories Culturals i Treballadors Estrangers) to the Ayuntamiento de Salt, October 04, 2010.

Gupta, Akhil, and James Ferguson. 1992. "Beyond 'Culture': Space, Identity and the Politics of Difference." *Cultural Anthropology* 7 (1): 6–23.

Gupta, Akhil, and Aradhana Sharma. 2006. "Globalization and Postcolonial States." *Current Anthropology* 47 (2): 277–307.

Hage, Ghassan. 2000. *White Nation. Fantasies of White Supremacy in a Multicultural Society.* New York: Routledge.

———. 2010. "Intercultural Relations at the Limits of Multicultural Governmentality." In *The Ashgate Research Companion to Multiculturalism*. Farnham, UK: Ashgate.

Hall, Stuart. 1979. "The Great Moving Right Show: The Politics of Thatcherism." *Marxism Today*, January: 14–20.

———. 2011. "The Neoliberal Revolution." *Soundings* 48: 9–28.

Hall, Stuart, Chas Crither, Tony Jefferson, John Clarke, and Brian Roberts. 1978. *Policing the Crisis: Mugging, the State, and Law and Order.* London: Macmillan.

Hall, Suzanne M. 2015. "Super-Diverse Street: A 'Trans-Ethnography' across Migrant Localities." *Ethnic and Racial Studies* 38 (1): 22–37.

Halliday, Fred. 1999. "'Islamophobia' Reconsidered." *Ethnic and Racial Studies* 22 (5): 892–902.

Harcourt, Bernard. 2001. *Illusion of Order: The False Promise of Broken Windows Policing*. Cambridge, MA: Harvard University Press.

———. 2008. "Borders of Punishment. A Critique of Immigrant Profiling." In *Criminalisation and Victimisation of Migrants in Europe*, edited by Salvatore Palidda. Genova: Diparteminto di Scienze Antropologiche, Università degli Studi di Genova.

———. 2011. *The Illusion of Free Markets: Punishment and the Myth of Natural Order.* Cambridge, MA: Harvard University Press.

Harvey, David. 1985. "The Geopolitics of Capitalism." In *Social Relations and Spatial Structure*, edited by Derek Gregory and John Urry. London: Macmillan.

———. 1989. "From Managerialism to Entrepreneurialism: The Transformation in Urban Governance in Late Capitalism." *Geografiska Annaler. Series B, Human Geography* 71 (1): 3.

———. 1996. *Justice, Nature, and the Geography of Difference*. Cambridge, Mass: Blackwell Publishers.

———. 2000. *Spaces of Hope*. Berkeley: University of California Press.

———. 2001. *Spaces of Capital: Towards a Critical Geography*. Edinburgh: Edinburgh University Press.

———. 2003. *The New Imperialism*. Oxford : Oxford University Press.

———. 2005. *A Brief History of Neoliberalism*. Oxford: Oxford University Press.

Heil, T. 2014. "Are Neighbours Alike? Practices of Conviviality in Catalonia and Casamance." *European Journal of Cultural Studies* 17 (4): 452–70.

Hepburn, Eve, and Ricard Zapata-Barrero. 2014. "Introduction: immigration policies in multilevel states." In *The politics of immigration in multi-level states. Governance and political parties*, edited by Ricard Zapata-Barrero and Eve Hepburn, 3–18. London: Palgrave Macmillan.

Herzfeld, Michael. 2018. "Anthropological Realism in a Scientific Age." *Anthropological Theory* 18 (1): 129–50.

Hilgers, Mathieu. 2012. "The Historicity of the Neoliberal State." *Social Anthropology* 20 (1): 80–94.

Holmes, Douglas R. 2000. *Integral Europe: Fast-Capitalism, Multiculturalism, Neofascism.* Princeton, NJ: Princeton University Press.

Home Office, Generalitat de Catalunya. 2010. Informe 2010 sobre la seguridad en Cataluña. Generalitat de Catalunya.

Huntington, Samuel P. 1996. *The Clash of Civilizations and the Remaking of World Order*. London: Penguin.

Hurtado Jordá, Jorge. 1996. *Implicaciones sociales de la economía sumergida. Una investigación sociológica.* PhD presented at Universidad Complutense de Madrid.

Hurtado Martínez, Maria del Carmen. 1999. *La inseguridad ciudadana de la transición a una sociedad democrática: España (1977–1989)*. Cuenca: Ediciones de la Universidad de Castilla-La Mancha.

IDESCAT. 2009. Moviments migratoris 2008.

Iglesias, Natalia. 2008. "Polémica en Salt por la retirada de antenas parabólicas." *El País*, May 14, 2008. Retrieved from https://elpais.com/diario/2008/05/14/catalunya/1210727254_850215.html.

Ilan, Jonathan. 2011. "Reclaiming respectability? The class-cultural dynamics of crime, community and governance in inner-city Dublin." *Urban Studies* 48 (6): 1137–1155.

Informatiu Anti-Aru. 2010. "Informatiu anti-aru nº1." *YouTube*, October 15, 2010, https://www.youtube.com/watch?v=DKlXBWj_F2o

J.B.M. 2008. "Pineda exigeix ajuda a Montilla per afrontar la «situació d'emergència» de la immigració." *Diari de Girona*, June 7, 2008.

J.N. 2010. "Torramadé vol convocar un referèndum sobre l'ARU." *El Punt*, August 12, 2010.

Julbe, Bàrbara. 2008. "Salt multará con 1.500 euros a los vecinos que no retiren las antenas de las fachadas." *20 minutos*, May 20, 2008. Retrieved from https://www.20minutos.es/noticia/380228/0/antenas/salt/fachada/.

———. 2010. "Las nuevas medidas sobre inmigración dividen a la población de Salt." *La Vanguardia*, December 22, 2010.

———. 2011. "Más policía para sofocar el estallido de disturbios en Salt." *La Vanguardia*, January 17, 2011.

King, Desmond. 1999. *In the Name of Liberalism: Illiberal Social Policy in the United States and Britain*. New York: Oxford University Press.

Koutrolikou, P.-P. 2012. "Spatialities of Ethnocultural Relations in Multicultural East London: Discourses of Interaction and Social Mix." *Urban Studies* 49: 2049–66.

"la Caixa" Foundation. 2013. Casal dels Infants. *Intervenció comunitària intercultural. 2013.* Quadern de la Plaça: Monografia Comunitària de Salt.

La Farga. 1981a. "Molts bars i poc cafes." *La Farga* 26, September 26, 1981.

———. 1981b. "La immigració al nostre poble, i marginació i esperança." *La Farga* 28, November 28, 1981.

La Vanguardia. 1999. "El Parlament expresa su 'enérgico rechazo' a los actos racistas." *La Vanguardia*, July 29, 1999.

———. 2011. "Vivir." *La Vanguardia*, September 9, 2011: 1–3.

La Vanguardia. Redacción. 2004. Normes de composició i funcionament de l'òrgan de participació ciutadana LAOS-SALT (Espai per a la Integració i la Convivència).

———. 2011. "Badalona suprime bancos públicos de barrios con alta inmigración para desalojar a inquilinos 'molestos'." *La Vanguardia*, September 15, 2011. Retrieved from https://www.lavanguardia.com/vida/20110915/54216338821/badalona-suprime-bancos-publicos-de-barrios-con-alta-inmigracion-para-desalojar-a-inquilinos.html.

LAOS-Salt. 2005. Acta LAOS-Salt 02/06/2005.

———. Town Hall Minutes. 31 January 2005.

———. 2006. Memòria de les Activitats 2005-06, LAOS-SALT.

Lees, Loretta. 2008. "Gentrification and Social Mixing: Towards an Inclusive Urban Renaissance?" *Urban Studies* 45 (12): 2449–70.

Lefebvre, Henri. 1991. *The Production of Space*. Edited by Donald Nicholson-Smith. Oxford: Blackwell.

Lentin, Alana. 2018. "Beyond denial: 'not racism' as racist violence." *Continuum* 32 (4): 400–414.

Lentin, Alana, and Gavan Titley. 2011. *The Crises of Multiculturalism: Racism in a Neoliberal Age*. London: Zed Books.

Leralta Piñán, Olga. 2005. "Ser inmigrante: factor de riesgo en el acceso a la vivienda'." *Documentación Social* 138: 157–72.

Lévi-Strauss, Claude. 1963. *Structural Anthropology*. New York: Basic Books.

Lewis, Oscar. 1969. "Culture of poverty." In *On understanding poverty: perspectives from the social sciences*, edited by Daniel Patrick Moynihan, 187–220. New York: Basic Books.

Li, Tania. 2014. "Fixing Non-Market Subjects: Governing Land and Population in the Global South." *Foucault Studies* 18: 34–48.

Libertad Digital. 2011. "El pueblo de Salt vive atemorizado." *Libertad Digital*, January 19, 2011. Retrieved from https://tv.libertaddigital.com/videos/2011-01-19/el-pueblo-de-salt-vive-atemorizado-6014924.html.

López, Antoni. 2004. "Convivencia amenazada. Una protesta vecinal contra la inseguridad aviva el debate sobre la inmigración en la ciudad gerundense de Salt." *La Vanguardia*, July 18, 2004.

López, Isidro, and Emmanuel Rodríguez. 2011. "The Spanish Model." *New Left Review* 69: 5–29.

López Sánchez, Pere. 1986. *El centro histórico: un lugar para el conflicto*. Barcelona: Geo Crítica: Edicions de la Universitat de Barcelona.

———. 1993. "Todos, mayoría y minorías en la barcelona olímpica. apuntes sobre el gobierno de lo social en la Ciudad-Empresa." *Economía y Sociedad* 9: 103–15.

Lovering, John. 1999. "Theory Led by Policy: The Inadequacies of the 'New Regionalism' (Illustrated from the Case of Wales)." *International Journal of Urban and Regional Research* 23 (2): 379–95.

Low, Setha M. 1999. "Introduction: Theorizing the City." In *Theorizing the City. The New Urban Anthropology Reader*, edited by Setha M Low. New Brunswick, NJ: Rutgers University Press.

———. 2000. *On the Plaza: The Politics of Public Space and Culture*. Austin: University of Texas Press.

de Lucas, Javier. 2016. "Refugiados e inmigrantes: Por un cambio en las políticas migratorias y de asilo." *Pasajes: Revista de pensamiento contemporáneo* 50: 92–113.

Lundsteen, Martin. 2010. *Espacio, capital y cultura en Premià de Mar.* MA Thesis presented at the Department of Social Anthropology, University of Barcelona.

———. 2015. *Espai, capital i cultura a Premià de Mar. el cas de la mesquita*. Barcelona: Pol·len Edicions.

———. 2018. "'El Moro'—Discovering the Hidden Coloniality of the contemporary Spanish/Catalan Society and Its Colonial Subjects." In *Postcolonial Europe: Comparative Reflections after the Empires*, edited by Lars Jensen, Júlia Suárez-

Krabbe, Christian Groess-Green, and Zoran L. Pecic, 197–219. London: Rowman & Littlefield.

———. 2020a. "Conflicts in and around Space. Reflections on 'Mosque Conflicts' through the Case of Premià de Mar." *Journal of Muslims in Europe* 9 (1): 43–63.

———. 2020b. "An Iron Fist in a Velvet Glove: Neoliberal Government of the Migrant Poor and Other in Salt, Catalonia." *Dialectical Anthropology* 44 (1): 1–17.

———. Forthcoming. "Postcolonial Subjects in the Mists of the Neoliberal State: A New Social Question?"

Lundsteen, Martin, and Miquel Fernández González. 2021. "Zero-Tolerance in Catalonia: Policing the Other in Public Space." *Critical Criminology* 29 (4): 837–852.

Lundsteen, Martin, and Irene Sabaté. 2018. "The Social Articulation of the Crisis and Political Mobilisation in Spain. Some Reflections on the Shortcomings of the New Social Movements." In *Inclusion and Exclusion in Europe. Migration, Work and Employment Perspectives*, edited by Olena Fedyuk and Paul Stewart, 43–59. Colchester: ECPR Press.

Lundsteen, Martin, Ubaldo Martínez Veiga, and Jaime Palomera. 2014. "Reproducción social y conflicto en las periferias urbanas del estado español." In *Periferias, fronteras y diálogos. una lectura antropológica de los retos de la sociedad actual*, 111–17. Tarragona: Publicacions URV.

Macleod, Gordon. 2001. "New Regionalism Reconsidered: Globalization and the Remaking of Political Economic Space." *International Journal of Urban and Regional Research* 25 (4): 804–29.

Macleod, Gordon, and Craig Johnstone. 2012. "Stretching Urban Renaissance: Privatizing Space, Civilizing Place, Summoning 'Community.'" *International Journal of Urban and Regional Research* 36 (January): 1–28.

Maluquer Sostres, Joaquim. 1963. *L'assimilation des immigrés en Catalogne*. Genève: Librairie Droz.

Mann, Michael. 1984. "The Autonomous Power of the State: Its Origins, Mechanisms and Results." *European Journal of Sociology*, 25 (2): 185–213.

Marle, F. Van, and S. Maruna. 2010. "'Ontological Insecurity' and 'Terror Management': Linking Two Free-Floating Anxieties." *Punishment & Society* 12 (1): 7–26.

Martín Corrales, Eloy. 2002. *La imagen del Magrebí en España: una perspectiva histórica, siglos xvi–XX*. Barcelona: Edicions Bellaterra.

Martínez Veiga, Ubaldo. 1989. *El otro desempleo: La economía sumergida*. Barcelona: Anthropos, 1989.

———. 1999. *Pobreza, segregación y exclusión espacial: La vivienda de los inmigrantes extranjeros en España*. Barcelona: Icaria.

———. 2001. *El Ejido: Discriminación, exclusión social y racismo*. Madrid: Los Libros de la Catarata.

———. 2004. *Trabajadores invisibles: Precariedad, rotación y pobreza de la inmigración en España*. Madrid: Los Libros de la Catarata.

Marx, Karl. 1970. *Marx's Critique of Hegel's Philosophy of Right*. Cambridge: Cambridge University Press. https://www.marxists.org/archive/marx/works/1843/critique-hpr/.

Mas, Oriol. 2010. “Els veïns demanen concreció i saber quins seran els habitatges afectats per l’ARU de Salt.” *El Punt*, July 1, 2010.

Mateo Dieste, Josep Lluís. 1997. *El “moro” entre los primitivos. El caso del protectorado español en Marruecos*. Barcelona: “la Caixa” Foundation.

Miles, Robert, and Malcolm Brown. 2003. *Racism*. 3rd ed. London: Routledge.

Mitchell, Don. 1997. “The Annihilation of Space by Law: The Roots and Implications of Anti-Homeless Laws in the United States.” *Antipode* 29 (3): 303–35.

Moncusí Ferré, Albert, Francisco Torres Pérez, and Hernán Fioravanti Álvarez, eds. 2018. *Barris i ciutats en clau pluricultural. Construcció del conflicte, experiències veïnals i gestió institucional*. Valencia: Neopàtria.

Monnet, Nadja. 2002. *La formación del espacio público: Una mirada etnológica sobre el casc antic de Barcelona*. Madrid: Catarata.

Morell, Marc. 2004. “El trabajo de la gentrificación. Un bosquejo en torno a la formación de un sujeto histórico urbano.” *Working Papers Series Contested_Cities* WPCC-14002: 1-20.

Moreras, Jordi. 2004. “Conflictos en Cataluña.” In *Atlas de la inmigración Marroquí en España*, edited by Bernabé López García and Mohamed Berriane, 1999–2000. Madrid: Taller de Estudios Internacionales Mediterráneos, UAM, OPI, Secretaría de Estado de Inmigración y emigración, Ministerio de Trabajo y Asuntos Sociales.

———. 2007. “Los inmigrantes marroquíes en Cataluña: ¿Candidatos permanentes a la integración?” In *Salud mental en el paciente Magrebí*, edited by Driss Moussaoui and Miquel Casas, 49-68. Barcelona: Editorial Glosa.

Nadal, Jordi. 2010. “Crearan una taula de convivència a Salt per posar fi a la crispació entre les diverses comunitats del municipi.” *El Punt*, March 02, 2010.

Nadal, Jordi, and Montse Barrera. 2010. “Uns 200 veïns es concentren davant de l’Ajuntament de Salt per reclamar seguretat i obliguen a suspendre el ple.” *El Punt*, February 23, 2010.

Nadal i Farreras, Joaquim. 1978. “La industrialització al Gironès: l’exemple de Salt.” In *Girona Al Segle XIX*, 175–98. Girona: Gòthia.

Narotzky, Susana. 1997. *New Directions in Economic Anthropology*. London: Pluto Press.

———. 2005. “The Production of Knowledge and the Production of Hegemony: Anthropological Theory and Political Struggles in Spain.” *Journal of the World Anthropology Network* 1: 35–54.

Olivier de Sardan, Jean-Pierre. 1995. “La politique du terrain.” *Enquête*, no. 1 (October): 71–109.

Oller, Sílvia. 2008a. “Especial Salt. L’entrevista: ‘Ens calen més diners’.” *La Vanguardia*, July 18, 2008.

———. 2008b. “Carta a corbacho.” *La Vanguardia*, October 10, 2008.

———. 2010. “Si no hay dinero ni trabajo, la gente roba.” *La Vanguardia*, February 25, 2010.

Oller, Sílvia, and Bàrbara Julbe. 2011. “Una calma que oculta tensión.” *La Vanguardia*, January 18, 2011.

Onyar, Narcis. 1984. “Salt y Sarrià, un año de independencia.” *La Vanguardia*, March 3, 1984.

de Orovio, Nacho. 1999. "Hijos del mismo barrio." *La Vanguardia*, July 18, 1999.

de Orovio, Nacho, and Francesca Rodríguez. 1999. "Respuesta tibia al racismo." *La Vanguardia*, July 28, 1999.

Ortuño Aix, José María. 2006. "Report on Islamophobia in Spain." In *Islamophobia Project Report. Securitization and Religious Divides in Europe*, edited by Jocelyne Cesari, 227–300.

Palomera, Jaime. 2013. *Reciprocity and Conflict: The Urban Poor in a Bubble-and-Bust Economy.* PhD presented at the Departament d'Antropologia Social i Cultural, Universitat de Barcelona.

———. 2014. "How Did Finance Capital Infiltrate the World of the Urban Poor? Homeownership and Social Fragmentation in a Spanish Neighborhood." *International Journal of Urban and Regional Research* 38 (1): 218–35.

Pasetti, Francesco. 2014. "Country report integration policies in Spain." *INTERACT Research Report 2014/30.* Retrieved from https://cadmus.eui.eu/bitstream/handle/1814/33231/INTERACT-RR-2014%20-%2030.pdf?sequence=1&isAllowed=y

Pastor, Xavier. 2011. "Un pla de gestió de conflictes per a Salt." *Diari de Girona*, January 25, 2011. Retrieved from https://www.diaridegirona.cat/girona/2011/01/25/pla-gestio-conflictes-salt/460573.html.

Peck, Jamie, and Adam Tickell. 2002. "Neoliberalizing Space." *Antipode* 34 (3): 380–404.

PERI de Barri Vell (2002/5799). Pla de Reforma Interior del Barri Vell, Salt. Ajuntament de Salt. July 2002. Retrieved from: http://ptop.gencat.cat/rpucportal/AppJava/cercaExpedient.do?reqCode=veureDocument&codintExp=204524&fromPage=load.

Pineda, Iolanda. 2010. "Entrevista con Iolanda Pineda." *El País*, February 26, 2010. Retrieved from https://elpais.com/politica/2011/01/21/actualidad/1295625600_1295633190.html.

———. 2012. "Salt: un laboratorio social." *Página Abierta* 218, enero-febrero. Retrieved from http://www.pensamientocritico.org/iolpin0312.htm.

Pinilla, Òscar. 2010. "La policia local de Salt ja ha detingut aquest any una trentena de persones per delictes contra la propietat." *El Punt*, February 17, 2010.

Playà Maset, Josep. 2010a "Alta tension en Salt." *La Vanguardia*, February 27, 2010.

———. 2010b. "El Transfondo del Paro. SALT." *La Vanguardia*, February 28, 2010.

Polanyi, Karl. 2001. *The Great Transformation. The Political and Economic Origin of Our Time*. Boston: Beacon Press.

Quesada, Juan Diego, and Rebeca Carranco. 2010. "Salt, una olla a presión." *El País* March 7, 2010. Retrieved from https://elpais.com/diario/2010/03/07/domingo/1267937553_850215.html.

Quijano, Aníbal. 2000. "Coloniality of Power and Eurocentrism in Latin America." *International Sociology* 15 (2): 215–32.

Ramon Mòdol, Josep. 2010. "Transformació urbana del centre de Salt" *Territori. Observatori de projectes i debats territorials de Catalunya*: http://territori.scot.cat/client/print/print_notice.php?IDN=2741

Ribas-Mateos, Natalia. 2004. *Una invitación a la sociología de las migraciones.* Barcelona: Bellaterra.

Roberts, Dorothy. 2014. "Complicating the Triangle of Race, Class and State: The Insights of Black Feminists." *Ethnic and Racial Studies* 37 (10): 1776–82.
Rodríguez, Francesca. 1999a. "Una batalla campal entre jóvenes acaba en ataques de tinte racista." *La Vanguardia*, July 14, 1999.
———. 1999b. "Erupción racista." *La Vanguardia*, July 15, 1999.
———. 1999c. "Miedo en Ca n'Anglada." *La Vanguardia*, July 16, 1999.
———. 1999d. "Primeras detenciones." *La Vanguardia*, July 17, 1999.
———. 1999e. "Once detenidos por los últimos enfrentamientos en Ca n'Anglada." *La Vanguardia*, July 19, 1999.
———. 2000. "Terrassa invierte en Ca n'Anglada para evitar su marginación." *La Vanguardia*, January 15, 2000.
Rodríguez Cabrero, G. 1991. "Estado de bienestar y sociedad de bienestar. Realidad e ideología." In *Un debate en la Europa actual*, edited by G. Rodríguez Cabrero, 9–46. Barcelona: Icaria/ FUHEM.
Rogaly, Ben, and Kaveri Qureshi. 2013. "Diversity, Urban Space and the Right to the Provincial City." *Identities* 20 (4): 423–37.
Roura, Jordi. 2000. "Salt agruparà totes les entitats que ajuden a la integració dels immigrants." *Diari de Girona*, January 23, 2000.
RTVE. 2011a. "Mi vecino es okupa." *Comando Actualidad*, January 13, 2011. Retrieved from https://www.rtve.es/alacarta/videos/comando-actualidad/comando-actualidad-vecino-okupa/986410/.
———. 2011b. "Salt. Margarita de 90 años vive rodeada de ocupas." *España Directo*. Retrieved from https://www.youtube.com/watch?v=4eFU8jG5Byo.
———. 2011c. "Salt, paraíso ocupa." *España Directo*. Retrieved from https://www.youtube.com/watch?v=0EVCSNCoSFo.
Sabaté, Irene. 2018. "To Repay or Not to Repay: Financial Vulnerability among Mortgage Debtors in Spain." *Etnografica* 22 (1): 5–26.
Sahlins, Marshall. 1993. "Goodby to Tristes Tropes: Ethnography in the Context of Modern World History." *The Journal of Modern History* 65 (1): 1–25.
Sánchez, Alex. 2010. "Carlos Martínez Shaw y la manufactura algodonera Catalana del siglo XVIII." In *Carlos Martínez Shaw, Historiador Modernista*, edited by Roberto Fernández, 103–22. Lleida: Universitat de Lleida.
Sandoval, Antoni F. 2002. "PSC, ERC e IC-V alertan de la situación de la educación en Salt." *La Vanguardia*, March 2, 2002.
———. 2007a. "Alta tensión en Salt." *La Vanguardia*, May 9, 2007.
———. 2007b. "Más del 63% de los niños nacidos en Salt son hijos de familias inmigrantes." *La Vanguardia*, May 19, 2007.
———. 2007c. "De campaña en Salt. Vecinos piden a Montilla soluciones para el problema de la inmigración." *La Vanguardia*, May 24, 2007.
Santamaría, Enrique. 2002. *La incógnita del extraño. Una aproximación a la significación sociológica de la 'inmigración no comunitaria'*. Rubí: Anthropos Editorial.
Santiago, Martí. 2011. "La policia fa una batuda a Salt i deté set persones per incomplir la llei d'estrangeria." *Diari de Girona*, October 15, 2011. Retrieved from https://www.diaridegirona.cat/girona/2011/10/15/la-policia-fa-una-batuda-a-salt-i-dete-set-persones-per-incomplir-la-llei-destrangeria/522415.html.

Santos, Boaventura de Sousa. 2014. *Epistemologies of the South. Justice against Epistemicide*. Abingdon, UK: Routledge/Taylor & Francis.

Scott, Mark, Darren P. Smith, Mark Shucksmith, Nick Gallent, Keith Halfacree, Sue Kilpatrick, Susan Johns, Peter Vitartas, Martin Homisan, and Trevor Cherrett. 2011. "Interface." *Planning Theory & Practice* 12 (4): 593–635.

Serra, Carles. 2006. *Diversitat, racisme i violència. Conflictes a l'educació secundària*. Vic: Eumo Editorial.

Shore, Cris, and Susan Wright, eds. 1997. *Anthropology of Policy: Perspectives on Governance and Power.* London: Routledge.

Síndic de Greuges. 2010. *Report Q-05778/2010.* Síndic de Greuges.

Smith, Darren P., and Louise Holt. 2007. "Studentification and 'Apprentice' Gentrifiers within Britain's Provincial Towns and Cities: Extending the Meaning of Gentrification." *Environment and Planning A: Economy and Space* 39 (1): 142–61.

Smith, Gavin. 2011. "Selective Hegemony and Beyond-Populations with 'No Productive Function': A Framework for Enquiry." *Identities* 18 (September): 2–38.

Smith, Neil. 1987. "Gentrification and the Rent Gap." *Annals of the Association of American Geographers* 77 (3): 462–65.

———. 1993. "Homeless/Global: Scaling Places." In *Mapping the Futures. Local Cultures, Global Change*, edited by J. Bird, B. Curtis, T. Putnam, and L. Tickner. London: Routledge, Chapter 6.

———. 1996. *The New Urban Frontier: Gentrification and the Revanchist City*. London: Routledge.

———. 2002. "New Globalism, New Urbanism: Gentrification as Global Urban Strategy." *Antipode* 34 (3): 427–50.

Soifer, Maya. 2009. "Beyond Convivencia: Critical Reflections on the Historiography of Interfaith Relations in Christian Spain." *Journal of Medieval Iberian Studies* 1 (1): 19–35.

Solanes-Corella, Ángeles. 2015. "Rights, immigration and social cohesion in Spain." *Migraciones Internacionales* 8 (2): 9–40.

Solé Arraràs, Ariadna. 2014. "Ritos funerarios islámicos trasnacionales entre Catalunya y Kolda (Senegal). La construcción de la transnacionalidad desde la práctica religiosa y ritual." *Revista de Estudios Internacionales Mediterráneos* 16: 1–16.

Soler, Albert. 1997. "Problemas de integración racial en una escuela." *La Vanguardia*, October 21, 1997.

Soler, Tura. 2011a. "La policia treballa per expulsar reincidents però no sempre pot." *El Punt*, January 20, 2011.

———. 2011b. "Els mossos del SAP vaticinen encara més violència a Salt." *El Punt*, January 20, 2011.

Southerton, Dale. 2002. "Boundaries of 'Us' and 'Them': Class, Mobility and Identification in a New Town." *Sociology* 36 (1): 171–93.

Spanish Ministry of Work and Immigration (MTI). 2007. *Plan Estratégico de Ciudadanía e Integración 2007-2010.*

Spanish Ministry of Work and Immigration (MTI). 2011. *Plan Estratégico de Ciudadanía e Integración 2011-2014.*

Stack, Carol. 1975. *All Our Kin: Strategies for Survival in a Black Community*. New York: Harper & Row Publishers.

Staeheli, Lynn A., and Albert Thompson. 1997. "Citizenship, community, and struggles for public space." *Professional Geographer* 49 (1): 28–38.

Staellert, Christine. 1998. *Etnogénesis y etnicidad: una aproximación histórico-antropológica al Casticismo*. Barcelona: Proyecto a ediciones.

Suárez-Navaz, Liliana. 2004. *Rebordering the Mediterranean: Boundaries and Citizenship in Southern Europe*. New York: Berghahn.

Szpiech, Ryan. 2013. "The Convivencia Wars: Decoding Historiography's Polemic with Philology." In *In a Sea of Languages: Rethinking the Arabic Role in Medieval Literary History*, edited by Susan Akbari and Karla Mallette, 135–61. Toronto: University of Toronto Press.

Swartz, Marc J., Victor Turner, and Arthur Tuden. 1972. "Introduction." In *Political Anthropology*, 1–48. Transaction Publishers.

Taberner, Pep. 2001. "Salt pide cambios en su mapa escolar para educar mejor a los inmigrantes." *La Vanguardia*, June 13, 2001.

———. 2003. "El precio del incivismo." *La Vanguardia*, October 28, 2003.

T.C.C. 2010. "L'equip de govern de Salt es queda sol en el projecte d´enderroc." *Diari de Girona*, September 21, 2010.

Thompson, Edward P. 1968. *The Making of the English Working Class*. Harmondsworth: Penguin.

Titley, Gavan and Alana Lentin. 2008. *The Politics of Diversity in Europe.* Strasbourg: Council of Europe Publishing.

Torramadé, Jaume. 2011. "La situación a Salt." Interview by Manuel Fuentes. *El Matí de Catalunya Radio, Catalunya Radio*, January 19, 2011. Audio, 1:03:41. https://www.ccma.cat/catradio/alacarta/el-mati-de-catalunya-radio-manel-fuentes/la-situacio-a-salt/audio/503170/.

Town Council. 2012. *Normes de composició i funcionament de l'òrgan de participació ciutadana LAOS-SALT (Espai per a la integració i la convivència).* Retrieved from https://dibaaps.diba.cat/vnis/temp/CIDO_bopg_2004_08_20040811_BOPG_20040811_026_027.pdf

Trillas, Joan. 2014. "La XVII Fira del Cistell de Salt tanca amb un èxit absolut." *El Punt AVUI+*, October 6, 2014. Retrieved from http://www.elpuntavui.cat/article/783066-la-xvii-fira-del-cistell-de-salt-tanca-amb-un-exit-absolut.html.

Turner, Victor. 1996. *Schism and Continuity in an African Society: A Study of Ndembu Village Life*. Classic Reprints in Anthropology. Oxford: Berg.

Uitermark, Justus. 2014. "Integration and Control: The Governing of Urban Marginality in Western Europe." *International Journal of Urban and Regional Research* 38 (4): 1418–36.

Vertovec, Steven. 2007. "Super-Diversity and Its Implications." *Ethnic and Racial Studies* 30 (April 2012): 1024–54.

VilaWeb. 2011a. "Augmenta la presència policíaca a Salt pels actes vandàlics." *VilaWeb*, January 16, 2011. Retrieved from https://www.vilaweb.cat/noticia/3835748/20110116/augmenten-actes-vandalics-salt.html

———. 2011b. "Preocupació a Salt per la mort del jove que empaitava la policia." *VilaWeb*, January 21, 2011. Retrieved from https://www.vilaweb.cat/noticia/3837965/20110121/tensio-salt-mort-jove-empaitava-policia.html.

Visa, Lluís, Ivanna Vallespín, Mercé Pérez Pons, Rebeca Carranco, and Antía Castedo. 2011. "La Cataluña que arde de noche." *El País*, April 19, 2011. Retrieved from https://elpais.com/diario/2011/04/19/catalunya/1303175238_850215.html.

Wacquant, Loïc. 2007. *Los condenados de la ciudad: gueto, periferias y Estado*. Buenos Aires: Siglo XXI Editores.

———. 2008a. *Urban Outcasts: A Comparative Sociology of Advanced Marginality*. Cambridge: Polity Press.

———. 2008b. "Relocating Gentrification: The Working Class, Science and the State in Recent Urban Research." *International Journal of Urban and Regional Research* 32 (1): 198–205.

———. 2008c. "Ordering Insecurity: Social Polarization and the Punitive Upsurge." *Radical Philosophy Review* 11 (1): 9–27.

———. 2009a. *Prisons of Poverty*. Minneapolis: University of Minnesota Press.

———. 2009b. *Punishing the Poor: The Neoliberal Government of Social Insecurity*. Durham NC: Duke University Press.

———. 2009c. "The Body, the Ghetto and the Penal State." *Qualitative Sociology* 32: 101–129.

———. 2012. "Three Steps to a Historical Anthropology of Actually Existing Neoliberalism." *Social Anthropology* 20 (1): 66–79.

Wacquant, Loïc, Tom Slater, and Virgílio Borges Pereira. 2014. "Territorial Stigmatization in Action." *Environment and Planning A: Economy and Space* 46 (6): 1270–80.

Wessendorf, Susanne. 2013. "Commonplace Diversity and the 'Ethos of Mixing': Perceptions of Difference in a London Neighbourhood." *Identities* 20 (4): 407–22.

Wetherell, Margaret, and Jonathan Potter. 1992. *Mapping the Language of Racism. Discourse and the Legitimation of Exploitation*. New York: Columbia University Press.

Wieviorka, Michel. 1998. Is Multiculturalism the Solution? *Ethnic and Racial Studies* 21 (5): 881–910.

Williams, Eric Eustace. 1944. *Capitalism & Slavery.* Chapel Hill: University of North Carolina Press.

Williams, Raymond. 1977. *Marxism and Literature*. Oxford: Oxford University Press.

Wimmer, Andreas, and Nina Glick Schiller. 2003. "Methodological Nationalism, the Social Sciences, and the Study of Migration: An Essay in Historical Epistemology." *International Migration Review* 37 (3): 576–610.

Wolf, Eric. 1982. "Introduction." In *Europe and the People Without History*, 3–24. Berkeley: University of California Press.

———. 2001. *Pathways of Power: Building an Anthropology of the Modern World*. Berkeley: University of California Press.

Wright, Erik Olin. 2010. *Envisioning Real Utopias.* London: Verso.

Ybarra, Josep-Antoni, Jorge Hurtado Jordá, and Begoña San Miguel del Hoyo. 2002. "La economía submergida en España: un viaje sin retorno." *Sistema: Revista de Ciencias Sociales* 168–69: 247–82.

Young, Jock. 1999. *The Exclusive Society: Social Exclusion, Crime and Difference in Late Modernity*. London: SAGE Publications.

Yuval-Davis, Nira, Georgie Wemyss, and Kathryn Cassidy. 2017. "Everyday Bordering, Belonging and the Reorientation of British Immigration Legislation." *Sociology* 52 (2): 1–17.

Zapata-Barrero, Ricard. 2003. "The 'discovery of immigration in Spain': the politicization of immigration in the case of El Ejido." *Journal of International Migration and Integration* 4 (4): 523–539.

Zhang, Li. 2001. *Strangers in the City: Reconfigurations of Space, Power, and Social Networks within China's Floating Population*. Stanford, CA: Stanford University Press.

Zino Torraza, Julio. 2006. "Inmigración y prácticas sociales discriminatorias." In *Flujos migratorios y su (des)control: puntos de vista pluridisciplinarios*, edited by Roberto Bergalli, 25–42. Rubí: Anthropos.

Zuloaga, Lohitzune. 2014. *El espejismo de la seguridad ciudadana. Claves de su presencia en la agenda política*. Madrid: Los Libros de Catarata.

STATISTICS

National Institue of Statistics, INE.

Observatori d'Empresa I Ocupació.

Statistical Institute of Catalonia—IDESCAT.

Index

M

N

R

S